TEACHING CROSS-COUNTRY
Skiing

Bridget A. Duoos
Anne M. Rykken

Human Kinetics

Library of Congress Cataloging-in-Publication Data

Duoos, Bridget A.
Teaching cross-country skiing / Bridget A. Duoos and Anne M. Rykken.
    p. cm.
Includes bibliographical references.
ISBN-13: 978-0-7360-9701-7 (soft cover)
ISBN-10: 0-7360-9701-5 (soft cover)
1. Cross-country skiing--Study and teaching. I. Rykken, Anne M. II. Title.
GV855.3.D86 2012
796.93--dc23
                2011028524

ISBN-10: 0-7360-9701-5 (print)
ISBN-13: 978-0-7360-9701-7 (print)

The web addresses cited in this text were current as of August 2011, unless otherwise noted.

Acquisitions Editor: Scott Wikgren; **Developmental Editor:** Ragen E. Sanner; **Assistant Editors:** Anne Rumery and Elizabeth Evans; **Copyeditor:** Pat Connolly; **Permissions Manager:** Dalene Reeder; **Graphic Designer:** Bob Reuther; **Graphic Artist:** Dawn Sills; **Cover Designer:** Keith Blomberg; **Photographer (cover):** Paul Philips/Competitive Image; **Photographer (interior):** Paul Philips/Competitive Image, unless otherwise noted; page 4, photo courtesy of Ahvo Taipale; page 8, photo courtesy of Fischer Sports; pages 12 (figure 2.5), 14, 49, 55, 56, 69, 111, photo courtesy of Anne Rykken; pages 12 (figure 2.6), 26, photo courtesy of Bridget Duoos; pages 45 (figure 3.24), 47, photo courtesy of Ann Schley, highwoodSTUDIOS. **Art Manager:** Kelly Hendren; **Associate Art Manager:** Alan L. Wilborn; **Illustrations:** Artwork drawn by and provided courtesy of Anne Rykken, unless otherwise noted; **Printer:** McNaughton & Gunn

Printed in the United States of America   10 9 8 7 6 5 4 3 2 1

The paper in this book is certified under a sustainable forestry program.

Human Kinetics
Website: www.HumanKinetics.com

United States: Human Kinetics
P.O. Box 5076
Champaign, IL 61825-5076
800-747-4457
e-mail: humank@hkusa.com

Canada: Human Kinetics
475 Devonshire Road Unit 100
Windsor, ON N8Y 2L5
800-465-7301 (in Canada only)
e-mail: info@hkcanada.com

Europe: Human Kinetics
107 Bradford Road
Stanningley
Leeds LS28 6AT, United Kingdom
+44 (0) 113 255 5665
e-mail: hk@hkeurope.com

Australia: Human Kinetics
57A Price Avenue
Lower Mitcham, South Australia 5062
08 8372 0999
e-mail: info@hkaustralia.com

New Zealand: Human Kinetics
P.O. Box 80
Torrens Park, South Australia 5062
0800 222 062
e-mail: info@hknewzealand.com

E5226

Contents

Basic Skills Index

This index lists the location of basic skills found throughout the book.

Games and Activities Index

This index lists the location of games and activities found throughout part II.

Lesson Finder

This finder charts the location of the lessons for chapter 4 as well as their accompanying reproducibles from part III.

Lesson number	Title	Page	Assessments and reproducibles
BEGINNER LEVEL			
1	Get Ready to Ski	53	▶ Boot Size Record, page 199 ▶ Pole Size Record, page 224 ▶ Ski Size Record, page 228 ▶ Boot Sizer: Boys and Girls, page 200 ▶ Boot Sizer: Men and Women, page 201 ▶ Pole-sizing directions, page 225 ▶ Ski-sizing directions, page 231 ▶ Get Ready to Ski station signs, page 207 ▶ Clothing Guide for Cross-Country Skiing, page 202
2	Moving Indoors	57	▶ Moving Indoors station signs, page 214 ▶ Skier Walk Assessment: Contralateral Arm and Leg Movement, page 187 ▶ On and Off: Putting Skis On and Taking Skis Off Assessment, page 179 ▶ Beginner Basic Skills Checklist, page 152 ▶ Beginner Basic Skills Rubric, page 154 ▶ Norwegian Words Related to Snow and Skiing, page 223
3	Outdoors Without Poles	61	▶ Beginner Basic Skills Checklist, page 152 ▶ Beginner Basic Skills Rubric, page 154
4	Shuffle, Shuffle, Glide: Developing Rhythm	63	▶ Shuffle, Shuffle, Glide: Weight Shift, page 185 ▶ Scooter Shift Challenge, page 182
5	Glide, Glide, Glide: Perfecting Rhythm	65	▶ Scooter Countdown, page 181 ▶ Shuffle Countdown, page 184 ▶ Scooter Arms, page 180
6	Introduction to Hills	67	▶ Uphill Herringbone Peer Evaluation, page 192
7	Adding Poles to the Glide	69	▶ Diagonal Stride With Poles Rubric, page 161 ▶ Double-Pole Fun Peer Evaluation, page 162
8	Snowplows!	71	▶ I Can Teach You the Snowplow Stop, page 165 ▶ Snowplow Turn Skills Rubric, page 190
9	Putting It All Together: Trail Time	73	▶ Beginner Basic Skills Checklist, page 152 ▶ Beginner Basic Skills Rubric, page 154 ▶ Kilometers Skied Record, page 213
10	I Can Ski Scavenger Hunt	75	▶ Beginner Basic Skills Checklist, page 152 ▶ Beginner Basic Skills Rubric, page 154

(continued)

Lesson Finder (continued)

Preface

Laughter, squeals, shouts, and other sounds of fun rise from the colorful group of students darting, gliding, and jumping with their cross-country skis on in the crisp winter air. You hesitate for a moment to catch your breath and survey the scene. You can hardly believe that this noisy, moving, active group of students is really your fourth-hour class—the same students who are usually so difficult to motivate. As you glance at your watch, you see that the class time has again flown by. You must now check the students' heart rates and then head back inside. Your students have smiles on their sweaty faces as they glide up to you and locate their pulse. You cannot help grinning as you look over the group and see that even the most difficult students have rosy cheeks, appear more relaxed, and are interacting with classmates. Wow! You hate to see this fun and successful ski unit end. You laugh as a few of the students scramble to find their loose ski and then race back to the gym door. Who knew that teaching cross-country skiing outside in cold temperatures during winter could be so much fun for both you and the students? You marvel at how active the classes have been during this unit and at the improvement in skill you have observed.

Would you like to have that sort of success when teaching an activity? You can. With help from *Teaching Cross-Country Skiing,* you will be able to improve not only your knowledge about classic cross-country skiing but also your own skiing skills. We have written this book for you—someone interested in teaching classic cross-country skiing skills to children and young adults. Cross-country skiing is an important activity to include in your curriculum for several reasons. Over the past several decades, physical education programs in the United States have shifted from focusing on team and dual sports to focusing on lifetime activities, sports, and fitness. Learning lifetime activities is vital to people's health and well-being. Cross-country skiing is an activity that provides enormous physical and mental rewards, and people can continue to participate in this activity throughout their lifetime. Because cross-country skiing is an easy-on-the-joints activity, people may continue to participate well into their 80s! Cross-country skiers do not experience the same pounding on the joints that runners do, making this activity much kinder to vulnerable knees and backs.

In addition, cross-country skiing provides the opportunity for your students to move, really move, their entire body—whether it's over a challenging and hilly terrain, on the flat when playing a game, or on a gently rolling ski track. Any desired workout intensity can be accomplished with cross-country skiing. Cross-country skiing is one of the best cardiovascular exercises; it uses the large muscle groups of both the upper and lower body and is rhythmic and continuous in nature. Whether your students are gliding down a ski track or chasing a fleeing skier they are trying to tag, they will soon be increasing their heart rate into their training zone—and they will have no problem keeping it there. In addition to providing the heart and lungs with a workout, cross-country skiing also requires extensive use of the arm, leg, abdominal, and back muscles.

What could be better than a winter activity that gets you and your students outside for a fun, energetic class session participating in a lifetime activity that builds cardiovascular endurance, increases strength, and improves balance? In addition, your students will stay toasty warm and will smile for the entire class time! Cross-country skiing enables you to provide just such an experience. Using the complete, detailed lesson plans in this book, you will be able to successfully add a classic cross-country ski unit to your curriculum and teach your students how to cross-country ski.

Unique Contributions

This book is unique in that the main focus is on a structured series of lesson plans appropriate for teaching children and young adults how to cross-country ski. No other book available on the market today provides this focus. In addition to the lesson plans, the book provides information that enables you to learn about how a ski works, which is critical to being able to teach ski skills. We have also included details on the critical features of important ski skills that will ultimately enhance teaching and improve student learning. Measuring student progress toward the lesson objectives will be easy and fun with the many assessments included for each lesson. This book makes it easy for you to add the wonderful lifetime activity of cross-country skiing to your school curriculum.

Book Scope

Teaching Cross-Country Skiing assumes that your students are new to the activity of classic cross-country skiing. The first 10 lesson plans in the book are for the beginner skier. In the first lesson, you begin class indoors, fitting skis and practicing basic ski skills. The second lesson moves the class outdoors to practice those basic ski skills on snow. In the remaining beginner lessons, students learn the diagonal stride technique, with and without poles. They also learn how to double pole, climb, and descend gentle hills. Many fun games and skill-testing activities keep students interested and highly engaged. Work on the diagonal stride continues in the 10 intermediate lessons. In these lessons, students also work to improve hill-climbing technique, and they practice using snowplow stops and turns to control speed and maneuver around obstacles when descending hills. The intermediate lessons provide challenges for students as they work to improve the diagonal stride; these challenges include increasing the length of the glide, shifting weight properly to commit to the gliding ski, and using the poling action for propulsion. Of course, skiers are also challenged as the distances skied gradually increase, and the lessons always include highly active games and activities that keep skiers moving. Other skills covered include performing the kick double pole (for moving up and over hills), skiing over bumps, and improving balance on one moving ski. In the 10 advanced lessons, distances skied are increased, and technique is refined. Students have fun learning the stem Christie, traversing steeper hills, and edging. Your skiers' diagonal stride will become a rhythmic, continuous motion kept up over hillier and longer trails.

Book Organization

Teaching Cross-Country Skiing is organized into three parts. In part I, you will find a brief history of skiing as well as information about why cross-country skiing is an important activity to include in your curriculum. This part also provides information on how to prepare for classic skiing, including details on choosing and fitting equipment and how to dress. You will also learn about the science of snow and skis, which will improve your understanding of how a ski functions. This understanding is critical to your success as an instructor and to your students' success as skiers. The lessons and supporting materials in this book focus on how to teach classic, or Nordic, cross-country skiing to children and young adults. Classic skiing is a traditional method of cross-country skiing that is an enjoyable, rhythmic activity and that also helps develop the balance and strength needed to be able to take part in other forms of cross-country skiing, like skate skiing. In chapter 2, you will learn about different types of skis, boots, and poles that can be used for cross-country skiing and how to select the most appropriate type of equipment for your program.

Part II focuses on teaching cross-country skiing. It provides biomechanical breakdowns of skills and helps you learn the critical features you need to be aware of when teaching a skill. This part includes the 30 lesson plans, 10 lessons each for the beginner, intermediate, and advanced levels. Also included in this part is a chapter that describes additional games and activities that you can use to supplement the ones provided in the lesson plans.

Part III gives you what you need to make teaching this unit a bit easier. You will find forms for assessing your students, suggestions for interdisciplinary lessons, and templates for recording kilometers skied and other activities—in short, material that will make your job easier!

Benefits for the Teacher

Teaching Cross-Country Skiing will enable you to improve your knowledge base about this lifetime activity so that you can successfully add a cross-country skiing unit to your curriculum. You will have a great time teaching this fun activity to your students. The complete lesson plans provided in this book are invaluable. They take you from instruction for the beginner skier to lessons for the advanced skier. We have provided everything you need to conduct an engaging class session . . . except the snow! The complete, detailed lesson plans and the supporting forms, charts, and assessments will make offering a cross-country ski unit an easy and exciting addition to your curriculum.

Unique Book Features

We have focused each structured lesson plan on accomplishing a lesson objective that will enhance your instruction of cross-country skiing. Each lesson builds on skills learned in the previous lesson, and the lesson design allows for review and practice of skills throughout the entire cross-country ski unit. These fun, fast-paced lessons allow students to engage in a high level of activity throughout the whole class period. Game play and a variety of activities are used to help teach and reinforce ski skills as well as build students' confidence in their ability to move on skis.

No other book on the market today provides you with such a well-defined and focused lesson plan that includes lesson goals, introductory activities, lesson focus, review, games, and assessment suggestions. The lessons even include sample dialogue that you can use to open and close each class session. Within these dialogues, instructions to the teacher are provided in brackets. In addition, the lessons are aligned with the National Association for Sport and Physical Education (NASPE) national standards and provide suggestions for interdisciplinary lessons that you can take to the classroom teacher. This book will also teach you about the physical benefits of cross-country skiing, the history of cross-country skiing, the interaction of skis and snow, and appropriate clothing and equipment selection for children and young adults. A biomechanical breakdown of the ski skills (including pictures) will give you a good look at the critical features of each skill that you will be teaching. Assessment forms and activity supplements—such as a chart for measuring boot size and ski length—are additional unique features of this book that will help you present a great skiing unit to your students.

PART I

Learning About Cross-Country Skiing

CHAPTER 1

An Introduction to Cross-Country Skiing

Cross-country skiing is an activity that dates back approximately 5,000 years. In the Scandinavian countries, remnants of short, wide skis have been found preserved in prehistoric bogs, and petroglyphs of skiers have been found carved into rocks. These artifacts show that early people used skis to move over the deep snow found in northern climates. The skis enhanced people's ability to hunt animals and provide food. This early means of transportation enabled people to travel greater distances. This brought people nearer to each other and had far-reaching effects on the lives of Scandinavians, including an increase in military effectiveness (Bays, 1980).

Eventually, changes in the ski binding allowed people to make more effective turns on hills. When Sondre Norheim (a Norwegian) wrapped a strip of osier around his heel to help keep his foot attached to the ski, skiing was changed forever. The improvement in the binding system enabled people to turn their skis more readily, made it easier to navigate steeper hills and mountain terrain, and allowed skiers to perform more daring moves. Skis used for fun and recreational activities became increasingly popular as equipment evolved through the years. Ski racing and ski jumping became common activities performed across the northern climates. When Scandinavians immigrated to the United States, they brought along their knowledge of skiing as well as the tools for making skis. Soon, people were skiing in the United States. Ski jumps were built, and ski races were held. More and more people discovered that being outside skiing during the winter months was not only fun, but also felt great and was good for their body.

As an instructor who teaches skiing to children and young adults, you are playing an important role in introducing young people to the benefits of exercising outside during the winter months. In addition, you are teaching your students about an activity that has been around for thousands of years—a wonderful activity that will undoubtedly be around for thousands more!

Benefits of Cross-Country Skiing

Cross-country skiing can be enjoyed by a wide range of students, from the youngest kindergartners to those secondary students who are

This young boy in Finland is ready to go skiing.

so difficult to please. This activity can challenge students who are in excellent cardiovascular condition, or it can provide a gentle workout in the appropriate training zone for students who are just getting into shape. Moreover, for the students who really don't care about "getting in shape," cross-country skiing can simply be a very fun activity. And while having fun, those students will still gain benefits related to cardiovascular fitness, strength, and balance. By getting your class outside during the winter months to exercise, you are showing your students that they can easily stay warm while out in cold temperatures. Cross-country skiing provides many benefits, including some great physical benefits.

The physical benefits of cross-country skiing are well known. If you look at Olympic cross-country skiers, you can see the positive effects on the body that result from training for cross-country skiing. The average elite female cross-country skier carries 11 percent body fat, and elite male skiers carry 5 percent. These percentages are well below the average for people who are considered to be athletic—17 percent for females and 10 percent for males (Fox, Bowers, and Foss, 1993). The high number of calories burned while skiing helps to keep skiers trim and lean. One hour of moderate cross-country skiing can burn approximately 470 calories for a 130-pound person and nearly 700 calories for a 190-pound person. Therefore, cross-country skiing is a great way to burn calories while having fun!

Cross-country skiing is also an efficient way to exercise a large number of muscles at once. Because skiers use ski poles as a means of propulsion, the upper body gets much more of a workout when cross-country skiing compared to when running or cycling. When a skier is using the diagonal stride, the biceps and triceps provide power to the ski poles. When the double-pole technique is used, the skier's core muscles, pectoralis major, deltoids, and latissimus dorsi are put to work. Of course, the leg muscles also do their fair share. The quadriceps (the muscle group on the front of the thigh) and the gastrocnemius (the large, powerful muscle on the back of the lower leg) provide the forceful "kick" and propel the skier forward. People who use cross-country skiing as a workout over several weeks will discover that the muscles

Fun Facts About the History of Cross-Country Skiing

- People living in the wintry climates of Norway and Sweden were the first to create and use cross-country skis.
- Remains of skis found above Sweden's Arctic Circle date back as far as 2000 B.C.
- The Scandinavian skiers drew pictures (called petroglyphs) on cave walls that showed them skiing.
- The early skiers probably used the long bones from animals as the first skis. They tied the skis to their feet using long, woody strips peeled off from trees and shrubs. It was not until many years later that people discovered that they could make skis out of the wood from trees.
- The early skiers used one long pole to help push them through the snow.
- The first ski race took place in Tromso, Norway, in 1776.
- Cross-country skiing is also called Nordic skiing because of where it got its start—in the northern Nordic countries.
- The Norwegians and Swedes used their skis for transportation, just as we use a bike or car today.
- In 1850, Norwegian Sondre Norheim—who lived in Morgedal, Norway—discovered that if he wrapped a long strand of osier around his foot and ski, he could easily make better turns on his skis.
- When people began making long wood skis with leather bindings that held their feet to the skis better, skiing became more fun. Skiers could now move faster and cover more distance.
- In 1830, people in Finland started using two ski poles.
- Beginning in 1825, many people left Norway and Sweden to come to the United States to live (Lovell, 1984). These people frequently chose to live in the northern states (such as Wisconsin, Minnesota, North Dakota, and South Dakota) because the weather and land were similar to their old home. They loved the snow, and they made skis to use for work and play.
- In 1849, many people headed to California hoping to find gold. Norwegian skiers brought their skis and used them when crossing California's Sierra Mountains. The most famous skier was John "Snowshoe" Thompson. Snowshoe became famous for delivering the U.S. mail for 20 years on his skis.
- Cross-country skiing has been included in the Olympic Winter Games since 1924. Cross-country skiers compete in races that cover various distances, from short sprint events to longer 30K (women) and 50K (men) races. They also compete in team relays, biathlons, and Nordic combined events that include cross-country skiing and ski jumping.

of their entire body increase in strength. As a result, cross-country skiing and other activities become easier.

Cross-country skiing involves the use of the large muscle groups of both the upper and lower body; therefore, during this activity, there is a large demand for oxygen to be supplied to these muscles. The body's ability to supply oxygen to the working muscles is referred to as $\dot{V}O_2$max. Because of the large number of muscles that are working hard when a person is skiing, $\dot{V}O_2$max measurements in skiers are

very high. Well-trained cross-country skiers have efficient cardiovascular systems; in fact, elite cross-country skiers have the highest recorded $\dot{V}O_2$max levels of any group of athletes (Saltin and Astrand, 1967).

Cross-country skiing on a regular basis has a tremendous effect on a person's cardiovascular system. In addition to gaining strength in the muscles of the upper and lower body, people who use cross-country skiing as a workout method over several weeks will also discover that their heart is stronger. A strong heart pumps

Cross-country ski racers are highly trained athletes.

more efficiently, sending out more blood to the muscles with each contraction. Through weeks of skiing, people often discover that their resting heart rate has decreased. Highly trained Olympic cross-country skiers have resting heart rates between 28 and 40 beats per minute. Compare that to the resting heart rate of the average person, which is 60 to 80 beats per minute! With the highly active lesson plans found in this book, you should have no problem raising your students' heart rates. In fact, some students may need to take short breaks to catch their breath and let their heart rate drop slightly so that it returns to the appropriate training zone. Younger children are very good at doing this naturally. If you have heart rate monitors, you should use them to check students' heart rates during and immediately after the lessons. You will be impressed with the amount of time your students are spending in their training zones!

The benefits of cross-country skiing extend beyond the physiological to overall general health and well-being. A lot of evidence exists (Fraioli et al., 1980) indicating that regular physical activity increases the release of mood-lifting endorphins in the body. After one of the energetic and fun lessons you lead, students will be smiling and laughing; they will be relaxed and in a better mood than when you started class. In addition, students will leave class with a sense of accomplishment, knowing that they have developed new skills in a fun activity. They will also know that they can use these skills beyond class time for many years to come. The results of a Finnish research study on the activity levels of boys and girls showed the benefits of cross-country skiing: Among boys, the proportion of persistent exercisers was highest for those who participated in cross-country skiing, jogging, and bodybuilding (Aarnio et al., 2002). By teaching cross-country skiing, you are providing students with fantastic exercise during class time, and you are also helping them learn an activity that many students will pursue outside of class. Cross-country skiing is an activity that students can do with their families, with friends, or alone. With help from the lesson plans in this book, you are the catalyst to make that happen!

Summary

So now that you are convinced of the value of including cross-country skiing in your curriculum, let's move on to some things you must consider when getting ready to ski. Everything you need to know about selecting equipment and clothing is covered in the next chapter.

CHAPTER 2

Getting Ready to Ski

Kick and glide, kick and glide! It is time to get ready to ski. That means you need to make decisions about the appropriate skis, poles, and boots for your students. When selecting equipment for children and young adults, you must consider many factors. One major decision is determining what type of skis are most appropriate for your program's needs—classic or skate skis, waxable or no-wax skis, and so on. To help your students learn good diagonal stride technique, you need to understand how various types of skis react to a skier's kick, how the ski interacts with snow, and how the ski glides. Getting ready for skiing also means being knowledgeable about how to dress in layers and how to choose appropriate cross-country ski clothing. Providing your students with guidance on how to stay comfortable while out skiing in a range of temperatures and weather conditions will be important to the success of your ski outings. After learning about all of these topics in this chapter, you will be ready to make the necessary decisions that will soon have your students out skiing.

Types of Skis

One of the first decisions you will make for your program is whether to purchase classic skis, skate skis, or combi skis (see figure 2.1). Before you purchase skis, you need to consider the age of the skiers and the availability of groomed ski tracks.

CLASSIC SKIS

Classic skis, also called diagonal skis, are used when performing the diagonal stride (either in groomed tracks or in ungroomed conditions). The diagonal stride is the technique used most often by beginner skiers, and it requires skiers to move their limbs contralaterally. Classic skis can be purchased with either a waxable or no-wax bottom. For younger elementary children, the length of the skis should be head height or less, while upper elementary and middle school students can handle skis that reach the wrist when the arm is stretched overhead (Flemmen and Grosvold, 1982). Classic skis are a good choice for the elementary ages as well as the middle and secondary levels. All skiers should learn how to correctly diagonal stride on classic skis so they develop the ability to balance and glide on one ski. The focus of this book is on teaching students how to diagonal stride using classic skis.

Classic skis are narrow and lightweight. They have a turned-up tip in the front and a flattened tail at the other end. Construction of the skis involves using a layering process that starts with a plastic such as P-Tex or polyethylene for the ski base. On top of the base is a core layer of foam, wood, or a honeycomb material. The sidewalls of the ski are a plastic or wood laminate. The top layer of the ski consists of a fiberglass laminate. All of these layers are glued together. This layering process makes the ski flexible and soft from tip to tail so that it can glide over the snow—but also rigid and strong enough to maintain camber. Manufacturers will add the brand name, color, and design on top of the laminate.

In between the tip and tail, an area of camber runs the length of the ski. When a diagonal ski sits flat on the floor, the tip and tail should be touching the floor, and the middle portion of the ski should be off the floor. You should see a slight upward curve that runs almost the full length of the ski and does not touch the floor. This is the ski's camber.

Ski bindings are attached in the center of the camber area. When the skier performs a kick, the ski will be pressed to the snow, and the fish scales or ski wax will grip the snow, propelling the skier forward. The binding is located so that the pivot point of the boot (the point where you can flex up onto the toes) is over the balance point of the ski. If a ski is too stiff, the skier will have a difficult time flattening the ski against the snow; as a result, the fish scales or wax will not grab the snow effectively to allow for a good kick.

After an effective kick, the skier should be able to glide. When a skier stands on top of the skis with his weight evenly distributed over the skis, the ski camber is slightly off the snow, allowing the skier to glide on the tips and tails of the skis. If the ski is very flexible and too soft for the skier's weight and strength, the wax or

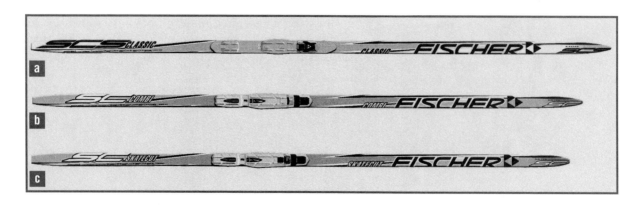

Figure 2.1 *(a)* Classic, *(b)* skate, and *(c)* combi skis.

fish scale area will continually drag on the snow and interfere with the skier's ability to glide.

SKATE SKIS

In groomed conditions, skiers use skate skis to move forward by putting the skis in a V position and pushing off from side to side. Skate skis are shorter than classic skis. Skate skis will need to have a glide wax applied from tip to tail on the bottom of the skis. Your students will probably want to try skate skiing because it is fast and looks like a lot of fun. However, you should reserve this experience for the middle and secondary students. Elementary students usually lack the necessary strength to perform the skate movements correctly for more than a few strides.

COMBI SKIS

A combi ski (short for combination ski) allows skiers to diagonal stride and skate ski on the same ski. The combi ski may seem like a good alternative to having both classic and skate skis; however, a combi ski will not successfully meet the demands of either type of skiing. A combi ski correctly fit for skate skiing will be too stiff to be a good diagonal stride ski. If the ski is correctly fit for diagonal striding, then it will be too soft for successful skating. Students will get frustrated when the ski does not enable them to successfully perform the needed technique.

Ski Characteristics

Now that you understand the techniques and equipment available, it is time to decide if you want waxable classic skis or waxless classic skis. You also need to consider ski camber and length. Your choices will hinge on the age of the skiers you are working with, the space available for waxing, and the length of your class periods.

WAXABLE AND NO-WAX SKIS

For waxable skis (see figure 2.2a)—that is, skis that require wax to be applied before use—you will need to pay attention to the air temperature (or snow temperature if you really want to get it right) before heading outside. Waxable skis are not a practical choice for elementary students, but they are certainly a good option for middle and secondary students. These older students can benefit from learning how to wax a ski correctly, and they may even enjoy doing it. In addition, waxable skis can be used in a wider range of temperatures. When considering waxable skis, you need to make sure that you have space available where you can set up an area for waxing. You must also determine whether your class periods are long enough for both waxing and skiing.

No-wax skis (see figure 2.2b) have a pattern embossed on the bottom side of the ski. This

Figure 2.2 Side-by-side comparison of *(a)* waxable and *(b)* no-wax skis.

pattern allows the ski to grip the snow when the skier kicks downward on the ski to flatten it. The pattern may be a fish scale design or grooves marked under the foot area (extending from slightly behind the heel to a spot forward of the toe). No wax means just that—you do not need to apply any wax to the bottom surface of the ski before using it. These skis will have the best grip when the snow temperatures hover around the freezing point. They will not work as well in extreme (very cold) temperatures. A no-wax ski would be the best choice for the elementary and middle school grades.

SKI CAMBER

If you set a cross-country ski on the floor and view it from the side, you will see that the tip and tail of the ski contact the floor (see figure 2.3a). The middle section of the ski (the part that will be under the foot of the skier) will be slightly off the ground. This is the camber of the ski. On a waxable ski, this camber area is the part that needs to be waxed. On a no-wax ski, this area will usually have a fish scale pattern. Take the time to explain to your students that the fish scales or patterns in the ski's kick zone help the ski to grab the snow and increase friction in that area. This will help students understand why you are asking them to kick down, which in turn, propels them forward.

Have students find and touch the kick zone of their waxless skis so they can feel the roughness of the fish scales or pattern created on the ski base. When the skier kicks, or applies downward pressure to the ski, the ski should flatten against the ground (see figure 2.3b). During the kick, the fish scales (or the wax if using waxable skis) press into the snow, providing the grip that allows the ski to move forward. Students need to understand this concept when learning how to diagonal stride.

You can have the students put their skis down parallel to each other on the gym floor and stand with their weight evenly distributed over both skis. While one student does this, a partner observes whether or not the camber has completely flattened out. The ski camber should remain off the floor, even if only slightly. Point out that this is how the ski works when the skier is gliding on snow. For the skier to glide fast, the fish scale or patterned area needs to be off the snow and not dragging in the snow. After the kick, the opposite ski should glide on its tip and tail (Gullion, 1990). Skis that are too soft for a student's strength and body weight will remain flattened to the snow throughout the phases of the diagonal stride, making gliding impossible.

While the skier is standing on both skis with weight evenly distributed, the partner should place an index card under the ski bottom beneath the skier's foot. The partner should try to slide the card forward toward the toe and then backward closer to the heel. Instruct students to shift all of their weight to one ski to see what happens while the partner is sliding the card

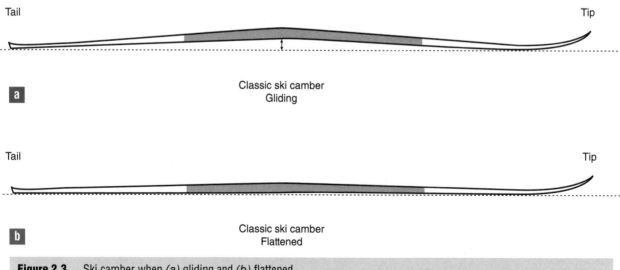

Tail

Tip

a

Classic ski camber
Gliding

Tail

Tip

b

Classic ski camber
Flattened

Figure 2.3 Ski camber when (a) gliding and (b) flattened.

from toe to heel. The ski should flatten against the floor just as it will flatten against the snow when the skier kicks. Shifting weight to one ski should trap the index card between the ski base and the floor.

Your students will have a better grasp of the diagonal stride once you have explained how the diagonal ski works with the snow. This will help beginner skiers move from shuffling or walking on skis to performing the kick and glide action characteristic of effective cross-country skiing.

The skier's degree of success in kicking or pushing against the snow has everything to do with Newton's third law of motion: action-reaction. This presents the perfect opportunity for you to collaborate with a science teacher. The science teacher can discuss the law of action-reaction and can conduct short lab experiments that will help students understand what happens when they kick on their diagonal skis. Point out that when they push down on the ski they are using their muscles to create the "action"—pushing against the snow and against the very large mass of planet earth. The "reaction" comes from the equal and opposite force applied to the much smaller skier from the snow and planet earth.

SKI LENGTH

Once you have decided on the type of ski that best suits your program goals, you need to determine the length of the skis that you will purchase. If the skis are too long for the skier, the student will have a difficult time learning proper technique and will become frustrated. A shorter ski will be easier to maneuver, especially for elementary students; however, for secondary students, a diagonal ski that is too short will hamper the skiers' ability to glide, which is an important part of the diagonal stride technique.

For elementary students, the length of classic skis should be at or very close to the student's height. If necessary, it is better to go with a shorter ski length rather than a longer one when working with younger children. For middle and secondary students, ski length can be determined by having the students stand with an arm outstretched overhead while wearing their tennis shoes. The tip of the ski should reach to the student's wrist. When using skate skis, the tip of the ski should reach to a spot several inches above the top of the skier's head. (See figure 2.4.)

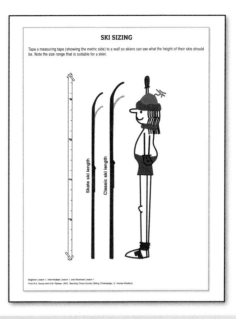

Figure 2.4 To help students see what the length of their skis should be, you can tape a measuring tape to the wall with the metric side visible. The light and dark ski tips indicate the range of length suitable for a skier. See page 231 for a reproducible version of this diagram.

Other Equipment

Selecting the proper skis for your students is important, but cross-country skiing requires other equipment as well. Your students will also need boots, bindings, poles, and appropriate clothing before they can join in on the fun. Just as there are classic skis and skate skis, there are also classic ski boots and skate ski boots. Major differences exist in the construction of the various types of boot, such as the height and stiffness of the boot. In this section, you will learn about these differences as well as the bindings that attach the ski boot to the ski. You will also learn about selecting the appropriate ski pole length for a skier and choosing clothing that will keep the active skier warm and comfortable.

BOOTS

As mentioned, ski boots come in either classic (also known as diagonal stride) or skate boots, and the type of boot used will depend on the type of skiing being done. Expect to see a European sizing on the boots. To make the boot-fitting process easier, you can refer to a shoe conversion chart such as the one found in chapter 7 of this book. Classic boots will generally have a lower cut to them (see figure 2.5a). Skating boots have higher and more rigid sides that allow for the effective transfer of force from the pushing leg to the ski when the skis are in a V position (see figure 2.5b). The fit of either type of boot is similar to that of a shoe; a thumb's width of space is needed at the toe so the toes can wiggle, and the heel should not slide up and down in the boot. Skiers should try the boots on with the heavier socks that they plan to wear when skiing.

BINDINGS

Bindings should be simple to operate. Remember that your students will be putting skis on and taking them off in the cold and snow. Having the same system of boots and bindings for all the students will help simplify things. Some bindings allow the skier to step into them by

lifting the heel up, pressing the toe of the ski boot into them (see figure 2.6a), and snapping them closed by pushing down on the bindings with the hands (see figure 2.6b). These bindings are easy to use for all levels of skiers. Bindings that release by pressing a pole tip into the front of the binding are another option. Stay away from the older three-pin binding systems. Your skiers will have more control with newer binding systems and will be able to get into and out of them by themselves.

POLES

Ski poles are used to help propel the skier forward. For many beginners, the poles are also important for maintaining balance. You must ensure that the poles are the proper length for each individual student. This is critical to the student's ability to use the poles correctly and

Figure 2.5 (a) A diagonal or classic ski boot and (b) a skate boot.

Figure 2.6 Bindings that allow students to (a) easily press the toes of their boots into the ski binding and (b) push the binding closed to secure boot and ski.

efficiently. Diagonal stride poles should reach to the armpit of the skier (Flemmen and Grosvold, 1982). Skate poles are considerably longer and should reach to the skier's mouth (Gullion, 1990). Ski poles can be fit to the students when they are wearing tennis shoes. Ski poles that are too long or too short will hamper the student's ability to master technique and may leave the skier with sore muscles. All poles should have adjustable straps that will accommodate a range of student hand sizes when the students are wearing mittens or gloves. (See figure 2.7.)

You may have difficulty convincing some of your students that their ski poles are not just for balance purposes. To emphasize the importance of the poles for improving the skiers' forward propulsion, you may want to revisit Newton's third law. Point out that the force applied to the pole is transferred to the snow and to planet earth, resulting in a reaction to the skier's push. Similar to the leg muscles when kicking, the arm and core muscles supply the force exerted along the axis of the pole. Skiers should plant the pole with their hand forward and with the pole angled backward, using the triceps to push on the pole. This will result in an increase in the skier's forward speed. Contrast this with an upright skier who holds the pole with the elbow bent to 90 degrees and plants the pole when it is in a vertical position. With the pole in this position, the skier will find it much more difficult to apply force, and the force that is applied will create a vertically directed reaction force. Once students get the feel of pushing off their poles, they will quickly discover the benefits of using the arms and poles correctly. As students become increasingly comfortable on their skis and are able to balance on one gliding ski, they should be able to effectively use the poles for propulsion, not strictly for balance.

WAX

Your older and more experienced skiers may ask about waxable skis, or you may choose to introduce this option to your students by showing them a pair of waxable skis. Maybe your program already has waxable skis available. If you have enough class time and the necessary space for ski preparation, waxable skis are a wonderful option. Therefore, you should learn about ski wax and the purpose it serves.

Ski wax comes in various degrees of softness and hardness, and it serves the same purpose as the fish scales or patterns found in the kick zone of waxless skis—that is, to increase the friction between the ski and the snow so that the ski grabs the snow more effectively. The hard ski waxes come in small, soft metal tins with a plastic cover. You can peel narrow strips of the tin away to expose the wax, making it easier to apply the wax to the ski base. Apply the wax to the ski base by rubbing it in the kick zone (see figure 2.8a); the kick zone runs from approximately 6 inches (15.2 cm) in front of the ski binding to approximately 2 inches (5.1 cm) beyond the heel of the ski boot. After applying the wax on that area, take a cork (see figure 2.8b) and repeatedly smooth the wax out to a glossy sheen, working the cork in one direction from the toe to the heel.

Hard waxes are rated for snow temperature and are color coded. Generally, red waxes are for warmer temperatures around 32 to 37 degrees Fahrenheit, violet waxes are used around freezing, blue waxes are for a temperature range of about 15 to 31 degrees, and green waxes are for temperatures of 14 degrees and below. Slight variations can exist in the color coding

Figure 2.7 To help students see what the length of their ski poles should be, you can tape a measuring tape to the wall with the metric side visible. See page 225 for a reproducible version of this diagram.

of various wax manufacturers; always read the label. The condition of the snow (whether it is fresh and new or has melted and refrozen) will also affect wax selection. Skiers usually depend on the air temperature when selecting wax for the day. If you want to be more accurate, stick a thermometer into the snow and leave it there for five minutes to determine snow temperature.

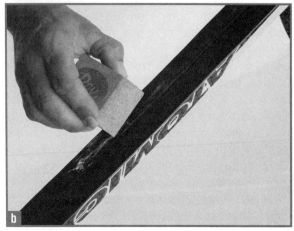

Figure 2.8 *(a)* Waxing a ski and *(b)* smoothing wax with cork.

Snow temperatures usually lag behind the air temperature by 3 to 5 degrees.

Softer waxes called klisters may be used in warm, melting snow or snow that has melted and refrozen. Klisters come in soft metal tubes similar to a toothpaste tube. These waxes are very sticky and gooey. Like the hard waxes, klisters come in different colors and are temperature dependent. However, manufacturers have developed a universal klister that will work for a wider range of temperatures on snow that has melted and refrozen.

The characteristics of the snow you will be skiing on should determine which type of wax you put on your skis. Freshly fallen snow on a cold, crisp day will still have the sharp points of the snowflakes, which makes it easier for the points to bite into a harder wax. When the snow has been on the ground for several days, the sun will melt those sharp snowflake points, or wind will tumble the snowflakes around, knocking off the points. As the snowflake starts to change from a pointy, sharp flake to a more rounded one (in a process called destructive metamorphism), you will have to choose a slightly softer wax. Warm, sunny days with temperatures hovering around freezing will mean that you need to use a softer wax so the rounded snowflake shape will have an easier time gripping the ski. Over time the snowflake deconstructs to the form of a rounded water droplet, and the softest waxes (the klisters) are then necessary. Snow that has melted and refrozen will require the use of a soft wax. (Refer to figure 2.9 to see snow in various degrees of melt.)

Waxing skis can be a complicated procedure or can be as simple as rubbing in a wax with a cork. Other options for waxing include hot waxing, using expensive fluoro waxes, or putting structure in the wax with special tools and paste waxes. You can visit your nearest ski shop to get the latest information on waxes. You may even

Figure 2.9 Fresh snow has sharp points that easily bite into a hard wax, while a soft wax allows a better grip for the melting snowflake.

want to attend a wax clinic. There is a great deal to learn about waxing, and you can make it as simple or as complicated as you like.

CLOTHING

Selecting the proper clothing for cross-country skiing can be difficult given the high physiological demands of skiing. Be aware that your students will become warm quickly once skiing activity begins—and they will cool off rapidly if they are standing around. Therefore, for the safety and comfort of everyone, you should keep instructions short. If students overdress, they will sweat and become uncomfortably warm. This will discourage students and will lead to the risk of hypothermia if the activity level drops and the skiers start to cool off. Elementary students will be too warm if dressed in the typical heavy jacket, snow pants, hat, and mittens. Have your students dress in layers, including a lightweight insulating layer, a slightly warmer middle layer, and a wind-breaking third layer. All skiers should wear a hat pulled over their ear tips to avoid frostbite; they should also wear lighter-weight gloves or mittens. Mittens will be warmer than gloves; however, big puffy mittens (the type often worn during downhill skiing) will be too warm, will cause very sweaty hands, and will make it difficult for skiers to handle ski poles.

Ski and Pole Handling

There are several methods to use when carrying skis and poles. Each teacher should select the method that works best for their class and the abilities of their students. One method that can be tried is to carry one ski and one pole in each hand. Another method would be to carry both skis in one hand and both poles in the other. In this method, teachers can use a supply of rubber bands to put on the tips and tails of the skis to hold the skis from twisting and turning. Once outside and ready to ski, skiers can put the rubber bands back in the teacher's basket, on the wrist around the outside of their mittens, or even in an empty pocket.

Summer Equipment Storage

When choosing equipment, you must keep in mind that you will need to store it. Following are several simple storage ideas that can help you organize skis, boots, and poles. These systems work well all year round. Make sure that ski racks are mounted at a height that will accommodate long and short skis. (See figure 2.10.)

Dress to Ski

- The key to dressing for skiing is to layer, layer, layer. Start out with long underwear. Depending on the conditions, add sweaters, coats, or shells.

- Skiers should always wear a hat! If you become too warm, you should unzip at the neck slightly, but you should leave your hat on.

- Fleece pants and coats topped with a wind shell will work for an amazing range of conditions.

- Skiers should stay away from cotton. Some of the new fabrics such as MTS and Capilene are just as soft as cotton, and they do a superior job of wicking moisture away from the skin.

- Downhill ski gloves are generally too heavy for cross-country. Mittens are great in especially cold weather, and they can be worn with lightweight liners to add warmth if necessary.

- The adult skier in the group should wear a backpack containing extra mittens, a hat, a face mask, a wind jacket, and, of course, healthy treats! Check out the Clothing Guide for Cross-Country Skiing in chapter 7 for more specifics about dressing for Nordic skiing.

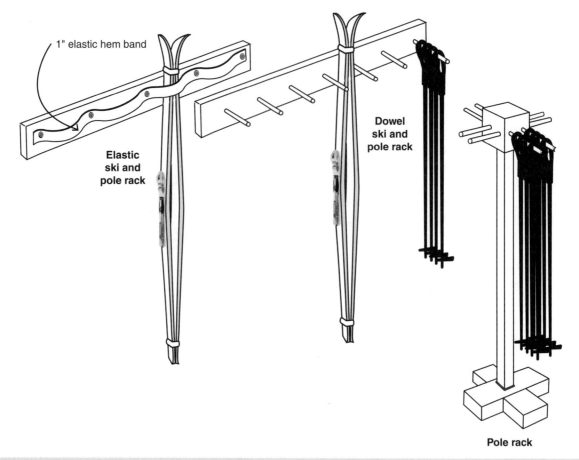

1" elastic hem band

Elastic
ski and
pole rack

Dowel
ski and
pole rack

Pole rack

Figure 2.10 Cross-country skiing equipment can be easily stored during the summer months. By using racks, you can keep your equipment organized and in good shape.

SKI STORAGE

Nowadays, cross-country skis require little maintenance. To keep skis performing at their best, you should keep the ski bases clean, whether they are waxable or no-wax skis. Things such as leaves, dirt, and sticky tree parts can build up on the ski base and slow down the ski.

At the end of your ski unit, you should prepare the skis for the summer by cleaning the bases and wiping off the tops and bindings.

For waxable skis, you should clean off the old wax. Use a bit of citrus-based ski wax remover and a scraper to clean the kick zone. Apply the cleaner, let it soak in for a few minutes, and then scrape from tip to tail in the kick zone until the wax is gone. If the glide zone has been waxed previously, melt a soft wax over the length of the ski and scrape it off from tip to tail while it is still warm. This will pull the dirt out from within the bases. Then, reapply a medium-temperature glide wax and leave it on the ski over

the summer. This protective coat of wax keeps the base from oxidizing and maintains the ski's gliding properties.

For no-wax skis, it is a good idea to wipe down the skis with wax remover before applying a medium-temperature glide wax for storage (similar to waxable skis).

After you have cleaned and renewed your ski bases, you should check the binding screws and put a small squirt of an all-purpose oil on the binding mechanism. Rubbing paraffin on the binding beneath the foot area will help reduce ice and snow buildup. If you have time, finish the job by waxing the top of the skis with a furniture wax, being careful not to get any of the spray on your base wax. This will help keep the snow off the top of the skis next winter.

Clean, waxed skis should be stored in a cool, dry environment where there is little fluctuation in temperature. Avoid storing them in direct sunlight. Ski ties (or rubber bands) should be placed on the tips and tails. Do not bind the skis closed with the camber compressed. To help keep dust and dirt off the skis, you can cover them with bags, sheets, or tarps.

By following these procedures, you will have your skis almost ready to go at the beginning of the next season. For skis that have been waxed with soft glide wax, you should scrape the glide wax off at the start of ski season. Several swipes with a plastic scraper will get the soft wax off; you can then brush the remaining wax off the base using a nylon brush.

BOOT STORAGE

The most important thing about storing boots is to make sure they are completely dry before packing them away. Loosening their laces, stretching out their tongues, and allowing them to dry for a few days will help this process. Boots can be stored on open, dry shelving or can be packed in large plastic storage bins. Organizing the boots by size when you put them away for the summer will save you time next fall.

POLE STORAGE

When storing ski poles, you should check for tears in the straps, cracks in the pole shaft, and missing or broken pole tips. Take the time to repair the poles before storing them so they are ready for the next ski season.

Summary

Skis, boots, poles, clothing; you are now ready to take your students skiing! As you have discovered, including cross-country skiing in your curriculum does require some planning. For starters, your department needs to have skis, boots, and poles that will fit students of various sizes. As a teacher, you need to understand how a ski is designed and how it interacts with the snow; you must understand how to kick and flatten the ski against the snow, resulting in a forward motion. Students should have this same understanding when learning the diagonal stride technique. For students to have an enjoyable experience in this highly active sport, they must dress in comfortable clothing that allows them to regulate their body temperature. As a teacher, you should now feel better prepared to gather the necessary ski equipment, make clothing recommendations to your skiers, and head outside to have some winter fun!

PART II

Teaching Cross-Country Skiing

CHAPTER 3

Basic Cross-Country Skiing Skills

Cross-country skiing over a variety of terrains—from rolling hills to steep and twisty trails—provides skiers with opportunities to use a multitude of ski skills. Cross-country skiers using classic skis and using the diagonal stride technique tend to use certain skills over and over again. Some of these skills are variations of other techniques (e.g., the kick double pole is a variation of the double pole). Many of the skills that classic skiers use are considered to be basic skills that are foundational to being a good skier with solid technique. These basic skills provide classic skiers with many ways of skiing across the snow and safely maneuvering over beautiful, demanding, and fun terrain. In this chapter, each of the basic skills is broken down into the critical features of body position and movement. The set of photos in the Critical Features sections that start each skill show an advanced student demonstrating the proper way to do each skill. In addition, details are provided on how the skills are commonly performed by young cross-country skiers at the beginner, intermediate, and advanced levels. Commonly seen errors for youth skiers at these three levels are discussed, and teaching hints are provided to help you teach the skill to young skiers. The photos in the beginner or intermediate sections show how a student of that level might do the skill, including some common errors that students of that level might make. This is to help you visually identify what level students are working at for each skill.

DIAGONAL STRIDE

The diagonal stride is the technique used most commonly when people are cross-country skiing on classic, or diagonal, skis. In this technique, the skier uses a kicking action followed by a weight shift to the gliding ski; after the weight shift, the skier quickly performs a poling action with the arm opposite the kicking leg. The diagonal stride can be done in groomed tracks at a slow to high speed. It can also be done across a wide open area of ungroomed and deep snow, but the movement will be considerably slower. The diagonal stride technique is very versatile, and the movement pattern is similar in nature to walking. These factors make the diagonal stride a popular technique that is easy to learn. See figure 3.1 for the diagonal stride critical features and technique biomechanics.

■ Critical Features

Start with the feet side by side.

Kick back and down with the right foot as the right arm swings forward and the left arm swings backward. Make sure the poles are angled backward.

Plant the right pole even with the left foot so you can push off the pole and glide on the left ski.

Return the right foot next to the left foot as you prepare to kick with the left foot. The left arm swings forward, the right arm swings backward, and the poles are angled backward.

Glide on the right ski. Then plant the left pole even with the right foot for the push-off, and return the left foot to a side-by-side position with the right foot, preparing for a right-leg kick.

Figure 3.1 Advanced-level skier performing the critical features of the diagonal stride.

◼ Beginner Skier

Figure 3.2 Beginner-level diagonal stride.

For beginner skiers, the diagonal stride technique (see figure 3.2) will more closely resemble a shuffling of both feet on the snow and will not have a distinct kick or glide phase. Many new or young skiers do not have the leg strength to dynamically balance well enough to shift their body weight over a gliding ski. Frequently, the young skier will slide the foot forward so that the foot moves in front of the knee. Poles will be used for balance purposes rather than for propulsion. The skier may flick the pole basket out ahead of the hand, and the pole plant may be vertical.

Common Errors

- Skiers use the poles for balance by planting the pole vertically and farther away from the body (see figure 3.2a).
- The foot slides in front of the knee (see figure 3.2a).
- No real kick is made; instead, the skier shuffles and slides the skis forward (see figure 3.2a).
- Body weight is not completely transferred to a gliding ski (see figure 3.2c).
- Skiers move the right arm and right leg forward at the same time.

Teaching Hints

- Watch skiers walk in the gymnasium. Make sure that they are using a contralateral arm and leg pattern while walking (as the right arm swings forward, the left leg should be stepping forward). This is the same pattern that the students will use when skiing; therefore, if they do not perform it correctly when walking, chances are they will not perform the motion correctly when on skis.
- Use a variety of ski games and activities to increase the students' comfort level on skis. Your students' confidence will improve once they learn how to control and steer their skis.
- Have the students spend lots of time using just one ski. Make sure that they frequently switch the foot that the ski is on. New skiers will soon be gliding on one ski without even thinking about it when playing a game or doing scooters.
- Don't use poles at all for the first six beginner lessons. Always have students spend part of every lesson skiing without poles, whether it is for a warm-up, drill, activity, or game.
- Encourage skiers to work on balance and leg strength at home. They can do this by standing on one foot when brushing their teeth or when watching TV.

continued ▶

Diagonal Stride (continued)

Activities and Games That Help Teach the Skill

If you have your skiers wear just one ski, they will be forced to shift their body weight over the gliding ski immediately after the kick. Changing the ski over to the other foot can be done quickly and easily, so students can practice gliding on both legs in a short amount of time. Game play using one ski is also a good way to teach skiers to steer and control their ski—and they often don't even realize they're learning it!

- Scooters—Make sure that skiers work both legs by switching the ski to the other foot.
- Jumping Jack Tag (see page 80)—No poles are used.
- Any of the tag games played with skiers on one ski

■ Intermediate Skier

Figure 3.3   Intermediate-level diagonal stride.

The intermediate skier can perform a kick and can glide on one ski, even if only for a short period of time (see figure 3.3). Intermediate skiers, who are usually a bit older than the typical beginner skier, will have increased leg strength and fairly good balance. Skiers at this level are able to perform the diagonal stride rhythmically; however, you should review the basics with them and encourage them to think about what they are doing. Skiers sometimes hurry to beat their friends or partners, and this can decrease their skill proficiency to the point where they are almost back to the beginner level. To help intermediate skiers improve their diagonal stride, you should use noncompetitive drills, games, and activities that the skiers will not rush through.

Common Errors

- Skiers straddle the tracks and do not commit completely to the gliding ski after the kick.
- Skiers are unable to continuously repeat the kick and glide rhythmically with their arms and legs working contralaterally.
- The pole is planted in front of the foot (see figure 3.3a).
- Skiers hurry because they are trying to beat their friends, and technique falls apart.
- Skiers do not use the poles for propulsion (see figure 3.3b).
- Poles are planted vertically rather than angled backward.

Teaching Hints

- Continue to have the students ski without poles for a part of every lesson. This helps improve balance and confidence.
- In activities with no poles, encourage skiers to swing their arms down the track by swinging their arms out in front of their body as their hands reach down the track.
- Encourage skiers to start with their feet side by side and to figure out which foot they will kick with first. Standing in place, they should slide that ski backward and then figure out which arm should be moved forward and which arm should be moved backward. Skiers should return their feet to the side-by-side position before they actually start the diagonal stride. Do not use poles.
- Tell skiers that if they lose the correct rhythm, they should stop, put their feet side by side, and then start again.
- When adding poles to the practice of the diagonal stride, go through the sequence introduced in Intermediate Lesson 4 (see chapter 4), where skiers start with the poles out of the snow and then slowly lower the poles to the snow. If they lose their diagonal stride rhythm, skiers pull the poles out of the snow and start again.

Activities and Games That Help Teach the Skill

- Slow-Mo Ski—This activity forces skiers to think about what they are doing in the diagonal stride movement. Once skiers get the correct feel and rhythm of the diagonal stride, the Slow-Mo Ski activity will continually challenge them to increase their glide phase. Practice this exercise without poles.
- Scooters—Skiers should work on scooters regularly. This exercise will help to improve skiers' balance and will force them to shift their body weight over the gliding ski. Stress the importance of the arms moving contralaterally, and make sure that skiers work both legs.

■ Advanced Skier

Advanced skiers will be confident in their ability to use the diagonal stride to move rhythmically and quickly from place to place. These skiers have increased leg strength and improved balance, which will improve their performance of the diagonal stride. They have an easier time committing their weight to the gliding ski, so the shift of body weight over the gliding ski should be visible. Advanced skiers will have discovered that using the poles for propulsion really makes a difference in their forward speed and momentum; therefore, they will plant the poles angled backward and in the area across from the foot.

Common Errors

- The skier's foot slips when performing the kick, resulting in a lack of forward propulsion.
- Skiers make a noisy, slapping sound when diagonal striding.
- The kick is executed late.
- Skiers do not fully commit to the gliding ski.
- Skiers "sit" with deeply bent knees.
- The pole plant is still slightly vertical.

Teaching Hints

- The kick should be made when the feet are side by side. If the feet are allowed to slide too far apart before kicking, the foot may slip.
- The kick should be downward, not backward.
- The kick should be done almost simultaneously with the pole plant. The kick will be started just slightly before the pole plant.
- Hips should be kept high and forward. Skiers shouldn't slump. The lean should start at the ankles.

Activities and Games That Help Teach the Skill

Continue to play games with skiers wearing just one ski. Make the playing area larger and make teams smaller so that skiers are forced to move greater distances with increased speed.

- Scooter count—Skiers should strive to reduce the number of scooter pushes made and should attempt to glide as long as they can. They should swing their hands down the track, reaching out in line with the ski.
- Slow-Mo Ski—Practice first without poles and eventually with ski poles. Skiers should be using the correct contralateral arm and leg pattern. They should be able to perform the slow-motion diagonal stride for at least 150 yards (137 m) without stopping.

DIAGONAL STRIDE UPHILL

As the name implies, the diagonal stride uphill technique is the diagonal stride done on an incline rather than on flat terrain. When a classic skier using the diagonal stride approaches a hill, the skier can continue to diagonal stride up the hill as far as possible. As the steepness of the hill increases, the glide phase of the diagonal stride will shorten, and the stride rate will increase. The poling frequency will also increase, and the skier will continue to push off of the poles for added propulsion up the hillside. The steepness of the hill may eventually force the skier to switch to a herringbone technique in order to finish the climb up and over the crest of the hill. The skier should then continue the motion forward by resuming the diagonal stride. Learning how to ski into a hill, transition to the herringbone, and return to the diagonal stride will serve your skiers well as they ski over all types of terrain. See figure 3.4 for the diagonal stride uphill critical features and technique biomechanics.

■ Critical Features

As the hill gets steeper, shorten your stride. The glide phase disappears, and the tempo increases.

Focus the eyes on the hill in front of the skis. With very bent elbows, plant the poles across from the heel or slightly farther back.

Push off the poles to help maintain continuous momentum up the hill.

Figure 3.4   Advanced-level skier performing the critical features of the diagonal stride uphill.

■ Beginner Skier

Figure 3.5   Beginner-level diagonal stride uphill.

When moving up a hill, beginner skiers will use a shuffling and sliding technique (see figure 3.5) that is similar to the technique used when diagonal striding on flat terrain. Make sure that the skiers' first uphill attempts are done on gentle and short hills that they will be able to move up successfully. Nothing is more frustrating for beginner skiers than repeatedly falling when trying to ski up a hill that is too steep for their skill level. Encourage skiers to pick up the pace as they move up the hill and to swing their arms energetically straight ahead up the hill. No-wax skis (which are normally used by beginners) will provide the needed grip to allow the skier to climb the hill. The challenge for the skier will be learning how to kick downward to effectively use that grip.

Common Errors

- The gliding foot slides out in front of the knee (see figure 3.5*b*).
- The pole plant is vertical (see figure 3.5*b*).
- Skiers slide backward.
- Skiers fall.

Teaching Hints

- Don't use poles.
- Encourage skiers to swing their arms vigorously.
- If necessary, have skiers shorten their stride and make the movement more like jogging uphill. This enables some beginner skiers to have more success in making it up the hill.
- Select gentle hills for the skiers' first attempts at diagonal striding uphill.
- Provide plenty of verbal encouragement and words of praise for good effort and when skiers are successful at making it up the hill.

Activities and Games That Help Teach the Skill

- Hill run—Encourage skiers to pick up the pace and jog up the hill without using poles.
- Hilltop retrieve—Make uphill practice fun by setting a small stuffed animal several strides past the top of the hill. Skiers will fetch the stuffed animal and return it to the bottom of the hill. Set multiple sets of parallel tracks up the hill, and allow plenty of space between tracks for skiers to perform a straight downhill run to the bottom.

■ Intermediate Skier

Figure 3.6   Intermediate-level diagonal stride uphill.

Intermediate skiers will be able to readily diagonal stride up gentle and moderate hills (see figure 3.6) using their ski poles. These skiers will still be using the poles for balance purposes some, if not all, of the time; however, skiers at this level will be starting to understand the importance of good poling action for forward propulsion. Some of your skiers will not be in very good aerobic condition, and these skiers may need to stop and catch their breath on moderate hills. Challenge your skiers to diagonal stride continuously up and over the hill, pushing off their poles with each stride.

Common Errors

- The poling action is used for balance purposes (see figure 3.6*a*).
- Stride length is too long.

continued ▶

Basic Cross-Country Skiing Skills   ■   **27**

Diagonal Stride Uphill (continued)

- Stride length is very short (see figure 3.6b).
- Stride rate is too slow.
- Skiers continue to straddle the two tracks and do not commit to a complete shift of body weight to the gliding ski.

Teaching Hints

- You should encourage skiers to push off the poles. The arms should be bent at pole plant, and the follow-through of the arm swing behind the body should be shortened.
- The stride length should shorten. This will probably happen naturally. If it does not, tell skiers to "hurry up the hill."
- The stride rate should increase. Encourage skiers to keep moving up the hill.
- The length of time spent gliding will decrease slightly. The steepness of the hill may cause this to happen without any instruction being necessary.
- You should review the diagonal stride technique and have students practice on the flat. Make sure that the skiers are able to shift their body weight to the gliding ski. Skiers must be able to commit to the gliding ski on the flat before they will be able to fully commit to the gliding ski in the diagonal stride uphill.

Activities and Games That Help Teach the Skill

- Hill run—Encourage skiers to pick up the pace and jog up the hill without using poles.
- Hill run with poles—Skiers should maintain a faster diagonal stride pace all the way up the hill.
- Pole and push—Encourage skiers to shout out "Pole" and "Push" as they perform the diagonal stride uphill, moving up and over the crest of the hill.

■ Advanced Skier

Advanced skiers will have discovered how much fun it is to power up and over the crest of a moderate hill using a strong diagonal stride technique. Skiers at this level will usually have no problem with starting the diagonal stride technique several strides away from the bottom of the hill and transitioning into the uphill technique as the hill steepens. For these skiers, aerobic fitness may be more of a limiting factor than the technique; some skiers may be forced to stop and catch their breath or to slow their pace.

Common Errors

- The pole is planted too far in front of the gliding foot.
- The poling follow-through behind the body is too long.
- The glide completely disappears, and skiers jog or run up the hill.

Teaching Hints

- The entire poling action should be shortened so that the pole plant is made across from the middle of the boot with the arm bent to approximately 90 degrees.
- The follow-through of the arm swing should be shortened.
- Skiers should use a snappy, quick action as they ski up the hill.
- Skiers should be sure to shift weight to the gliding ski, even if the glide is shorter than the glide done on the flat.

Activities and Games That Help Teach the Skill

- Up and over—Skiers start several strides from the hill bottom; they should get into a good diagonal stride rhythm before they are actually climbing the hill. As the hill steepens, skiers transition to a shorter stride; a faster, shorter poling action; and a glide with a weight shift. When skiers are nearing the crest of the hill, encourage them to make it up and over the hilltop. They should then transition back to using the same diagonal stride technique used on the flat.
- Cardio builder—Repeat the previous drill several times with a straight downhill tuck in between climbs.

DOUBLE POLE

For the double-pole motion, the skier has the feet side by side, swings both arms forward at the same time, plants the poles, and pushes off of them. This push results in a powerful surge forward and increases the skier's speed. The double pole is a great technique to use for picking up speed when skiing on flat terrain. It can also be used when at the crest of a hill to gain added momentum over the top of the hill and into the downhill. Children have an easy time learning how to perform the double pole, so this technique can be taught to beginner skiers. Skiers may also use the double pole as a way to take a break from the alternate arm action of the diagonal stride. See figure 3.7 for the double pole critical features and technique biomechanics.

■ Critical Features

Position the feet side by side.

Extend the arms in front of the body with slightly bent elbows and with the poles angled backward.

Bend at the waist, crunching the core, until the back is almost parallel to the ground.

As you complete the push on the poles, weight is on the heels, and the skis shoot forward. Begin to recover by swinging the arms forward in preparation for the next push.

Figure 3.7 Advanced-level skier performing the critical features of the double pole.

continued ▶

Double Pole (continued)

■ Beginner Skier

Figure 3.8   Beginner-level double pole.

Most beginner skiers are able to successfully perform the double-pole technique (see figure 3.8). Because both skis remain side by side throughout the motion, the skier maintains a wide base of support and has increased stability. Fewer skiers will fall when double poling compared to when using the diagonal stride, which requires skiers to dynamically balance on one ski. For these reasons, the double pole is one of the easiest techniques to teach the beginner skiers and one of the easiest for them to learn. Having a group of young skiers who are able to move from one location to another using the double pole will be very helpful for your classes. Beginner skiers have fun with this motion, and they are proud of their ability to use the double pole to move on skis.

Common Errors

- The skier flexes only slightly from the waist (see figure 3.8*a*).
- The feet slide apart instead of remaining side by side (see figure 3.8*b*).
- The knees are straight throughout the motion (see figure 3.8).
- Skiers flick the ski poles out in front of them (see figure 3.8*c*).

Teaching Hints

- Have the skiers practice bowing from the waist so they flex forward to the point where the back is almost parallel to the snow.
- Demonstrate to the skiers what happens when the ski poles are flicked out in front of the body so that the poles are planted far in front of the body and angled forward. When the poles are planted in this manner, it is difficult, if not impossible, to apply any force on the poles that will help move the skier forward. An effective pole plant is done with the poles angled backward and poles planted.
- Mixing another game or activity in with double-pole practice will make sure students' core muscles are not overtaxed.

Activities and Games That Help Teach the Skill

- Dangling arms—Without using poles, skiers stand on their skis with feet side by side. With slightly flexed knees, the skiers bend forward at the waist, allowing their arms to dangle freely from the shoulder joint. Their hands should be hanging directly above their toes.
- Double pole for distance—In Beginner Lesson 7, skiers will be challenged to see how far they can glide after performing five double-pole pushes.
- 10 poles—This time, skiers get to see how far they can go in 10 double-pole pushes.

■ Intermediate Skier

Figure 3.9   Intermediate-level double pole.

Intermediate skiers are able to easily perform the double-pole motion (see figure 3.9), and they are starting to understand when to use it most effectively. Be sure to teach these skiers how they can diagonal stride toward the top of a hill and then, at the crest of the hill, can switch to using a few powerful double poles to jettison themselves over the hilltop. With repeated practice of this move, intermediate skiers will understand how to effectively pick up speed into the downhill. Using the double pole on flat terrain will also help intermediate skiers increase speed and build arm strength. When out skiing with your students, you should mix using the diagonal stride and double-pole action. Point out opportune times for the skiers to switch to the double pole.

Common Errors

- The pole plant is too far forward of the feet or too far behind the feet (see figure 3.9*a*).
- The body does not lean forward from the ankles at the start of the action (see figure 3.9*a*).
- The skier does not use the abdominal muscles to crunch the upper body while poling.
- Skiers are not bending at the waist as much as they think they are.
- The arms are not swung back into pole-planting position (see figure 3.9*d*).

continued ▶

Double Pole (continued)

Teaching Hints

- The pole plant should be slightly in front of the feet, with poles angled backward and elbows bent.
- You can tell skiers to crunch their abdominal muscles as they do when performing a curl.
- Skiers should bend until they are looking at their knees.
- After making the push on the poles, skiers can relax their arms (remember the arm-dangling activity) as they swing their arms forward in the recovery phase, preparing to plant the poles again.

Activities and Games That Help Teach the Skill

- Double pole for distance—Let your skiers see how far they can glide after performing 5 double-pole pushes. Try again with 10 pushes. In chapter 7, you will find assessment forms that can be used to record multiple trials of this activity.
- Stride, double pole, stride—Skiers practice diagonal striding, then transition to the double pole for several pushes, and then transition again to the diagonal stride.

■ Advanced Skiers

Advanced skiers will fly across the snow with powerful double-pole pushes. Increased arm strength, muscular endurance, and knowledge of when to use the double pole will be evident in the advanced skier's technique. Skiers at this level will have a good feel for when they should use the technique over uneven terrain, flat terrain, and as they are moving over the crest of a hill. The tempo of the double pole will be faster for these skiers, and they will have a more aggressive appearance. The arms will swing forward in unison, and the elbows will be slightly bent. In the traditional double pole, the skier will reach out with the entire body angled forward. The skier will bend at the waist so that the back becomes nearly parallel to the ground. The knees will have a slight bend in them. A version of the double pole that is currently in vogue involves using a greater knee bend (causing a "bouncing" appearance) and a faster turnover of the poling action.

Common Errors

- The torso angle and pole angle are vastly different throughout much of the double-pole motion.
- The pole plant is not angled backward as much as it should be.
- The skier's hands and pole grips do not pass below knee level.
- Body weight remains on the toes after the poling action.

Teaching Hints

- The torso angle should closely approximate the pole angle throughout much of the double-pole action.
- The poles should be planted angled backward so that the force transmitted to the poles will result in a reaction that moves the skier forward. A more vertical pole plant wastes energy because force is exerted in a downward motion. Force exerted downward in the poling action is not productive in producing the reaction force that propels the skier forward.
- The elbow joints are extended at pole plant, and the elbows then flex to approximately 90 degrees. The elbows then extend again in the follow-through.
- The skier's body weight should shift toward the heels as the skier is finishing the crunch action. Weighting the heels will help the skis to scoot forward.

Activities and Games That Help Teach the Skill

- Stride, double pole, stride—Skiers practice diagonal striding, then transition to the double pole for several pushes, and then transition again to the diagonal stride.
- Hilltop double pole—Skiers start several strides back from the crest of the hill. They take several diagonal strides to reach the hilltop and then transition to several double-pole pushes before assuming a tuck position for a fast downhill run.
- Downhill double pole—Skiers practice their double pole on a slight downhill. Before the skiers lose all of their momentum in the glide phase of the last pole push, they should transition to the diagonal stride.

HERRINGBONE

Skiers of all ages and abilities love going down hills, any size hill, over and over again. That means the skiers will also have to go *up* that hill; therefore, skiers must learn how to safely and quickly position their skis in a way that enables them to climb a hill, regardless of how gentle or steep the hill is. Beginners should initially be taught how to ski into a hill using the diagonal stride technique. The diagonal stride uphill will enable skiers to move up gentle to moderately steep hills. But when the incline of the hill increases and the climb becomes more challenging, cross-country skiers will need another technique to get them to the top of the hill. Angling the skis outward into a V position, or herringbone, and stepping up the hill will allow the skier to progress up and over the crest of the hill. As the steepness of the hill increases, the skier will need to edge the skis (tilt the ski onto its edge) in order to keep from slipping or sliding backward. Using the poles to push off the hillside will provide additional forward momentum that will help carry the skier to the hilltop. See figure 3.10 for the herringbone critical features and technique biomechanics.

■ Critical Features

With head up and eyes looking at the hilltop, push off the inside edge of the right ski and push off the left pole as you step up the hill with the left ski.

Step up the hill with the right leg as you climb. Weight has shifted to the left ski, which is now planted. Push off the right pole and the deep inside edge of the left ski as you climb the hill, maintaining a wide V pattern with the skis.

Step up the hill with the left leg. The tail of the left ski will clear the right ski as you continue the contralateral arm and leg pattern. Be sure to continue using the strong ski edging that allows for an effective push off the ski and prevents you from slipping backward.

Figure 3.10   Advanced-level skier performing the critical features of the herringbone.

continued ▶

Herringbone (continued)

■ Beginner Skier

Beginner skiers are eager to climb hills (see figure 3.11), even if it is only so they can race down the slope! They love to play on hills, so reminding them of the fun time they will have going down the slope will make the work of climbing up the hill easier. Start herringbone practice on flat terrain without the ski poles before moving to a gentle uphill. Beginners may need to watch several demonstrations of the herringbone and may need numerous practice tries before they are able to herringbone uphill with no problems.

Figure 3.11 Beginner-level herringbone.

Common Errors

- The skier does not use the poles for uphill propulsion (see figure 3.11*a*).
- The skier has trouble stepping up the hill (see figure 3.11*b*).
- Skiers slip backward down the hill.
- One ski is edged, and the other ski slips.
- Skiers step on the tail of the other ski.
- The skier falls.

Teaching Hints

- Start your beginner skiers on the flat and teach them how to duck walk. In the duck walk, the ski tips are wide apart, and the tails are close together in a V position. Allow skiers to walk around so they can experiment with how far apart their skis need to be and how large a forward step they need to take so that the skis do not cross or hit the inside of the skier's leg. Practice without using ski poles.
- Once skiers have mastered the duck walk on the flat, show them how to set the ski down on the inside edges of the skis by rolling their ankles in slightly when duck walking. Continue practicing on flat terrain and encourage skiers to forcefully tromp the ski edge into the snow with each step.
- Make sure that students' first attempts to herringbone up a hill are done on a gentle hill, without using poles. Encourage skiers to duck walk up the hill with the skis set on the inside edge.
- Tell skiers to take a *step up the hill* so that their skis will be farther apart as they step. This will help skiers avoid crossing the tails of the skis.

Activity That Helps Teach the Skill

Ups and downs—Provide many opportunities for skiers to practice the herringbone, making sure that you have a variety of fun activities for them to try on the way down the hill. Teach them how to do a straight run down the slope in a balanced skier's slouch and how to assume a skier tuck position.

■ Intermediate Skier

Figure 3.12 Intermediate-level herringbone.

Intermediate skiers frequently experience similar problems to those that the beginner skiers have when herringboning up a hill (see figure 3.12). These problems often appear when the skier is fatigued or when the hill is of a moderate to steep slope. Intermediate skiers should be using ski poles when herringboning and should be pushing off the poles as they climb. Intermediate skiers will have the strength to move up a moderate hill nonstop, and they will be able to combine the herringbone technique with the diagonal stride. Skiers should be able to start a diagonal stride several strides from the base of the hill and continue the diagonal stride uphill into the hill before feeling the need to transition to the herringbone. Once they have moved up and over the top of the hill, skiers should transition back to a diagonal stride and continue skiing. Depending on their aerobic fitness, intermediate skiers may have to stop and catch their breath once they have taken several herringbone steps uphill.

Common Errors

- Skiers slip backward down the hill.
- One ski is edged, and the other ski (the nonedged ski that is positioned on the ski base) slips.
- The pole plant is upright (see figure 3.12*a*).
- Ski poles are not used for propulsion up the hill (see figure 3.12).
- Skiers stare at their skis.

Teaching Hints

- Before moving to the hill, skiers should review the technique of setting the inside edge of each ski into the snow by practicing the duck walk and V position on the flat. Skis will slip down the hill if the V position is narrow or if the skis are not set on the inside edge of the ski.
- Skiers may have an easier time edging the ski that is on the stronger side of their body; the ski on the weaker side may stay flat on the snow, causing the skier to slip. Have your skiers repeat "Stomp, clomp" or "Edge, edge" as they pick their skis up, take a step up the hill, and firmly set the inside ski edge in the snow.
- The ski poles should be used in the same pattern as for the diagonal stride (and should be angled backward) so that when the step is taken up the hill with the right ski, the skier is pushing off the left pole. To encourage skiers to use their arms and poles properly, have them repeat out loud "Push, step, push, step" as they climb the hill.
- You should remind skiers to look up the hill. This causes skiers to raise their head and moves their center of gravity backward slightly.

continued ▶

Herringbone (continued)

Activities and Games That Help Teach the Skill

- Knee Ski—Skiers will learn how to do the Knee Ski in Intermediate Lesson 7. This is a fun way to move down the hill by kneeling on your skis. Once at the bottom of the hill, skiers will want to practice their herringbone to get to the top of the hill so they can try this activity again.
- Miss Me, Please!—This is another challenging activity from Intermediate Lesson 7. It involves a downhill run in which skiers lift a ski off the snow to avoid hitting the stuffed animal placed in the track. Again, skiers will eagerly practice their herringbone on the way up to the top just so they can ski downhill.
- Slalom course—Use a broad, moderate hill that has space to set up a slalom course and includes enough room off to the side for skiers to herringbone up. If there is plenty of space, make several slalom courses that range from easy (with fewer flags spaced farther apart) to the Olympic slalom course (with more flags set closer together). When going downhill is so much fun, skiers don't mind the practice they get by herringboning up the hill.

◼ Advanced Skier

Advanced skiers will be able to herringbone easily up moderate to steep hills, even in a variety of snow conditions. These skiers have learned how to effectively push off their poles, step up the hill, and consistently edge their skis. Therefore, progress uphill is steady for these skiers. When advanced skiers have problems with the herringbone, those problems are often caused by fatigue or by trying to race up the hill.

Common Errors

- The skier plants a pole between the skis and ends up tripping.
- The poles are not used for propulsion.
- The skier tires half to three-quarters of the way up the hill.

Teaching Hints

- All skiers occasionally make the mistake of planting a pole between the skis rather than outside of the skis. This usually happens when a skier is fatigued. Practice the herringbone when skiers are warmed up but still fairly fresh.
- When practicing, skiers can repeat out loud "Push, step, push, step" or "Push, edge, push, edge" as they perform the herringbone, making sure that they are really pushing off the poles. Once the skiers discover how helpful the pole push is when climbing, they will try to always execute good pushes.
- You should provide an opportunity for skiers to get their heart rate into their training zone during each ski lesson. Most skiers will probably have their heart rate in their zone for the majority of the lesson; however, for the well-conditioned students, you may need to encourage increased repetitions or distance in order to help them reach and maintain the appropriate heart rate.

Activities and Games That Help Teach the Skill

- Hill repeats—On a broad, moderate to steep hill, set up a slalom course that leaves plenty of room off to one side for skiers to herringbone up. Skiers will want to ski the slalom course, and the only way to do that is to climb back up the hill. Getting skiers to complete multiple hill climbs is easy when the skiers are able to ski a fun, challenging slalom course.
- Fast climbs—Skiers race each other while performing the herringbone up a moderate to steep hill. Conduct a challenge ladder so that all skiers will get multiple chances to move up the hill rapidly. Although having students race and hurry in performing a skill is usually not good for technique, this activity is guaranteed to get the heart rates into the training zones. After several weeks of performing fast climbs, skiers will have an easier time moving up hills without stopping to rest.

SNOWPLOW STOP

Although becoming a good cross-country skier requires people to learn a variety of ski skills, the most important thing may be learning how to ski under control at all times. This means that cross-country skiers must learn how to control their speed and must be able to stop on a variety of terrains (hill or flat) and in all types of snow conditions. For skiers to do this, they must learn the snowplow wedge position. Skiers can initially learn the snowplow wedge on the flat. They can then practice it on gentle hills and gradually move to steeper hills. The snowplow wedge is used to control speed in a downhill run, so beginner skiers should practice sliding their skis from a straight (downhill run) position to a gentle snowplow wedge, which will slow their descent. Practice should also include moving the skis into a wider snowplow position in which the skis are edged to provide increased braking power, resulting in a snowplow stop. As skiers become increasingly proficient with the snowplow stop, practice should also include stopping gradually as well as stopping very quickly. The snowplow stop is a technique that beginner skiers can readily learn and must be taught! See figure 3.13 for the snowplow stop critical features and technique biomechanics.

■ Critical Features

From the parallel ski position in a downhill run, slide the skis into a wide V position with ski tips together and tails spread. Keep the knees and ankles flexed, the hands held low and in front of the body, and the ski poles angled backward. This results in a snowplow stop.

Figure 3.13 Advanced-level skier performing the critical features of the snowplow stop.

■ Beginner Skier

The beginner skiers will be excited to learn how to perform snowplow stops (see figure 3.14), because this means that they can now maneuver on hills, safely control their speed, and come to a stop when they want to. Because of the skiers' eagerness to learn how to stop, they are receptive to practicing the technique on the flat before trying it on a gentle hill. Begin by having the skiers practice alternating between the snowplow (pizza slice) position and the straight ski (french fries) position on the flat. Providing many opportunities for beginners to practice the snowplow stop on gentle hills will yield quick results. Snowplow practice should be done without the poles.

Common Errors

- Skiers use a narrow V position (see figure 3.14).
- The shoulders and hands are raised (see figure 3.14).
- The skier flexes forward at the waist as the skis are slid into the V position.
- The skier starts to turn rather than maintain a position headed straight down the hill.
- The skis slide way too far apart; the skier does the splits and ends up sitting down.
- The skis cross.
- The skier doesn't stop.

Figure 3.14 Beginner-level snowplow stop.

continued ▶

Snowplow Stop (continued)

Teaching Hints

- Skiers should bend their knees and sit slightly as they are sliding their skis into position.
- The skier needs to maintain even amounts of pressure on both skis as the skis are slid into the V position. Putting increased pressure on one ski will cause the skier to turn.
- The skier will need to make the leg muscles work to control the distance the skis are moving apart. Practice the snowplow position on the flat so the skiers can see and feel how far apart their legs will need to be.

Activities and Games That Help Teach the Skill

- Pizza, French Fries!—On a gentle slope, skiers start gliding downhill and then respond to the teacher's command of "Pizza!" by sliding their skis into the snowplow stop position. When the teacher calls out "French fries!" the skiers return their skis to the straight ski position and continue gliding downhill.
- Red Light, Green Light—This game gives students repeated opportunities to practice moving from a downhill run to a snowplow stop. Skiers start at the top of the hill and begin their downhill run when the traffic controller calls out "Green light!" When the traffic controller calls out "Red light," skiers must quickly perform a snowplow stop.

■ Intermediate Skier

Intermediate skiers have gained confidence through repeated practice of the snowplow stop. These skiers are able to control their descent using a narrow snowplow position that slows their speed, and they can come to a complete stop using a wider snowplow position (see figure 3.15). Intermediate skiers are ready to work on increasing the amount of edging they use on the inside edge of their skis. With practice, they will discover how quickly they can stop when they apply increased pressure on the inside edges of the skis while in the snowplow position.

Figure 3.15 Intermediate-level snowplow stop.

Common Errors

- Skiers place uneven amounts of pressure on the skis, causing the skiers to start to turn as they are trying to stop.
- The skier does not bend the knees to help absorb the force of stopping.
- Skiers have difficulty coming to a complete stop because the V position of the skis is too narrow or because the skis are not edged.
- Skiers fall forward from the waist when they come to an abrupt stop.

Teaching Hints

- The snowplow V position needs to be wide enough so that the ski tips are angled inward and the ski tails are well separated.
- Skiers must apply sufficient force on the inside edges of the ski to create enough friction to stop their movement.
- Skiers should "sit" into the stop by bending the knees to help absorb shock. The upper body should remain upright.

Activities and Games That Help Teach the Skill

- Cone stop—Set up plastic cones randomly and offset from each other all over a moderate hill. Once skiers start their downhill run, they perform a snowplow stop whenever they come to a cone. After stopping, they move their skis to a parallel position and start to move downhill again.
- Red Light, Green Light—Refer to the directions provided in the previous Beginner Skier section.

- Whistle stop—Have skiers spread out at the top of a moderate hill. Skiers should assume the skier's slouch position and begin a downhill run. When the teacher blows a whistle, the skiers should immediately perform a snowplow stop. When the teacher blows the whistle a second time, skiers should resume their descent. Repeat the whistle blows and fast snowplow stops until all skiers reach the bottom of the hill.

■ Advanced Skier

Advanced skiers are able to easily perform the snowplow stop. They can stop quickly by edging the skis once the skis are in the snowplow position. Because of increased leg strength, these skiers can apply steady pressure to the inner edges of the skis. The advanced skier is able to execute a snowplow stop on moderate to steep hills and under a variety of snow conditions.

Common Errors

- Skiers do not begin to stop until they are too close to the spot where they intended to stop.
- Skiers are not controlling their speed and are moving very fast before they start the snowplow stop.
- On icy, steep, or difficult hills, skiers do not put enough pressure on the inside edges of the skis to come to a complete stop.

Teaching Hints

- Teach your skiers to ski under control at all times. Talk with skiers about their responsibility to ski safely and respectfully.
- Provide a variety of opportunities for skiers to practice their snowplow stops on increasingly steeper hills and under a wide range of conditions.

Activity That Helps Teach the Skill

Speed stops—Start waves of four or five skiers down a moderate hill. When the teacher suddenly calls out "Stop" or blows a whistle, skiers use the snowplow stop to stop as quickly as possible. When the teacher calls out "Go," skiers should begin to ski downhill. Repeat until all skiers are at the bottom of the hill. Emphasize quick snowplow stops with deep edging.

SNOWPLOW TURN

The snowplow turn is a fun technique that gives beginner skiers a boost in confidence and improves their ability to maneuver on hills and around corners with increased safety. Learning how to ski safely down a hill includes controlling speed as well as being able to turn to avoid other skiers or objects. Once skiers have become comfortable with sliding their skis into a snowplow wedge and performing a snowplow stop, they are ready to use the snowplow wedge position to perform snowplow turns. Once the snowplow turn is mastered, skiers will be thrilled with their accomplishment and will be ready to tackle linked snowplow turns and hillier terrain. See figure 3.16 for the snowplow turn critical features and technique biomechanics.

■ Critical Features

Slide the skis into a narrow V position with tips together and tails spread; the skis should be on a slight inside edge. Keep the knees and ankles bent, the weight balanced over both skis, and the hands in front of the body with poles angled backward off the snow. Once in this position, initiate the turn.

Rotate the knee and foot in the direction of the turn, and shift weight to the inside edge of the uphill ski (the ski opposite the turning direction—to turn to the left, weight is put on the right ski). Keep the hands and poles quiet, and glide around the turn.

As you head in the new direction, move from the inside edge to the flat of the uphill ski, and evenly distribute weight over both skis. You are now ready to link a snowplow turn in the other direction.

Figure 3.16 Advanced-level skier performing the critical features of the snowplow turn.

■ Beginner Skier

Figure 3.17 Beginner-level snowplow turn.

Many beginner skiers are able to steer their skis easily in one direction but have problems turning to both the right and the left. Leg strength may play a role in the skiers' ability to control the skis. Beginner skiers will also maintain a wider snowplow position, which helps them with their balance. The ski tips may be a bit farther apart than what you will observe in a more advanced skier.

Common Errors

- The skier is able to turn in one direction but not the other (see figure 3.17).
- The arms are used to steer (see figure 3.17*a*).
- The hands are held unevenly (see figure 3.17*b*).
- The skis cross.
- The skier doesn't turn, but rather comes to a gradual stop.
- The legs are straight with little or no knee bend.

Teaching Hints

- Have students practice moving into the snowplow V position on the flat before moving to a gentle hill. This practice will help beginners get the feel of maneuvering, steering, and controlling the length of the ski they are working with.
- If skiers have problems with the ski tips crossing, tell the skiers to increase the width of their V by moving the ski tails slightly farther apart.
- Have skiers practice on a gentle hill with plenty of space widthwise. Space the skiers out so that each skier has more than adequate space to maneuver.
- Make sure that skiers practice both right- and left-hand turns.
- Encourage skiers to steer with their knees and feet by pointing them in the direction they want to go.
- Instruct skiers to bend at their knees, not at their waist, so that the upper body remains upright.
- Teach skiers to keep their arms and hands quiet, with elbows bent and hands slightly in front of the body.

Activities and Games That Help Teach the Skill

- Copycats—Let skiers watch you perform a snowplow turn and then have them try the move. Let each student have a turn skiing immediately behind the teacher or another skier who can perform snowplow turns so that the student can follow in the leader's path.
- Slalom course—Set up a short slalom course of three or four cones well spaced out on a gentle hill. Have skiers practice linking their snowplow turns in both directions.

■ Intermediate Skier

Figure 3.18 Intermediate-level snowplow turn.

continued ▶

Snowplow Turn (continued)

Intermediate skiers will have improved confidence levels because they are able to link snowplow turns and move down a moderate hill by turning back and forth across the hill (see figure 3.18). Through practice, the intermediate skier will have discovered just how wide the snowplow wedge position needs to be to allow for a successful turn. Skiers at this level have improved balance, and they may have learned that they can maintain a slightly higher downhill speed with a narrower snowplow position.

Common Errors

- The skier uses excessive flex at the waist (see figure 3.18*c*).
- The skier edges the skis too aggressively, resulting in the skier coming to a stop rather than gliding around a turn.
- Skiers are able to complete one turn but not two or more linked turns.
- Skiers are able to complete one or two snowplow turns at a higher speed, but then they are unable to control their speed to make a third turn.

Teaching Hints

- Skiers should spend plenty of practice time experimenting with the amount of edging they need to use in order to allow the skis to turn rather than stop.
- When skiers perform snowplow turns using a narrower V position of the skis, the turn will be done on a flatter ski and will allow the skiers to pick up speed. However, by the time the skiers have completed several linked turns, they may have increased their speed enough to be out of control. Encourage these skiers to use a slightly wider V shape, to increase their knee bend, and to increase the edging on the inside of the ski.
- Skiers will need to practice and experiment with the appropriate width of the snowplow V to determine the position that allows them to effectively turn the skis. Too wide of a V will result in edging that causes the skis to brake. A narrow V will allow the skis to pick up speed, which does help with turning the skis; however, if the speed becomes too great, the skier may feel out of control and either fall or resort to a straight downhill run.

Game That Helps Teach the Skill

Slalom course—Slalom courses are always a fun way to challenge your skiers to perfect their snowplow turns. Make the course more difficult than a beginner's course by adding cones or flags for the skiers to turn around and by moving the cones closer together.

■ Advanced Skier

Advanced skiers are not only able to make snowplow turns, but they can easily link many turns together as they wend their way down a moderate to steep hillside. Skiers at this level can make linked snowplow turns that are close together in a variety of snow conditions. They use the move to control their speed and to ski under control. Some of the advanced skiers may be doing snowplow turns that are starting to resemble a stem Christie.

Common Errors

- Skiers attempt to steer with their shoulders.
- Skiers pick up speed and cannot link more than a couple turns.

Teaching Hints

- The upper body should be kept relatively quiet; skiers should use the lower body to steer during the turn.
- If skiers pick up too much speed as they complete several turns, they need to increase the width of their V position so that they increase the amount of edging they are doing.

Game That Helps Teach the Skill

Super slalom course—Try the slalom course on a steeper hill, and increase the number of flags to ski around. Putting the flags closer together will force the skier to make tighter and quicker linked turns. Let skiers have multiple runs at the course, and record the number of turns they complete on each run.

Additional Basic Skills and Terms

DEAD BUG

Falling down is part of learning how to ski, so you should help your students learn how to fall safely and how to get up quickly. The dead bug (see figure 3.19) is one method that skiers can use to untangle their skis and stand up. In this maneuver, skiers mimic a dead bug lying on its back with four legs in the air. To do this, skiers fall to the side or back with their rear end hitting the ground first. They then roll onto their back and lift the skis overhead, untangling the skis by making them parallel. The skiers then roll to one side, keeping the skis parallel while slowly lowering them to the ground. The skiers are then able to move onto one knee and use their hands to help push themselves into a standing position.

Figure 3.19 Dead bug.

FALL LINE

The *fall line* (see figure 3.20) is a term that Nordic and alpine skiers frequently use when discussing hills. This term will be helpful when you are teaching skiers how to traverse a hill, sideslip, and perform a fast downhill tuck. The fall line is an imaginary line that runs the straightest route down a hill. If you were to stand at the top of the hill and give a ball a gentle push, gravity would move the ball down the hill in the straightest possible path—the fall line. When skiers want to go as fast as they can, they will assume a tight skier's tuck position and align their skis downhill with the fall line. Young skiers enjoy the thrill of a speedy trip down the fall line, and they will want to repeat the experience.

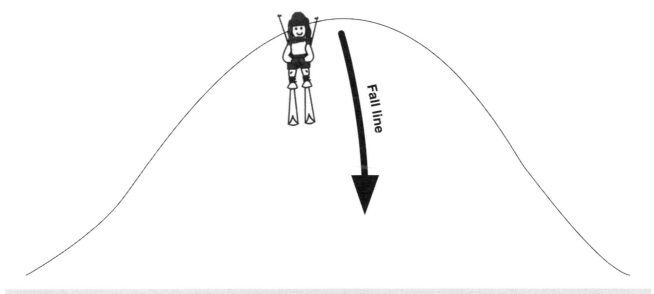

Figure 3.20 The fall line runs the straightest route down the hill.

continued ▶

Additional Basic Skills and Terms (continued)

FRENCH FRIES

When gliding down a hill, skiers position their skis so they are parallel to each other. This is called the french fries position (see figure 3.21). The skis remain flat on the snow, and the skier assumes a skier's slouch (all-purpose sport stance) with slightly bent knees and with the hands held in a relaxed position at the skier's sides. When the skis are in the french fries position, the skier will rapidly pick up speed while descending the hill. Point out to skiers that their bent knees will act as shock absorbers and help them ski over bumps on the hill without falling.

Figure 3.21 French fries position.

KICK DOUBLE POLE

For the kick double pole (see figure 3.22), the skier uses the same initial movement as for the double pole (described earlier), but a kick is added to the movement. This kick helps to quickly propel the skier down the track. As the skier's arms start to swing forward to plant the poles, the skier moves one of his feet backward and performs a kick (similar to when diagonal striding). Skiers will feel a surge of forward momentum when they kick. Getting the timing down for the kick may be challenging for some students. Some skiers may have one foot slide back slightly when they perform the double pole. Encourage these skiers to continue the kick with this foot as they are poling. Skiers can reduce fatigue by alternating kicking legs or by combining the kick double pole with the double pole.

Figure 3.22 Kick double pole.

SIDESLIPPING

Sideslipping is a handy skill that skiers can use when they find themselves on a hill that is too steep for them to ski straight down (see figure 3.23). Sideslipping allows skiers to slide under control down the hill. To perform this technique, skiers stand with their skis perpendicular to the fall line of the hill. They edge the skis by rolling their ankles inward toward the hill; this keeps the skis from sliding. Next, they roll their ankles back to a neutral position so the skis are positioned on the flat ski bottom. At this point, skiers may need to push on the uphill ski pole to start sliding downhill while still keeping the skis perpendicular to the track down the hill—the skiers are sliding down the hill sideways. Skiers control the downward descent by edging the skis (to slow the sideslip) or moving to the flat ski bottom (to increase sideslipping speed).

Figure 3.23 Sideslipping

SIDESTEPPING

Sidestepping is a technique that can be used to move up a steep hill (see figure 3.24). Some students may find it easier to sidestep up the hill rather than use the herringbone. When learning the sidestep, students can begin by practicing indoors and then move outside to practice on flat ground in the snow. Practice should include sidestepping to the right and left. Keeping the skis parallel, the skier lifts the right ski, moves it approximately 6 inches (15.2 cm) to the right, and sets it down. The skier then picks up the left ski and brings it to a parallel position alongside the right ski. This pattern is repeated. Skiers should also practice performing the sidestep to the left. Once skiers are able to easily sidestep in both directions, they are ready to work on sidestepping up a slight to moderate hill. They should begin with skis perpendicular to the fall line. Skiers repeat the same sidestepping pattern used when on the flat, but they keep the skis edged to avoid sideslipping.

Figure 3.24 Sidestepping.

SKI SCOOTERS

For ski scooters (see figure 3.25), skiers remove one ski and use that free foot to push off the ground (kick downward and backward) on the side of the ski track so they can glide on the ski. Skiers should swing their arms in a contralateral pattern, reaching down the track with their hands.

Figure 3.25 Ski scooters.

continued ▶

Additional Basic Skills and Terms (continued)

SKIER SLOUCH

To get into the skier slouch position (see figure 3.26), students should stand tall with muscles clenched and then gradually relax until their body is slumped slightly. The shoulders are rounded, the knees and ankles are bent, and the upper body is relaxed. The hands should hang loosely at the sides and slightly to the front.

Figure 3.26 Skier slouch.

SKIER STRIDE POSITION

The skier stride position (see figure 3.27) mimics the position of the body when a skier is performing the diagonal stride. This position is similar to a lunge. When the right leg is forward, the left leg is back. At the same time, the left arm is forward, and the right arm is back. This position is used when performing scooters, when playing some freeze tag games, and, of course, when diagonal striding!

Figure 3.27 Skier stride position.

SKIER'S TUCK

Skiers assume the skier's tuck (no poles) by bending the knees and moving into a crouch position (see figure 3.28). In this position, skiers should rest their forearms on their thighs, keeping their hands low and touching just in front of the knees. Skiers use the skier's tuck position when making a straight run down the hill; the skis are kept parallel, and the skiers use their knees as shock absorbers while moving over bumps (moguls). Skiers should straighten their body and use a snowplow stop to control their speed at the bottom of their descent.

Figure 3.28 Skier's tuck.

STAR TURN

To perform a star turn, the skier turns in a clockwise circle by keeping the tails of the skis together and lifting and moving the tip of the right ski approximately 6 inches clockwise (see figure 3.29). The skier sets down the right ski and brings the tip of the left ski to a parallel position alongside the right ski. The skier then lifts the right ski tip and repeats the sequence, continuing to alternate right and left skis until the skier has completed a circle.

Figure 3.29 Star turn.

TRAVERSE

When traversing a hill, skiers move at a slight diagonal, almost perpendicular to the fall line of the hill (see figure 3.30). They start at one side of the hill with their skis perpendicular to the fall line. Skiers should edge the skis by rolling their ankles and knees inward to the uphill side of the slope. The skiers can angle their skis slightly downhill while still maintaining a largely perpendicular position. They push on their poles to start moving. Skiers cut across the hill, and when they reach the other side, they make a snowplow turn and head back across the hill in the direction they just came from. The skiers should continue to zigzag back and forth across the hill until they reach the bottom.

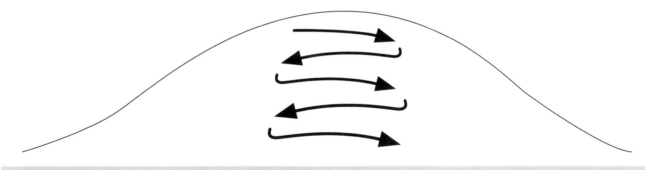

Figure 3.30 Traverse.

CHAPTER 4

Lessons

Skis, boots, poles! Now that you have a better understanding of Nordic skiing and the equipment used by cross-country skiers, it is time to glide into the lessons you will be leading your students through.

The lessons are divided into beginner (first year), intermediate (second year), and advanced (third year) levels. Each level contains 10 lessons that use a skill progression to teach a variety of skills for cross-country skiing. You will be teaching your students everything from how to carry their skis, to falling safely and getting up, performing the diagonal stride, climbing up hills, gliding down, controlling speed, and stopping at the bottom. Your students will gain confidence with snowplow turns, snowplow stops, double poling, step turns, and much more.

Each lesson includes sample dialog in the Set Induction and Closure sections with teaching instructions provided in brackets to help guide you through teaching classic cross-country skiing. Each lesson also includes suggestions for games and activities that will help improve your students' ability to balance on a moving ski, change direction, and control their skis. These games and activities are not only fun, but will also increase your students' heart rates and improve their overall confidence on skis. Be sure to include them in every lesson you teach; the students love them!

Some of the lessons, games, and activities require handouts, station signs, or other lesson aids. You will find these in reproducible form in part III of this book.

Assessment

Assessment plays an important role in your teaching and in your students' learning. When planning a lesson, you need to determine the objectives or goals of the lesson. This is an important step in defining the lesson and providing the lesson with structure and direction. The skill progression, activities, and games included in each ski lesson all contribute to accomplishing the objectives for that lesson. The only way to determine if these objectives have been reached is to do some form of assessment. During each ski lesson, you should use the suggested formative assessments for that lesson because they will provide important feedback regarding student progress. For each lesson, you will be referred to forms and charts that break down each skill, making assessment easier for you.

You should also use peer assessment from time to time. This is a great activity that not only aids you with the assessment process, but also helps students learn the biomechanics of the skill being assessed. The Basic Skills Checklists included for each level can also be used as summative assessment at the end of the ski unit (see chapter 6 for checklists).

Being prepared to conduct assessments outside will make the entire process easier for you and your students. Having plastic clipboards for teacher use, for pairs of students, or at stations will help keep paperwork dry. The clipboard can also be slipped into a plastic bag if it will be put on the snow. Crayons or pencils tied to the clipboard will be easier to hold with mittens on and will not freeze.

FORMATIVE ASSESSMENT

Formative assessment is done during the lesson or the unit. This type of assessment provides information about how the students are progressing toward accomplishing the goals and objectives of the lesson. You can use this information to determine whether any changes need to be made to the lessons in order to ensure that students reach the objectives. Once a formative assessment is completed, you should review the results and determine if you need to reteach, review, or spend additional time practicing the skill that was assessed. You may need to adapt the next lesson to reflect the students' current ability to execute the skill. Formative assessments done by students—in the form of self-assessments or peer assessments—can also be used to engage students fully in the lesson. These student assessments are great motivators. You may also use the results of assessments to place students of similar skills into groups for teaching or grading purposes.

Many of the assessments found in chapter 6 are formative. Depending on the length of your ski unit, you may want to repeat the assessments, either as a way to review a skill or to determine if improvement has occurred. Students will enjoy the opportunity to try an assessment again once they have had a chance to spend more time practicing the skill. Many of the assessment forms have space to record more than one trial, so the assessments can easily be administered several times.

SUMMATIVE ASSESSMENT

Evaluation at the end of a lesson—or more commonly at the conclusion of a unit—is called summative assessment. This type of assessment reflects the progress that students have made over the course of the unit. Typically, this information is used to compare students with each other or against standards set before the unit began. Summative information indicates if the students have achieved the goals or made progress toward accomplishing the goals. This information is often made public and supplied to school administrators to prove teacher accountability for student outcomes. Again, you can use the Basic Skills Checklists in chapter 6 to assess student progress toward achieving competency and proficiency when performing the basic ski skills. All of the assessments in chapter 6 will provide skiers with interesting challenges and provide teachers with important feedback that can be used to increase and measure student learning.

Once an assessment has been completed—regardless of whether the assessment is formative or summative—you need to make adjustments to your instructional process to ensure that students are indeed learning and that lesson objectives are accomplished. After you have taught the lessons once, you can also make adjustments to the assessments. These adjustments should help ensure that the assessments fit your teaching style, the length of the class period, the length of the cross-country ski unit, and the level of your students. You should also reflect on the assessment outcomes after every lesson and plan adjustments to the upcoming lessons as appropriate.

The assessments in chapter 6 provide you with a variety of methods for assessing numerous important skills for cross-country skiing. If desired, you can use just portions of the Basic Skills Checklists; for the intermediate and advanced lessons, you will be directed to use specific parts of the checklists. A class and student version of the checklists are provided so you can record information about one student per sheet or list the entire class on one sheet.

Self-assessments and peer assessments are also useful summative assessments. If students are unfamiliar with assessing themselves or others, you may need to take time to teach students how to do this. Initially, you should limit the number of items being assessed; you can gradually increase this number as the students increase their comfort level with this form of assessment. Testing their own skills is often highly motivating for students, so you should consider letting students administer the assessments more than once to measure progress on skill acquisition. Another good idea is to create individual student files that students can use for storing their assessment results. This will engage students and encourage student responsibility for improving their skill level, and it will also provide you with important documentation of student work.

The assessments in chapter 6 include several unique forms of assessment that require students to analyze a ski skill or use their observation skills while watching another skier. Students are then asked to draw a picture of a specific ski skill, paying particular attention to important critical features of the technique. Many of the assessments ask the students to list important critical features that they would focus on if they were teaching a cross-country ski skill to a friend. These assessments are highly engaging, and they encourage students to use higher-order thinking skills.

Interdisciplinary Ideas

Ideas for interdisciplinary lessons are included in the lesson plans. These ideas can be used as is or can be modified. Interdisciplinary lessons enrich your students' experience in the cross-country ski unit by expanding on the material you are covering in class. Collaborating with the classroom teachers also lets the other teachers see the importance of what you are doing in your class.

■ **Lesson 1**—For the younger students, the math teacher can help develop a lesson on measuring. The lesson could also cover how to convert inches to centimeters (skis are usually measured in centimeters).

■ **Lesson 2**—You can work with the science teacher to design a lesson about how snowflakes are formed. The lesson can cover how different weather conditions cause different types of snowflakes to form and what happens to snowflakes as they fall to earth. Continue this lesson by discussing the destructive metamorphism and constructive metamorphism that snowflakes experience once on the ground.

Younger students can learn more about snowflakes by folding and cutting out paper snowflakes for an art project.

By using the list of Norwegian words related to snow and skiing, you or the language teacher can teach students fun words to describe snow in the Norwegian language.

■ **Lesson 3**—The science teacher or physics teacher will be interested in helping you teach students about the law of action-reaction. You can explain how a ski flattens against the snow when the skier kicks. You can also describe the important role that the fish scale pattern or ski wax plays in gripping the snow, allowing for a ground reaction force that moves the skier forward.

■ **Lesson 4**—In this lesson you can turn to the science or physics teacher to help teach a lesson about the way skis are designed with camber and flex and how a skier glides on the tips and tails of the skis after performing a kick. Learning about the smooth bottom of the ski's tips and tails and how different these areas are from the kick area of the ski will help skiers to better understand how they glide on their skis.

■ **Lesson 5**—Working with the history teacher, you can design a lesson about Snowshoe Thompson. This will provide students with an interesting glimpse into the history of skiing as well as U.S. history. Snowshoe Thompson was born Jon Tostensen on April 30, 1827, in the Telemark region of Norway. This area of Norway is considered the birthplace of skiing and gives us the name for the Telemark ski turn. Jon immigrated to the United States in 1837, and as a young adult, he became a miner who delivered mail over the mountains during the gold rush.

■ **Lesson 6**—The history teacher can help you design a lesson about the Birkebeiners. This will provide a fascinating lesson on the history of skiing. Refer to the book *The Race of the Birkebeiners* (Lunge-Larsen, 2001) for a good synopsis of the interesting story of Baby Hakon and his rescue in 1206. The story involves traveling on skis over the mountainous Norwegian terrain.

■ **Lesson 7**—Connect with the reading or history teacher to have students read the book *Snow Treasure* (McSwigan, 2005). This tale of how children helped move nine million dollars worth of gold bullion on their sleds and skis in 1940 is an interesting story of courage and is full of adventure. Even though the appropriate reading age is 8 to 11, the story is a fascinating one for all ages and one that the middle school students, high school students, and adults would also enjoy.

■ All levels of skiers will enjoy learning about the cross-country ski events that are included in the Winter Olympics. Not only do skiers race long and short distances over difficult terrain, but they also take part in biathlons and Nordic combined events. The classroom or geography teacher could do interesting lessons about these challenging cross-country events.

The reading or history teacher can help with lessons for upper-level students that involve reading *Skis Against the Atom* (Haukelid, 1989). This book is Knut Haukelid's account of his experiences as a Norwegian resistance fighter. The story spans the time that Germany occupied Norway (from 1940 to 1945) and tells the tale of how the Norwegians destroyed the Nazis' "heavy water" facility in Norway. Students can read this story to learn the role that skis played.

Upper-level students can also learn to make their own skis with lessons from the industrial arts teacher. They can make skis from pine boards that are trimmed and shaped; the boards are bent with steam to create camber and an upturned tip. This is a fun project that will yield a usable pair of skis for the student. Teachers can refer to "Cross-Country Skis, the Easy Way" by George Mustoe and "Cross-Country Skis Norwegian Style" by Richard Starr (both appear as chapters in *Fine Woodworking on Bending Wood*).

■ **Lesson 8**—The science or biology teacher can help explore heart rate response to exercise. You can design lessons in which the students learn about the structure of the heart and how it responds to various intensities of exercise. These lessons would complement the heart rate records that the students are keeping based on their ski lessons. The information covered could also extend to the role of muscles in creating movement and how dependent muscles are on having the heart pump blood to them. Upper-level students can learn about $\dot{V}O_2$max, estimate their own $\dot{V}O_2$max level, and learn how they can improve it.

The art teacher can create lessons that incorporate painting pictures of skiers and making paper mache artwork related to skiing. You should make sure that correct ski techniques are depicted in this artwork.

■ **Lesson 9**—The biology teacher can help with lessons on nature for the younger skiers. This age group could take a winter nature tour and look for animal prints, birds, and other wildlife. Older skiers can ski out to the school's nature area or ski at a regional park to study winter wildlife and flora. The math teacher can assist students with a lesson on converting kilometers and miles.

■ **Lesson 10**—The art teacher can help students design and create ski-themed snow sculptures for the entire school to enjoy. You should ensure that correct ski technique is incorporated into the snow sculptures. Including a lesson on orienteering will be fun for all levels of skiers. Orienteering skills can be taught during a fall lesson, and then once there is snow cover, ski orienteering (Ski-O) skills can be taught. The geography teacher will be able to help teach the map-reading skills that students need in order to successfully read a Ski-O map.

■ **Cross-country ski stories**—The books mentioned in the previous lesson ideas are all interesting reading regardless of your age. Each of the books tells a story in which skis played an important role beyond the recreational use that we are most familiar with today.

GET READY TO SKI

This lesson is primarily used to prepare students for the rest of the ski lessons. Students will be doing ski, boot, and pole fittings at stations set up around the gym. If there is time at the end of class, the physical activity portion of the lesson will involve learning or playing games that students will later be playing on snow. Refer to chapter 5 to select a relevant activity. You can distribute copies of the Clothing Guide for Cross-Country Skiing handout. Students should take these home for their parents to read. This information should also be put on the department's website and should be sent in an e-mail to parents a week before the class moves outside.

■ NASPE Content Standard

Standard 1

■ Equipment

Tape, video player, video about cross-country skiing

ASSESSMENTS AND REPRODUCIBLES

- Boot Size Record, page 199
- Pole Size Record, page 224
- Ski Size Record, page 228
- Boot Sizer: Boys and Girls, page 200
- Boot Sizer: Men and Women, page 201
- Pole-sizing directions, page 225
- Ski-sizing directions, page 231
- Get Ready to Ski station signs, pages 207-210
- Clothing Guide for Cross-Country Skiing, page 202

■ Preparation

Suggested site: gymnasium. Set up station signs (see figure 4.1).

- Station 1: Boots—Photocopy several boot sizers (for boys and girls or men and women, depending on the age of your class) and tape them to the floor. Post the boot size record on the wall.
- Station 2: Poles—Photocopy several pole-sizing charts and tape them to the wall along with a copy of the pole size record.
- Station 3: Skis—Photocopy several ski-sizing charts and tape them to the wall along with a copy of the ski size record.

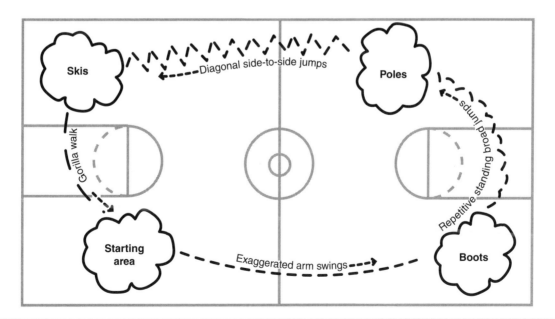

Figure 4.1   Station setup for Get Ready to Ski.

continued ▶

Fitness Development

Students should use the following locomotor skills to move between stations:

1. From the starting area to the boots station, students use an exaggerated arm swing while walking (see figure 4.2). They should walk energetically, swinging the arms forward and backward with an exaggerated arm swing.

2. From the boots station to the poles station, students use repetitive standing broad jumps (see figure 4.3). They should perform standing broad jumps—one right after the other—using good form.

3. From the poles station to the skis station, students use diagonal side-to-side jumps (see figure 4.4). Students start with feet together and perform a standing broad jump angled slightly forward and to the right. They then repeat the jump, angling slightly forward and to the left. Students should continue this pattern until they reach the next station.

4. From the skis station to the starting area, students use the gorilla walk (see figure 4.5). To perform the gorilla walk, students first assume the all-purpose sport stance, or skier's slouch (see figure 3.26, page 46). They lean forward from the ankles until they start to fall forward and have to take a step forward to catch themselves. Students repeat this action until they reach the next station.

Here are some other locomotor movements that could be done between stations:

- Forward bounding leap—Students leap through the air by taking off on the right foot and landing on the left foot. Then they repeat the leaping action, this time taking off with the left foot and landing on the right foot. Students continue this pattern until they reach the next station.

- Hopping—Students take off on the right foot, spring energetically into the air, and land on the right foot. They repeat this action with the left foot. Students continue this pattern until they reach the next station.

Figure 4.2   Exaggerated arm swing while walking.

Figure 4.3   Repetitive standing broad jumps.

Figure 4.4   Diagonal side-to-side jumps.

Figure 4.5   Gorilla walk.

Goal

Having all students find boots, skis, and poles of the correct size for them

Set Induction

[Make a short presentation about cross-country skiing using pictures, video, and other available resources. If possible, have a ski coach, a member of the high school ski team, or a parent who skis come to class to help introduce students to the sport of cross-country skiing. Then introduce the lesson's activity as follows.]

Today we are going to be figuring out the right size skis, boots, and poles for each of you. You can see the equipment at the stations set up around the gym. At each station, you'll find size identification charts that tell you what length skis and poles will work best for you and what size ski boot you will need. You will be working with a partner to help each other determine the right size. At each station, you will also find a chart for recording your size. Make sure you put your name and size on that chart before moving on to the next station. Please leave the equipment at the station when you move on to the next station. When you move from station to station, you will use the movement that the sign at that station tells you to do. You will be using exaggerated arm swings (see figure 4.2), repetitive standing broad jumps (see figure 4.3), diagonal side-to-side jumps (see figure 4.4), and the gorilla walk (see figure 4.5).

Activity

Students move from station to station, fitting equipment and recording sizes on charts.

Boots

Use the Boot Sizer: Boys and Girls chart to help students determine their boot size. Students should record their sizes on the Boot Size Record chart. Most ski boots are sized in European shoe sizes, so you should explain to students that their boot size may be marked with a different number than they are accustomed to. Boots should feel comfortable, like a comfortable walking shoe. The student's toes should not rub on the front, and the student's heels should not slip up and down in the back. Boots that are too large will be awkward to ski in. If boots are too constrictive, the feet will not stay warm. Make sure that students lace their boots up all the way so that no laces are left dangling.

Poles

Use the pole-sizing chart to help students find the right size for their poles. Students should then record the size on the Pole Size Record chart. Remember the following:

- Poles must have adjustable straps.
- Classic poles should reach to under the arm when the skier is standing on the floor (see figure 4.6).
- If poles are too long or too short, the skier will have difficulty mastering the technical skills necessary to become competent in cross-country skiing.

Figure 4.6 Appropriate pole length for classic skiing.

continued ▶

Skis

Use the ski-sizing chart to help students find the right size for their skis. Students should then record the size on the Ski Size Record chart. Remember the following:

- Classic skis should reach to just below the wrist of the skier's outstretched arm (see figure 4.7).
- If the skis are not the correct length, the skier will have difficulty mastering the technical skills necessary to become competent in the sport.

■ Assessment

Check to make sure that each student has recorded a ski boot size (in the European number), ski length, and pole length on the equipment size charts found at each station.

■ Closure

Who can tell me a good way to choose the correct length of ski to use? Let's have everyone stand up and put their right foot forward. Which arm should also be forward? Now put your left foot forward. Which arm should be forward? This is the same motion we will be using when we are outside on our skis. In our next class session, we are going to practice putting our skis on, and we'll learn some skills that we will eventually be doing outside on the snow. Don't forget to use the Clothing Guide for Cross-Country Skiing handout to get ready for when we do move outside. When you come to class next time, you should check the Boot Size Record chart, find your boots, and put them on. Have a great day. I will see you next time!

Figure 4.7 Appropriate ski length for classic skiing.

Interdisciplinary lesson ideas related to math.

MOVING INDOORS

In this lesson, the students will be putting on boots and skis, and they will perform basic movements indoors that will eventually be used outside. This experience provides an opportunity to familiarize students with equipment and movement patterns while in a warmer and less slippery environment. Students will work through a progression of exercises without equipment before moving on to a series of movements completed at stations with equipment. Refer to chapter 7 for station signs (pages 214-220).

■ NASPE Content Standards

Standards 1, 5

■ Equipment

Floor tape, objects for obstacle course (hula hoops, swim noodles, shoe boxes, long jump ropes, cones, limbo poles)

ASSESSMENTS AND REPRODUCIBLES

- Moving Indoors station signs (Choose the "Taking Skis Off and Walking With Skis and Poles" that best works for your classroom.), pages 214-221
- Skier Walk Assessment: Contralateral Arm and Leg Movement, page 187
- On and Off: Putting Skis On and Taking Skis Off Assessment, page 179
- Beginner Basic Skills Checklist, pages 152-153
- Beginner Basic Skills Rubric, pages 154-160
- Norwegian Words Related to Snow and Skiing, page 223

■ Preparation

Suggested site: large carpeted area or gymnasium. Tape markings on the floor and put up station signs (see figure 4.8). Set out boots and skis in two locations in the gymnasium; the equipment should be placed in a row from smallest to biggest. Make sure that the boots and bindings match and that you know how to use them. Make sure that skis are free of any wax on the bottom.

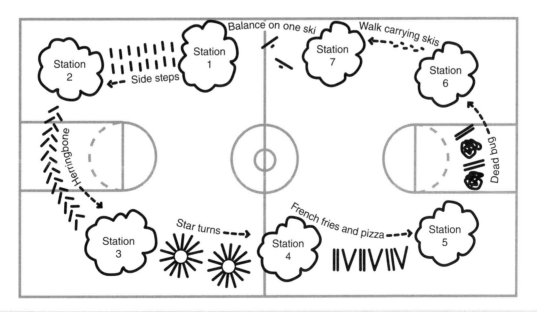

Figure 4.8 Gym floor layout for station signs.

continued ▶

Fitness Development

With skis on, students will be challenged to perform coordinated movements such as the star turn, the herringbone, and the snowplow wedge position. Because this activity is taking place indoors and not on a hill (where the snowplow and snowplow turn are normally done), skiers will put their skis into a snowplow position, or wedge shape, while standing on the floor.

Goals

- Developing control of the body without equipment
- Developing control of the body with equipment

Set Induction

Hello, skiers! Today we are going to be practicing many of the ski skills that will help make you a good skier when we go outside to ski on snow. The first thing we will do today is to find your ski boots and put them on. Once everyone has their ski boots on, we will practice walking and moving our arms and legs just as we will when skiing. We are also going to practice ski skills such as sidestepping, herringboning, star turns, french fries and pizza (snowplow wedge), and everyone's favorite, the dead bug! When everybody has their boots on, I will tell you about the stations I have set up. Let's get started!

Activities

Skier Slouch

Do this activity without skis.

1. Students perform a skier slouch (see figure 3.26, page 46). When students assume this relaxed, all-purpose sport stance, they are moving their body into position to initiate the kick in the diagonal stride technique.
2. Students progress to walking while swinging their arms in a contralateral motion. In a contralateral motion, the right arm swings forward as the left leg steps forward. The left arm swings forward as the right leg steps forward. Students continue walking around the room or gym, down the halls, and through your imaginary indoor "ski trails" while using a relaxed arm swing.

Bindings

Explain and demonstrate how to put boots in bindings (see figure 2.6, *a* and *b,* page 12). Have students practice several times until they are comfortable and capable of putting boots in bindings themselves. If possible, get some additional adults to help with this activity.

What to Do if You Fall

With skis on, students practice falling down and getting up:

1. Students sit in a fallen position.
2. Next, they lie on their back, with legs up and skis parallel (like a dead bug!).
3. Students then roll to one side and put their skis down.
4. Students move to a squatting position, supporting themselves with their hands on the floor.
5. From the squatting position, the students stand up.

This method works well when on flat ground; however, when on a hill, skiers must be certain that their skis are perpendicular to the slope of the hill.

Stations

Students work at and between stations, performing ski skills that they will be using when they begin skiing outside on snow. If the activity is not being done on carpet or a mat, you should discourage sliding on skis. These indoor activities will familiarize students with the activities they will encounter on snow during the next lesson. At each station with tape markings, skiers should follow the tape.

- Station 1: Sidestepping (see page 45). Figure 4.9 shows how the sidestepping pattern would appear when done in snow.
- Station 2: Herringboning (see page 33). Figure 4.10 shows how the herringbone pattern would appear when done in snow.
- Station 3: Star turn (see page 47). Figure 4.11 shows how the star turn pattern would appear when done in snow.
- Station 4: French fries and pizza (snowplow wedge position; see page 37). To perform this pattern, skiers put their skis into a snowplow position, or wedge shape. They will not actually perform a snowplow stop. Figure 4.12 shows how the french fries and pizza pattern would appear when done in snow.
- Station 5: Dead bug (see figure 3.19, page 43).
- Station 6: Students take off their skis and carry them with their poles to the next station. Students should hold one ski and one pole in each hand as they move to the next station. (Teachers may choose to teach the method where both skis are carried in one hand and both poles are carried in the other.)
- Station 7: Students put skis on and balance on one ski.

Repeat the stations if time allows.

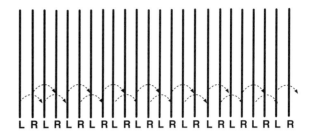

Figure 4.9 Sidestepping pattern.

Figure 4.10 Herringbone pattern.

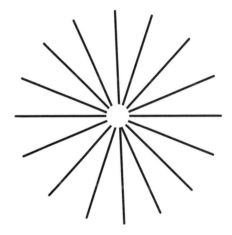

Figure 4.11 Star turn pattern.

Figure 4.12 Pizza and french fries pattern.

continued ▶

■ Games

Before starting these games, demonstrate how to carry skis safely.

1. Please Pass the Skis—Skiers stand in a circle, an arm's length apart from each other. The skiers put on skis, then take them off and pass them to the skier on their right. This continues until all skiers get their own skis back.

2. Follow the Leader—Have the students follow you and repeat your actions. Walk around carrying your skis properly. Stop, put the skis on, take three steps, take them off, carry them farther, and put them back on. Take big steps, tiny steps, and backward steps. Make star turns and then walk in a herringbone pattern. Sidestep to the right and left. Repeat.

3. Dead bug—Students practice falling and getting back up.

4. Obstacle Course—Set up a series of obstacles for skiers to sidestep over, go around (cones), go under (limbo poles), and go through (hula hoops). Use swim noodles with the ends set on shoe boxes to create a "balance beam" for skiers to step over. Skiers can also step over long jump ropes or step onto a stack of mats.

5. Role Playing—Lead skiers through an imaginary activity that requires them to sidestep several times, hop up and down, bend down, and stand on one foot. Take a trip to the jungle and step over a river or step high to avoid a gigantic spider. Or venture across the desert discovering interesting plants to ski around and huge sand dunes to step up. Let students contribute to the story by suggesting plants, animals, or land features that they imagine seeing.

■ Assessment

You can assess students as they perform the exaggerated "skier walk," keeping their arms and legs moving contralaterally. For this evaluation, use the Skier Walk Assessment: Contralateral Arm and Leg Movement form. Have each student demonstrate putting skis on and removing them. Assess the students by filling out the On and Off: Putting Skis On and Taking Skis Off Assessment form. You can also use the Beginner Basic Skills Checklist or the Beginner Basic Skills Rubric to assess some or all of the skills practiced when students are working at the stations.

■ Closure

Who would like to demonstrate how to carry your skis? Who can show us what a herringbone on skis looks like? What are two things to remember when you fall down and act like a dead bug to help you get up? In our next class session, we will be going outside to try the skills you learned today on snow. Next time, when you come into the gym for class, please find ski boots that fit and put them on. Have a great day, and I will see you next time!

Interdisciplinary lesson ideas related to science, language, and art.

OUTDOORS WITHOUT POLES

In this lesson, students will be on skis and will be outside working on skills that they previously practiced inside. Students will gain familiarity with how skis work on snow and how to control their skis. They will practice basic ski skills.

■ NASPE Content Standards

Standards 1, 5

■ Equipment

Cones

ASSESSMENTS AND REPRODUCIBLES

- Beginner Basic Skills Checklist, pages 152-153
- Beginner Basic Skills Rubric, pages 154-160

■ Preparation

Groom a track, or prepare a track by skiing over the same path repeatedly to compact the snow, setting a firmer trail. Flatten snow in a large area for games. Note: Deep snow will make skiing difficult for new skiers, so you should ski in as much track as you can ahead of time. In the game area, flattening the snow will make participation easier for everyone.

■ Fitness Development

Students will improve their aerobic fitness and flexibility.

■ Goal

Developing familiarity with being on skis

■ Set Induction

Hello, skiers! Today we are going outside to use all of the ski skills you worked on during the last class session. Does anyone remember the names of those skills? That's right, sidestepping, herringbone, french fries and pizza (or snowplow wedge shape), star turns, and the dead bug! We will not be using our poles today, so please leave them inside. Let's go outside and put our skis on, and then we are going to practice the skier's slouch before we ski the trail I have made.

[Students locate skis and put boots on. Move the class to an outdoor meeting area.]

■ Activities

1. Students practice assuming the skier slouch (see page 46).
2. Students progress to skiing with arms swinging in a contralateral motion. They should ski around the field or ski on trails using proper arm and leg movements.
3. After a review of the techniques, students practice the following:
   - Sidestepping (see page 45). Figure 4.9 on page 59 shows what the tracks of sidestepping will look like in the snow.
   - Herringbone (see page 33). Figure 4.10 on page 59 shows what the tracks of the herringbone will look like in the snow.
   - Star turns (see page 47). Figure 4.11 on page 59 shows what the tracks of star turns will look like in the snow.
   - French fries and pizza (snowplow wedge position; see page 37). Figure 4.12 on page 59 shows what the french fries and pizza pattern will look like in the snow.
   - Dead bug (see figure 3.19, page 43).

continued ▶

4. **Get to Other End of Short Field**—This activity allows skiers to experiment with the arm and leg actions. Make no corrections; only offer praise and advice for getting up when skiers have fallen. Once everyone has reached the end of the field, form a large circle and lead the group through several stretching activities, such as a skier stride (assume a lunge position, then repeat with the other leg), toe touches with slightly bent knees, overhead triceps stretches, and side bends. Finish with jumping jacks (see figure 4.13).

Figure 4.13 Jumping jacks on skis.

■ Games

Play simple games that allow and encourage skiers to fall down and then get up again. While playing these games, skiers will naturally learn to turn and move on their skis.

- Simon Says—Depending on class size, form one or more circles and appoint a Simon (leader) for each circle. Simon gets to tell the other players what to do by saying, for example, "Simon says make pizza!" The players should follow this order by executing the pizza pattern. If the leader fails to say "Simon says" and just says something such as "Make pizza!" the skiers should not follow orders. Leaders can choose from the ski skills practiced in this class session.

- Red Light, Green Light—Skiers stand in a row at the end of the playing area. One skier is the traffic controller; this skier stands in front of the group with her back to the row of skiers. The traffic controller calls out "Green light!" This gives the other skiers permission to ski as far forward as they can before the traffic controller calls out "Red light!" When she calls out "Red light," the traffic controller turns around quickly and tries to spot skiers who are still moving. Any skiers caught moving must return to the start line.

- Tag—Use cones to mark off a playing area. Designate one or two people to be It, and give them a brightly colored fabric square or a short section of a swim noodle to identify them as It. When a person who is It tags another skier, the person hands off the noodle and is no longer It.

■ Assessment

You can use the Beginner Basic Skills Checklist (found on page 152) throughout the lesson. This checklist helps you look for several critical features for each of the skills that skiers are working on.

■ Closure

Skiers, we had a busy class time today. We practiced many cross-country ski skills, which we will review right now. Spread out a bit and give yourself some personal space. One of the skills we practiced was like a piece of pizza. Let's see if everyone can move their skis into the shape of a piece of pizza. What is another name for the pizza skill? That's right, a snowplow wedge. When I point my arm, I want everyone to sidestep in the direction I am pointing. Ready? Go! [Point in one direction.] Ready? Go! [Change directions.] Let's finish our review by having everyone do a star turn, first going clockwise. Now change directions and go counterclockwise. Skiers, I am impressed with how well everyone followed directions today. Thank you for being good listeners! In our next class session, we will be practicing the diagonal stride technique. Have a great day!

Interdisciplinary lesson ideas related to science and physics.

SHUFFLE, SHUFFLE, GLIDE

Developing Rhythm

By now, students have gotten a taste of what moving on skis is like. They will now begin to develop a classic diagonal stride technique. The diagonal stride is fundamental in cross-country skiing. A good diagonal stride is characterized by rhythm, efficient kicks, strong poling, and gliding on one ski at a time. This lesson helps students further develop the basic strides that they learned in lessons 2 and 3.

■ NASPE Content Standards

Standards 1, 2, 5

■ Equipment

Cones, small stuffed animals, hula hoops, and long ropes with wooden handles and a loop at one end

ASSESSMENTS AND REPRODUCIBLES

- Shuffle, Shuffle, Glide: Weight Shift, page 185
- Scooter Shift Challenge, page 182

■ Preparation

Ski or groom parallel tracks the width of a football field in a space different from the one used for the previous lesson (which has probably been obliterated). If new space is not available, repair the previously used track by skiing over it a couple of times, redefining the parallel tracks. If this can be done the night before, the track will have time to "set up" better.

■ Fitness Development

Students will improve their aerobic fitness.

■ Goals

- To begin feeling comfortable gliding on skis, not just walking on them
- To be able to "shuffle, shuffle, glide" for 50 to 100 yards (46 to 91 m)
- To be able to do ski scooters on each foot

■ Set Induction

Hello, cross-country skiers! Today we are going to be working on the diagonal stride technique. I will demonstrate what this looks like for you right now. Notice that I am not using my poles. We are going to be practicing today without our poles. [Demonstrate the technique by going back and forth in front of the students several times.] Now it's your turn. I am going to put several of you at each set of tracks. To begin, you will get into your skier slouch and walk down the track while swinging your arms straight down the track. Let your skis slide without lifting or stepping. Wait when you get down to the other end. Ready? Go!

continued ▶

■ Activities

Choose one or two of these activities, depending on time.

- Students perform ski scooters (see page 45).
- On a flat area with multiple sets of parallel tracks, students perform the "shuffle, shuffle, glide" movement. They should emphasize the short, forceful kick needed to propel them forward and achieve the glide (see figure 4.14). Instruct the skiers to say "Shuffle, shuffle, glide" out loud as they perform the movement.

Shuffle.................................shuffle...............................glide!

Figure 4.14 Shuffle, shuffle, glide.

■ Games

The following activities and games will further reinforce the goals of this lesson:

- Obstacle Course—Set up a series of obstacles for skiers to sidestep over, ski around, ski under, and ski through. The course should be set up on flat terrain with a slight incline included.

- Skijoring—With a rope and wooden handles, skiers take turns pulling each other to experience the sensation of gliding. Tie a loop at one end of the rope that is large enough to fit loosely around the waist of the pulling skier (see figure 4.15). The pulling skiers should remove their skis, and the skier being pulled should hold the wooden handles. Using a 6-foot (183 cm) length of thick rope knotted at either end will also work.

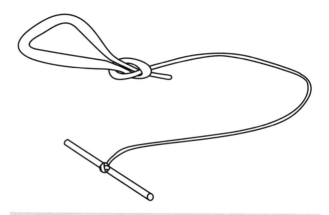

Figure 4.15 Skijoring rope.

- Hot Sand—As skiers move across the flat, they pretend they are barefoot on hot sand and yell "Ouch, ouch!" They lift their knees high, and their skis come off the "hot sand."

- Apple Picking—While gliding down a hill, skiers pick up objects from the snow. When skiers get to the bottom, they drop the object in a bucket. They ski around the bucket before skiing back up the hill.

- Simon Says—You (the teacher) should start as the first Simon and choose skills that the class has worked on; disguise the skills as something silly. Then let the students take turns being Simon.

- Hokey Pokey—Students stand in a circle and perform movements while singing to the tune of the Hokey

Pokey: "You put one foot in, you put one foot out, you put one foot in, and you shake it all about. You do the Hokey Pokey, and you turn yourself around. That's what it's all about!" Players use their feet, arms, head, and whole self. They finish with everyone sliding into the center to circle up for one last rousing round. Be sure that everyone has adequate space.

- Freeze Tag—Within a marked field, skiers use one ski only and no poles. One player is It. This player skis around and tries to catch someone. When the player touches another skier, the caught skier freezes on one foot and must balance until another skier tags him (to unfreeze him). If the group is large enough, have two players be It at a time, or have two games going on simultaneously.

Assessment

Observe skiers as they perform the "shuffle, shuffle, glide." Record your evaluations using the Shuffle, Shuffle, Glide: Weight Shift assessment form. Look for an actual glide in which the skier transfers weight to the gliding ski. You can also observe skiers as they perform scooters. Look for a transfer of weight to the gliding ski, and use the Scooter Shift Challenge form to record your assessment.

Closure

Today, skiers, we worked on your diagonal stride technique. We did this by practicing balancing on one ski. Let's see everyone stand on one ski and pick up one ski off the snow. Now switch legs and balance on the other ski. What words did I ask you to say out loud when we practiced skiing back and forth in the tracks? That's right: "shuffle, shuffle, glide." In our next class session, we will continue to work on our diagonal stride and practice the "shuffle, shuffle, glide." I also have several new games for us to play. Have a great day!

Interdisciplinary lesson ideas related to science and physics.

GLIDE, GLIDE, GLIDE

Perfecting Rhythm

This lesson will be similar to the previous lesson, reinforcing and advancing the kick and glide components of the classic ski technique. In this lesson, better balance is required because skiers will shift weight from ski to ski. No poles are used in this lesson.

NASPE Content Standards

Standards 1, 2, 4, 5

Equipment

Cones, Nerf ball

ASSESSMENTS AND REPRODUCIBLES

- Scooter Countdown, page 181
- Shuffle Countdown, page 184
- Scooter Arms, page 180

Preparation

Prepare multiple sets of parallel tracks on flat terrain.

Fitness Development

Students will improve their aerobic fitness and leg strength.

Goal

Improving kick efficiency and achieving longer glides by working to lower the number of scooter kicks and shuffles needed between glides

Set Induction

Hello, skiers! Today we are going to continue practicing our diagonal stride technique. Last class session, we worked on performing the "shuffle, shuffle, glide" and scooters. We'll now try to improve our ability to balance on one ski while the ski is moving. This is not easy to do, so practicing the "shuffle, shuffle, glide" and scooters will help us improve. We will start with several of you at each set of tracks. Each of you will have a partner. You'll do the "shuffle, shuffle, glide" from here to the cones at the other end. Remember to say the words out loud as you are doing the action. When one partner gets to the first cone, the second person can start. Once both of you get to the other end, one person can start back. Ready? Let's go!

Activity

Create an out-and-back track or loop. Have skiers complete the following in the order given:

1. Ski down and back using a "shuffle, shuffle, glide" movement.
2. Ski down and back again using a "shuffle, shuffle, glide, glide" movement.
3. Ski down and back again using a "shuffle, glide, shuffle, glide" movement.
4. On the way down, count the number of shuffles it takes to reach the end. Try to reduce the number of shuffles used on the return trip.
5. Repeat the trip down and back once again, trying to reduce the number of shuffles even further and extending the length of the glide.

continued ▶

If skiers have decreased the number of shuffles used for this exercise, they have probably increased the efficiency of their kick. The shuffle has naturally evolved into a kick, and the skiers are extending the length of time they are gliding on one ski. The goal is to have skiers shift their body weight to the gliding ski after performing a powerful kick.

Next, work on scooters.

1. Scooters—Students work on scooters. Encourage skiers to get set before starting this action. They need to think about which leg they will kick with and which arm needs to move forward.

2. Students repeat scooters with the other foot. Remind skiers to think about the arm and leg movement before they perform it.

3. Students perform scooters with both skis on. Emphasize correct arm swing. This exercise is good practice for developing an effective glide, and it lets the skier get the feel of how a good kick results in a powerful forward glide. Set up cones 10, 15, and 20 yards (9.1, 13.7, and 18.3 m) apart on multiple sets of parallel tracks. Let skiers repeatedly ski the distances while trying to maintain correct arm and leg action for each distance. Use the Scooter Arms assessment form to assess student progress.

Figure 4.16 Double scooter fun.

■ Games

- Scooter Soccer—Use cones or poles to mark a soccer field and goal. With one ski off, players try to move the ball down the field, passing the ball with their hands, not their feet. They try to score a goal. Players can only move the ball by passing to a teammate and may not ski with the ball or kick the ball. Players score by throwing the ball between the cones or poles that mark the goal. Skiers can change the foot that they have the ski on.

- Sharks and Minnows—This popular tag game is also known by many other names, such as Fish Across the Ocean and Fishes and Whales. The sharks stand in the middle of the playing area. The minnows spread out along the free zone (at one end of the playing area). When the sharks call out "Shark attack!" the minnows ski to the other free zone at the opposite end of the playing area to escape the sharks. If a minnow is tagged, that person becomes a shark and helps the other sharks catch the remaining minnows. Game play continues until all minnows have been tagged by the sharks.

- Double Scooters—Skiers work with a partner. One partner removes the right ski, and the other partner removes the left ski. Skiers hold on to their partner's waist for balance (see figure 4.16). The skiers should

be positioned so that their pushing feet are placed on the outside of the track. Once they reach the end of the track, skiers should remove their skis and put them on the opposite foot. They then repeat the scooter pushes on the way back. Skiers are striving for strong, coordinated pushes.

■ Assessment

Check for a transfer of weight to the gliding ski as skiers perform the "shuffle, glide" exercises. Use the Scooter Countdown or Shuffle Countdown assessment to assess the skiers' ability to decrease the shuffles and increase the gliding distance. Use the Scooter Arms assessment to look for correct arm swing when skiers perform scooters.

■ Closure

Skiers, today I saw that many of you were able to glide for a longer time on one ski. What helped you glide farther on your ski? That's right . . . having good balance helped. So did using the correct arm swing. Let's have everyone stand in the skier stride with the right leg forward and the left leg back in a lunge position. Which arm should be forward? Yes, you are correct; the left arm should be forward. In our next class session, we will work on the herringbone technique, and I will teach you how to walk like a duck! Have a great day!

Interdisciplinary lesson ideas related to history.

INTRODUCTION TO HILLS

Now that the skiers have acquired some skills, adding the ability to go up and down hills will allow them to explore a variety of ski trails and terrain. Hills may scare some skiers, but starting on a gentle slope that everyone can handle will relieve the fear for most. And the fun begins!

■ NASPE Content Standards

Standards 1, 2, 3, 5

■ Equipment

Cones, short swim noodle (or fabric square), assortment of Beanie Babies or other small stuffed animals (or yarn balls), plastic ice cream pails

ASSESSMENTS AND REPRODUCIBLES

- Uphill Herringbone Peer Evaluation, page 192

■ Preparation

Prepare several tracks up a gentle slope that starts from a flat area. Make sure there is enough space for skiers to herringbone up the hill to the top, turn, and ski straight down the hill in tracks.

■ Fitness Development

Students will improve their strength.

■ Goals

- Learning how to herringbone up an easy hill without using poles
- Being able to glide down a slight hill in a balanced position without poles

■ Set Induction

Hi, skiers! Today we will work on what all of you have been waiting for . . . hills! We have worked on herringboning on the flat; now we are going to use the herringbone technique to climb up hills. Let's have everyone stand with their skis in a herringbone position. That's right, stand with your skis in a V shape so your ski tips are apart and the ski tails are together. Give yourself some personal space and let's try duck walking. We are going to diagonal stride over to the hill. Then I'll have you practice starting your duck walk on the flat and moving up a small hill. Once we have learned how to herringbone on a small hill, we will try a bigger hill. We are also going to practice how to go down the hill. Let's go!

■ Activities

1. Skiers herringbone up the hill (see figure 3.11, page 34). They start the herringbone walk on the flat and gradually move up a gentle hill, continuing until they reach a flat area. Skiers should stand upright, looking at the top of the hill. This keeps the body's weight evenly distributed over the middle of the ski, which helps the skier maintain balance and avoid sliding backward. If skiers are slipping, encourage them to edge the skis slightly inward, to use a more upright position, and to take shorter steps. Skiers should step up the hill with their skis. Taking a moderate-sized step up the hill will help keep the skiers from crossing their skis.

2. Next, skiers glide down the hill. From the flat landing area, skiers face downhill in the skier's slouch (see figure 3.26, page 46), standing flat-footed on their skis; the legs are relaxed and bent at the knees and ankles, and the hands are in front of the body. A couple of small steps should get the skiers to the edge of the slope and down the hill for a fun ride!

continued ▶

3. Skiers repeat the uphill climbs and downhill runs as time allows. Skiers can also experiment with these variations on the downhill:

- Ski down on one foot.
- Shift from ski to ski.
- Kneel on the front of the skis, holding the tips.
- Squat on the skis.
- Place their hands in various locations, such as in the air, on their head, or on their hips.
- Stand tall, then get small, and then stand back up tall.

4. Skiers ski a short course that includes slight and moderate uphill sections that challenge the skiers to use the herringbone.

Games

- Beanie Pick-Up—Space out five or six Beanie Babies alongside the downhill ski tracks at intervals on both sides of the track. Place an ice cream pail at the bottom of the ski track. Place a cone at the top of the hill next to the ski track. Skiers pair off into teams of two; the teams start at the hill bottom. On "Go!" the first teammate herringbones to the hilltop, goes around the cone, gets in the ski track, and skis downhill; while going down the hill, the skier picks up the Beanies on one side of the track (see figure 4.17). At the hill bottom, the skier drops the Beanies into the pail, and the next teammate starts to herringbone up the hill. On the way down, this skier picks up the Beanies on the other side of the track. At the bottom, the skier drops the Beanies into the pail. If any Beanies are left on the hill, the first teammate herringbones up, goes around the cone, and starts downhill, collecting Beanies on the way. Teammates take turns until all of the Beanies have been collected.

- Downhill Ta-Da!—Partners work together to put together a routine of various actions (ski on one foot, shift from ski to ski, and other variations that they practiced earlier) that they can perform simultaneously as they ski downhill. Once teams have practiced, they demonstrate their routines to the rest of the class.

- Pizza Tag—Use cones to mark the playing area. In this tag game, skiers can avoid being tagged by making a pizza slice with their skis (snowplow wedge shape) when about to be tagged. Skiers must keep moving within the game area as they attempt to avoid being tagged by the skier who is It. Skiers may stay in one spot for a count of five, but they must run in place when not skiing. To identify the taggers, have them carry a brightly colored fabric square or a short swim noodle. Change taggers frequently. No poles are used. The game can also be played with skiers wearing just one ski; skiers are allowed to pause for five seconds, but they must perform jumping jacks if they are staying in one spot.

Assessment

Use the Uphill Herringbone Peer Evaluation checklist to assess the herringbone skill. This assessment form can also be used for evaluations by the teacher.

Closure

Skiers, we all got a good workout today climbing the hill. Who can tell me one thing that you should do when performing a herringbone up a hill? What will help you climb the hill? Yes, that is correct . . . taking a step up the hill helps you, as does edging your ski by turning your foot in so you are on the inside edge of the ski. Who had fun going down the hill? What was your favorite way to go down the hill? In our next class session, we will be learning how to use the poles. Have a great day!

Figure 4.17 Beanie Pick-Up.

Interdisciplinary lesson ideas related to history.

ADDING POLES TO THE GLIDE

By now, skiers should have overcome their initial fear of skiing without poles. Learning to ski without poles should have given the students a tremendous boost to their confidence and their balance. Today, they will be excited to be able to use their poles; however, they may actually find them to be a hindrance. Once they learn how useful poles can be, they will be quite happy to have them.

■ NASPE Content Standards

Standards 1, 2, 5

■ Equipment

Cones, 6-inch (15.2 cm) lengths of ribbon or small flags, 4- to 6-inch (10.2 to 15.2 cm) balls

ASSESSMENTS AND REPRODUCIBLES

- Diagonal Stride With Poles Rubric, page 161
- Double-Pole Fun Peer Evaluation, page 162

■ Preparation

Prepare parallel tracks set in long, fairly straight lengths.

■ Fitness Development

Students will improve their aerobic fitness and upper-body strength.

■ Goals

- Being able to consecutively double pole at least five times without stopping
- Learning how to use poles when diagonal striding on the flat

■ Set Induction

Hello, skiers! Today we are going to learn how to use ski poles, first for double poling—a powerful and fast way to move—and then for the diagonal stride. First, let's work on holding the pole correctly by putting your entire hand through the pole's strap, from the bottom up. [See figure 4.18a.] Pretend that your hand is a rabbit and that he is popping his head out of his hole as you move your hand up and through the open hole made by your ski pole strap. Now move your hand down slightly and, with the strap between your thumb and index finger, grasp the strap and the pole together. [See figure 4.18b.]

[Demonstrate the rabbit popping out of a hole. In this demonstration, the hand is the rabbit, and the pole strap forms a hole for the hand to move through from the bottom up; hence, the rabbit (hand) pops out of the hole. Using this visual encourages students to move their hand from

Figure 4.18 *(a)* Putting the hand through the bottom of the pole strap; *(b)* grabbing the strap and pole together.

continued ▶

the bottom of the strap upward and then slightly downward before they grasp the pole. This movement puts the strap into the correct position on the hand.]

Let's get started with double poling. I am going to demonstrate double poling back and forth a few times so you can see what it looks like. [Demonstrate the technique.] OK, now it is your turn. Let's put four people at each set of tracks. When the person in front of you gets to the cone, you can go ahead and start your double pole.

■ Activities

1. **Double poling** (see page 30)—Have students practice double poling back and forth on a long, flat track a few times. Remind skiers to compress quickly and deeply for a more powerful glide.

2. **Double pole for distance**—Establish a starting line with cones, flags, or tempera paint at one end of multiple sets of parallel tracks on flat terrain. The goal of this exercise is to have skiers perform a powerful double-pole push and glide as far as they can before making another double-pole push. Ask skiers to double pole five times and mark their ending point with a flag or short piece of colorful ribbon. Skiers return to the starting line and repeat the five double poles, striving to beat their original mark. For the second trial, skiers should move their marker to the new spot where they ended.

3. **10 poles**—Repeat the previous challenge, but this time skiers complete 10 double-pole pushes. They use a flag or ribbon to mark the spot where they stopped gliding.

4. **Diagonal stride**—Students should now realize the powerful benefits that poles can provide. To help students introduce poles into their diagonal stride, have the students try these steps:
   a. Skiers kick and glide down the track (and back) while holding their poles at midshaft; they swing their arms as they have learned to do in previous lessons (see figure 4.19).

Figure 4.19 Holding the poles at midshaft.

b. Next, skiers ski down and back while holding their poles at the top, with their hands in the straps. They just lightly tap the pole tips in the snow as they kick and glide, still emphasizing the kick and long glide as previously learned.

c. Now, skiers hold the poles at the grips, with their hands in the straps. They ski down and back, planting their poles completely in the snow and continuing their kick and glide.

5. **Stride-Stride-Glide Drill**—Using poles, skiers follow this sequence: stride-stride-glide, then stride-stride-glide, gliding now on the opposite leg. Skiers center their body weight over their gliding foot, moving their weight completely over the ski. Using shorter strides with a quicker tempo will help skiers keep their balance. Continue this drill until skiers are able to ride the gliding ski 10 times without losing balance.

6. **Two-Step Glide**—Skiers wear both skis for this drill, and they start the drill on flat terrain. The skiers stride along the snow with an even tempo, and they begin to count their strides. Then they start to glide longer with every third stride, riding the gliding ski as long as possible before taking the next step. Skiers should use this cadence: stride-stride-glide, stride-stride-glide.

If students are having trouble coordinating their swing with their poles, you can have them take a step back and practice the diagonal stride using proper, yet exaggerated, arm swing. They should first practice this without poles, then with poles, repeating as necessary.

■ Games

- **Dribbling Skiers**—Use multiple sets of parallel ski tracks. For each skier, place a small ball in the track in front of one ski tip. The ball should be bigger than a tennis ball so the ski doesn't roll over it. Skiers push the ball down the track while doing the diagonal stride; then they repeat the drill with the other leg. You can create a relay out of this exercise.

- **Pole Jungles**—Set up a maze of poles on flat terrain to match the group's abilities. A random pattern requires skiers to make many changes to negotiate the poles. Skiers will use their diagonal stride to complete a variety of tasks, such as turning around four poles, entering next to a red pole and leaving next to a blue one, doing the course backward, turning twice on one leg, and following another person. To further challenge the skiers, try setting the maze up on a hill.

- **Ski Tour**—The group goes for a ski using the diagonal stride with poles. Encourage skiers to try the double pole when skiing on the flat.

■ Assessment

- Double pole—Use the Double-Pole Fun Peer Evaluation checklist to assess the students' double-pole form. Look for the following: pole plant next to the foot, hands approximately at shoulder level with poles angled backward, torso compressing, back parallel to the ground, poles extended.
- Diagonal stride—Use the Diagonal Stride With Poles Rubric to assess the students' diagonal stride technique. Look for the following: poles held correctly, poles planted even with the foot and angled backward, and contralateral arm and leg movement.

■ Closure

Skiers, do any of you have tired arms today? We certainly gave our arms and core a good workout today, didn't we? Move so you have personal space and let's see everyone go through the double-pole action right where you are standing. Who can tell me one thing you must remember to do when performing the double pole? Yes, that's right; the poles need to be angled backward. What else do you need to do? Correct, you should swing your arms backward after you have pushed on the poles. Next class session, I will have another challenge for you. We are going to be diagonal striding up a hill and practicing using our poles when diagonal striding. See you next time!

Interdisciplinary lesson ideas related to reading.

Beginner

SNOWPLOWS!

It's time to tackle a slightly steeper hill and work on skills related to climbing a hill and controlling speed when descending. Skiers will be using the diagonal stride technique to ski straight up a hill. They will then use a snowplow wedge position to control their speed as they are coming down the hill.

■ NASPE Content Standards

Standards 1, 2, 5

■ Equipment

Cones, bright fabric square or short swim noodle

ASSESSMENTS AND REPRODUCIBLES

- I Can Teach You the Snowplow Stop, page 165
- Snowplow Turn Skills Rubric, page 190

■ Preparation

You need a large flat area with parallel tracks. Start on a flat area and lay tracks up a slightly steeper hill than previously used.

■ Fitness Development

Students will develop strength.

■ Goals

- Learning how to diagonal stride uphill using poles
- Learning how to use a snowplow stop to control speed when gliding down a hill
- Learning how to perform a snowplow turn

continued ▶

Set Induction

Hi, skiers! Today we will be working on improving our diagonal stride, and we will learn how to diagonal stride up a hill. We will also work on controlling our speed when coming down a hill by learning how to do a snowplow stop and snowplow turn. Are you ready? Let's get started by practicing the diagonal stride, using poles, in the tracks on a flat area. We'll ski back and forth three times, first without our poles and then using our poles.

Activities

1. Skiers ski back and forth several times in the large, flat area without using poles. Then the poles are added. Skiers should hold the poles at midshaft and swing them parallel to the ski track while skiing back and forth several times. Next, skiers hold the poles correctly and ski back and forth several times without putting the poles in the snow. On the next trip down the track, skiers should slowly lower the poles in the snow when they feel ready. If they lose the correct rhythm of "kick, glide, pole," skiers should pull the poles out of the snow and start over again with poles out of the snow.

2. Diagonal stride uphill (see chapter 3, page 26)—Skiers should start by practicing the diagonal stride at the base of the hill (on the flat) while facing uphill.

3. Snowplow stop (see figure 3.14, page 37)—Have skiers practice the snowplow stop.

4. Snowplow turn (see figure 3.17, page 40)—Once skiers have experimented with the snowplow stop, they will be eager to try the snowplow turn and may even have done several of these turns when practicing the stop. Conduct this practice on a gentle to moderate hill that is broad enough to provide plenty of space for turning skiers. Skiers should first practice without ski poles.

5. Linked snowplow turns—Once skiers have mastered snowplow turns in both directions, you can challenge the skiers to try connecting two turns to make an S shape as they are gliding downhill. When skiers are nearing the completion of one turn, they should release the ski edges and allow the skis to flatten out before beginning the next turn. Make sure skiers have plenty of space to experiment with linking snowplow turns.

Games

- Skier's Stride Freeze Tag—Mark the playing area with cones. This tag game is an old favorite in which a tagged person "freezes" in place until "unfrozen" by someone. When a skier is tagged, the skier should assume a frozen skier stride position (right arm forward, right leg back; see figure 4.20). To keep the

Figure 4.20 Frozen skier stride.

game lively, have more than one skier be It. Identify the skiers who are It by having them hold a bright ski hat or short swim noodle. Using only one ski will help beginner skiers to move more easily. No poles are used.

- Snowplow Red Light, Green Light—Play Red Light, Green Light on the hill. Skiers must use snowplow stops to stop when the traffic controller calls out "Red light!"

Assessment

Watch each student perform a snowplow stop. Look for bent knees, low hands, and ski poles angled backward. Students should be able to come to a gradual stop when moving down a moderate hill. Use the student assessment form, I Can Teach You the Snowplow Stop, to evaluate students' understanding of this technique. Assess the snowplow turns by using the Snowplow Turn Skills Rubric or the Intermediate Basic Skills Checklist.

Closure

Skiers, we had a good workout today, didn't we? Who can tell me one thing that you need to do when performing the diagonal stride up a hill? That's correct, shortening your stride will help you move up the hill. Did you have fun learning how to do a snowplow stop and snowplow turn? What shape do your skis need to be in to help slow you down when gliding down a hill? Next class session, we will ski some trails, and you will be challenged to use all of the ski skills you have learned. See you next time!

Interdisciplinary lesson ideas related to science and art.

PUTTING IT ALL TOGETHER

Trail Time

By now, most of the basic cross-country ski skills have been introduced; however, this has been done quickly. Some of your skiers will be successful, and some may be struggling. Use this lesson to practice all of the skills covered in the previous lessons. If you have the opportunity to venture out to a local ski trail, this would be an excellent day to do that. Students can test their new skills in the real world of a groomed ski trail, traversing flats and gentle to moderate hills.

Figure 4.21 is a map of a ski trail area. For this lesson, you should take students to a groomed ski area that has marked trails. At such areas, you may see a map (similar to the one in figure 4.21) that shows the route and distance of each of the trails at that area. Figure 4.22 shows the signs that you may also see along the trails; these signs indicate the level of difficulty of the trail. This is important information for you to be aware of because of safety issues. You would match the skill level of your skiers to the difficulty of the available trails. The signs included in figure 4.22 are universal signs that you will find at many groomed ski areas across the United States. Most ski areas use such signs.

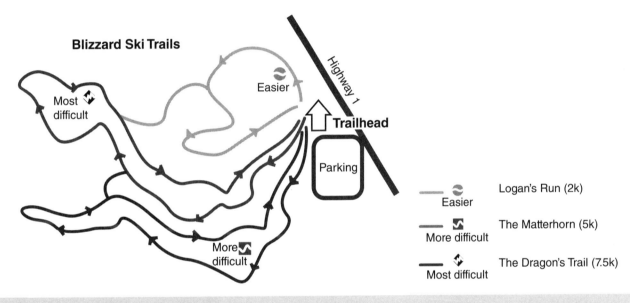

Figure 4.21 Ski trail map.

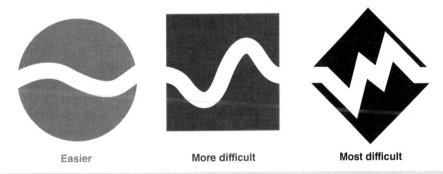

Figure 4.22 Trail difficulty signs.

continued ▶

■ NASPE Content Standards

Standards 1, 2, 4

■ Equipment

Trail map if going to a local ski trail; cones or flags if creating your own trails

ASSESSMENTS AND REPRODUCIBLES

- Beginner Basic Skills Checklist, pages 152-153
- Beginner Basic Skills Rubric, pages 154-160
- Kilometers Skied Record, page 213

■ Preparation

If the trail used for the previous day's activity is not in good shape, create a new loop that can be done easily in 15 minutes, combining flats, gentle hills, and turns.

■ Fitness Development

Students will improve their aerobic fitness and their strength.

■ Goal

To reinforce proper technique for performing the diagonal stride, double poling, and moving uphill and downhill for an assigned time period (based on the length of class)

■ Set Induction

Hello, skiers! Today we will be going for a distance ski over a trail that will require you to use all of the ski skills you have learned. You will be challenged with going up hills and going down hills. Let's get started by taking the first 10 minutes to do a warm-up loop using the diagonal stride and double pole. After we finish our warm-up, I will lead you on the trail I have created for you. Let's go!

■ Activity

Ski!

■ Assessment

The Beginner Basic Skills Checklist and the Beginner Basic Skills Rubric may be used to assess student progress. If you will be checking skills today, plan ahead so you can position yourself in a location where you will be able to observe all students performing the same skill. The Kilometers Skied Record can be used to record time, distance covered (in continuous activity), and 10-second heart rate counts taken before and after skiing the distance.

■ Closure

Skiers, did you have a good time today? What was the most difficult part of what we did today? What was the easiest? Skiing on a trail requires that you use all of the ski skills that we have been working on these past weeks. I hope you enjoyed our ski today. Next class session, we will use our ski skills to do a scavenger hunt. See you then!

Interdisciplinary lesson ideas related to science.

I CAN SKI SCAVENGER HUNT

For this lesson, the students will be using the skills they have learned over the past weeks to move over a variety of terrain in search of items on their scavenger hunt list. During this fun and engaging activity, skiers will use most of the skills they have learned. You will be pleased at how adept your students are with their newly learned skills!

▪ NASPE Content Standards

Standards 1, 2, 3, 5, 6

▪ Equipment

Cardstock, items to stash for the scavenger hunt, beanbags

ASSESSMENTS AND REPRODUCIBLES

- Beginner Basic Skills Checklist, pages 152-153
- Beginner Basic Skills Rubric, pages 154-160

▪ Preparation

On cardstock, print a list of items that are found in the area where you are skiing. These items may include acorns, an oak leaf, a maple leaf, a piece of tree bark, a bird's feather, and a tall weed. If you are having a difficult time compiling a list from things found in nature, you may want to stash things around your ski area for the students to find. Items that can fit into a pocket—such as a beanbag, tennis ball, or foam ball—will be easy to see and carry.

▪ Fitness Development

Students will improve their aerobic fitness.

▪ Goal

To ski around a large area using a variety of skills

▪ Set Induction

Hello, skiers! Today we are going to have a fun time doing a scavenger hunt. While on the hunt, you will be using all of your ski skills. But first, we'll start by warming up with everyone in a large circle, facing inward. You should have your skis on, but we won't use poles. I will lead you through several warm-ups. Let's get started!

▪ Activity Warm-Ups

- Jumping jacks—Yes, you *can* do jumping jacks on skis (see figure 4.13 on page 62).
- Skier stride—Keeping one ski in place, skiers slowly slide their other ski forward into an exaggerated stride, or lunge. They keep the forward knee over the toe of the boot that they slide forward.
- Jungle!—Position the skiers in a large circle, facing inward (with skis on but no poles). Take your class on an imaginary trip through a jungle. Start the trip by marching into the jungle (use an exaggerated arm motion, making sure that the action is contralateral to the legs as they are lifted off the ground). Sidestep over the river, turn using a star turn, and ski several strides off the circle when you see a leopard coming at you. Fall down when you trip over a huge vine, roll to your back to perform a dead bug, and then drop your parallel skis to the side and stand. Sidestep quickly to get away from a monkey that is chasing you. Let the students contribute what they see in the jungle before you return safely back to school.

continued ▶

- Circle Tag—Number off by twos around the circle, and have the twos move back three strides, still keeping the circle shape. The teacher stays in the inner circle and points to either the right or left. Skiers quickly sidestep in the direction indicated and try to tag the skier to their side. After the skiers take two or three sidesteps (see figure 4.23), the teacher should quickly change directions.

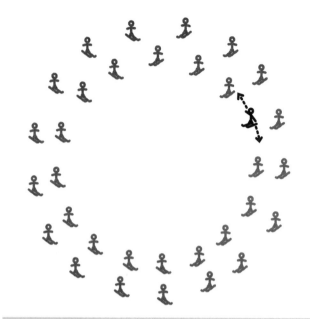

Figure 4.23 Circle Tag.

■ Activity

Scavenger hunt.

■ Game

Circle Relay—Skiers will ski in four sets of tracks around a large oval. Divide the class into relay teams (four skiers on each team), and space team members around the track at the north and south ends and the east and west sides on the track. Start the relay at the north end of the track, skiing clockwise. The starting skier carries a beanbag with her to hand off to her teammate. Skiers complete their leg and then stay where they just finished. Complete several laps around the track to determine a team winner.

■ Assessment

Observe skiers as they are collecting objects during the scavenger hunt. Position yourself so you are able to observe one or two of the skills that you have taught them, such as the herringbone, snowplow stops, the double pole, or the diagonal stride. Use the Beginner Basic Skills Checklist or the Beginner Basic Skills Rubric to record your assessment.

■ Closure

Skiers, what techniques did you use during the scavenger hunt? If you fell down, how did you stand back up? Did anyone remember to use the dead bug to stand back up? How many of you used a snowplow to stop? Show me the position your skis should be in when snowplowing. That's right, a pizza or pie shape. Well skiers, today is the last day we will be cross-country skiing . . . until next year! I hope you enjoyed learning how to ski, and I hope you will go skiing during the rest of this winter.

Interdisciplinary lesson ideas related to art and science.

GET READY TO SKI

For this lesson, you will be indoors getting all of the students sized for their skis, boots, and poles. You will be using the same setup used in Beginner Lesson 1, so the majority of the students should be familiar with how to size their equipment correctly. This makes the process go smoothly. Once everyone has equipment, you can review how to put the skis on and take them off. You can then discuss carrying methods and the basic skills.

■ NASPE Content Standards

Standards 1, 5

■ Equipment

Tape

ASSESSMENTS AND REPRODUCIBLES

- Boot Size Record, page 199
- Pole Size Record, page 224
- Ski Size Record, page 228
- Boot Sizer: Boys and Girls, page 200
- Boot Sizer: Men and Women, page 201
- Pole-sizing directions, page 225
- Ski-sizing directions, page 231
- Get Ready to Ski station signs, pages 207-210 (see Beginner Lesson 1 for full descriptions)
- Beginner Basic Skills Checklist, pages 152-153 (used here to help you review)
- Draw Me! handout, page 163

■ Preparation

Suggested site: gymnasium. Put up station signs on the walls. Put skis, boots, and poles at their respective stations.
- Station 1: Boots—Photocopy several boot-sizing charts and tape them to the floor.
- Station 2: Poles—Photocopy several pole-sizing charts and tape them to the wall.
- Station 3: Skis—Photocopy several ski-sizing charts and tape them to the wall.

■ Fitness Development

Students will use exaggerated locomotor skills to move between stations. Here are some of the movements that may be used:
- Exaggerated arm swing while walking
- Repetitive standing broad jumps
- Hopping
- Diagonal side-to-side jumps
- Forward bounding leaps
- If all else fails, run!

■ Goals

- Fitting all skiers with skis, boots, and poles
- Reviewing with skiers how all of the equipment works
- Having skiers successfully perform all of the basic skills

continued ▶

■ Set Induction

Hello, class! Today we are going to start our cross-country ski unit. Remember the fun we had last year when we went skiing? Who can tell me one thing you remember about cross-country skiing? To get ready to go outside and ski next class session, today we will practice putting on our boots and skis, and we will review how to carry our skis. We will also practice star turns, sidestepping, the herringbone, and the dead bug.

At each station, you will find a chart for recording your size. Be sure to put your name and size on that chart before moving on to the next station. Let's get started! I am going to number you off into groups of three and send each group to a station. One, two . . .

■ Activities

1. Skier slouch (see page 46)—Without skis, students stand tall with their muscles clenched and then gradually relax until they assume the skier slouch position.

2. Skiers progress to walking while swinging their arms in a contralateral motion. They should continue walking around the room or gym, down the halls, and through your imaginary indoor "ski trails" while using a relaxed arm swing.

3. Explain and demonstrate how to put boots in bindings (see figure 2.6*a* and *b,* page 12). Then have the skiers practice several times until they are comfortable and capable of putting boots in bindings themselves. If possible, get some additional adults to help with this activity.

4. With skis on, skiers practice the dead bug (see page 43). This method works well when on flat ground; however, when on a hill, skiers must be certain that their skis are perpendicular to the slope of the hill.

■ Games

- Sharks and Minnows—Refer to Beginner Lesson 5 (page 65) for the rules to this fun game.
- Traffic Lights!—Students (skiers) start spread out behind a line at one end of the gym. One person (the traffic controller) stands in the middle of the gym floor with his back to the group. When the traffic controller calls out "Green light!" skiers take ski strides, swinging their arms contralaterally and moving across the gym as if they are on skis. They continue until the traffic controller calls out "Red light!" Then the skiers freeze in their skier stride position and try to maintain balance. The traffic controller quickly turns around and tries to spot any skiers who are still moving or losing their balance. Caught skiers must return to the starting line and begin their ski across the gym again.

■ Assessment

To help review, you can reuse the Beginner Basic Skills Checklist to assess the students' ability to perform basic skills (star turns, sidestepping, herringbone, dead bug) and to carry skis and poles in an organized manner. Students should be proficient at the basic skills. Use the Draw Me! assessment to make sure that students understand the correct arm and leg position when doing the skier slouch walk and when diagonal striding.

■ Closure

How many of you have longer skis than last year? How about bigger boots? Great! You've grown! Everyone stand up so we can review the arm swing we learned last year. Feet shoulder-width apart, back hunched over a bit—now swing your arms in a relaxed back-and-forth effort. Now, let's keep this up, but do it standing on one leg. [After a few seconds, instruct students to switch legs while the arms continue to swing.] Great! We are going to continue these next time on skis, outside. Next class session, we will review some skills that we learned last year, such as the star turn, sidestepping, and herringbone. When you come to class next time, you will check the Boot Size Record chart, find your boots, and put them on. Have a great day, and I will see you next time!

Interdisciplinary lesson ideas related to math.

BASIC SKILLS ON SNOW

In this lesson, you will be outside leading your skiers through the basic skills that you practiced during the previous indoor lesson. Because the students practiced and became competent performing these skills on snow in the beginner lessons (you can review the skills using the Beginner Basic Skills Checklist, page 152), most students will quickly adapt to being back on snow. If you have time, you can use the Intermediate Basic Skills Rubric or the Intermediate Basic Skills Checklist for either teacher or peer assessment. You may also use the Scooter Skills Partner Checklist. During this lesson, you will be challenging the class to perform scooters: With one ski on, skiers push off with the booted foot and then glide on the ski. Skiers should be able to increase the distance they can glide on one ski compared to what they did in the beginner lessons. Improved balance and increased leg strength will help the skiers perform great scooters. Make sure that all skiers are using contralateral arm and leg motions.

■ NASPE Content Standards

Standards 1, 2, 4, 6

■ Equipment

Music player, Hokey Pokey music, cones

ASSESSMENTS AND REPRODUCIBLES

- Beginner Basic Skills Checklist, pages 152-153
- Intermediate Basic Skills Checklist, pages 166-168
- Intermediate Basic Skills Rubric, pages 169-176
- Scooter Skills Partner Checklist, page 183
- Norwegian Words Related to Snow and Skiing, page 223

■ Preparation

You need a groomed or skied-in ski track on a large flat area.

■ Fitness Development

Students will improve their aerobic fitness and flexibility.

■ Goals

- Reviewing the following basic skills on snow: star turns, sidestepping, dead bug, herringbone on the flat (done on flat ground), scooters right and left, diagonal stride without poles. (See chapter 3 for detailed information on all of these skills.)
- Learning how to perform the 180-degree kick turn.

■ Set Induction

Hi, skiers! Are you ready to go outside today and practice all of your ski skills? I see that everyone has their ski boots on. Today, we will first practice the skills that we practiced inside last class session—star turns, sidestepping, herringboning, and the dead bug. We are also going to practice our scooters with both legs. Do you remember scooters from last year? Who can tell me how you do a scooter? Who can tell me which ski track you will put your ski into before you start the scooter? I also have another turn to teach you today that is lots of fun. You may feel like a pretzel when we are done with this turn! I call it the 180 degree! We have much to cover today, so let's go outside and get started.

continued ▶

Activities

- Star turns (see page 47)—On a flat, groomed area, skiers should find personal space and practice star turns clockwise and counterclockwise.

- Dead bug (see page 43)—Students practice the dead bug. Before starting, make sure that everyone's mittens are tucked in their sleeve cuffs.

- Pole hopping—Lay down a series of poles, ropes, or paint lines on the snow about 12 inches (30.5 cm) apart. Have the skiers take turns sidestepping over them, moving to the right and left.

- Thousand steps—Skiers experiment with many little sidesteps rather than big ones.

- Changing Directions—Groups of skiers sidestep in one direction, and then the leader calls a change in direction. The leader will speed up the changes to help skiers develop quick reflexes. The leader can offer directions with her arms so that skiers have to look up rather than look at their feet.

- Herringbone (see page 35)—On a flat, groomed area, skiers practice duck walking without poles. Next, they practice duck walking with the poles, letting the arms swing as they would when walking with an alternating, contralateral movement. Move to a slight hill and let skiers walk up the hill.

- Ski scooters (see page 45)—With the ski on the left foot, skiers practice the kick and glide, moving back and forth in the tracks several times. Skiers then switch the ski to the right foot and continue practicing their scooters.

- 180-Degree Kick Turn—Have skiers all face the same direction with skis parallel. Keeping their skis flat on the snow, skiers twist their upper body to the right, planting both poles outside the left ski. Here comes the pretzel part: The skiers pick up the right ski and turn the leg outward, turning just the right leg until the ski is pointing in the opposite direction from where it started. Skiers then bring the left leg and left pole around at the same time to face the new direction, ending with skis parallel.

Games

- Turn on Three—Skiers must turn on the count of three no matter what. Try this in pairs (with one skier behind the other counting) or in synchronized groups.

- Banana, Gorilla—While sidestepping, skiers move the first foot and call out "Banana!" Then the other foot (the gorilla) moves up to eat the banana. While moving this second foot, the skiers call out "Gorilla!"

- Jumping Jack Tag—Depending on the size of your group, you can have one, two, or three people be It for this tag game. The skiers who are It can carry a brightly colored hat, fabric square, or swim noodle to help identify them. When a skier is tagged, the skier must run in place while at the same time waving her arms over her head and shouting, "Free me! Free me!" For this skier to be freed, a free skier must face the tagged skier, and together they must complete five jumping jacks. Once this is completed, the skiers can ski off. Change taggers frequently. Play without poles and with skiers wearing just one ski.

Assessment

Teacher assessment can be done using the Intermediate Basic Skills Rubric. Let partners work with each other to go through the Scooter Skills Partner Checklist.

Closure

It looks like all of you had a good workout today. I can tell that you are working hard on your scooters. Who can tell me what happens when you are doing a scooter and you push hard with one foot and shift your weight to the gliding ski? Who can tell me what letter of the alphabet your skis are shaped in when you herringbone? Who can tell me the name of the movement I am doing? [Perform a sidestep.] What is the name of this movement? [Do a star turn.] Next class session, we will be working on the diagonal stride, and we'll see if we can get a good rhythm down without using our poles. Have a great day!

Interdisciplinary lesson ideas related to science, art, or language.

DIAGONAL STRIDING WITH RHYTHM BUT WITHOUT POLES

This lesson will be a challenge for some of your skiers. The goal is for students to use the correct rhythm when diagonal striding without using ski poles. You will need to review the correct contralateral arm and leg position (when the right leg is forward, the left arm is forward) with your skiers before they put on their skis. Putting on skis should be easy for them to do by now. Skiers will be challenged once a glide becomes a part of the total movement. Balancing on a gliding ski without the use of poles is not easy to do. Your skiers will get better at this as they practice scooters on the right and left foot and play games that require balancing on a gliding ski without the use of poles. Students who have difficulty balancing on the gliding ski will also have trouble achieving the correct diagonal stride rhythm. These students may rush the glide or even skip it altogether, making the skill look more like running on skis.

■ NASPE Content Standards

Standards 1, 2

■ Equipment

Skis, boots, cones, white yarn balls (or any soft and squishy ball that will not freeze)

ASSESSMENTS AND REPRODUCIBLES

- Intermediate Basic Skills Checklist (Diagonal Stride No Poles section), page 166
- Intermediate Basic Skills Rubric (Diagonal Stride No Poles section), page 169
- No Poles Kick and Glide for Distance Challenge, page 222

■ Preparation

You need a groomed or skied-in ski track on a large flat area, along with an area of flattened snow for games. Multiple straight tracks set parallel to each other will allow students to have maximum practice time.

■ Fitness Development

Dynamic balance will be emphasized in this lesson.

■ Goals

- To use contralateral limb action while diagonal striding without ski poles
- To kick and glide properly by holding the glide phase with the arms in the appropriate position

■ Set Induction

Good morning, cross-country skiers! During our last two class sessions, we practiced a few of the basic ski skills that you learned last year when we had our cross-country ski unit. Today, we will work hard on perfecting the diagonal stride. Who remembers what the correct arm and leg position looks like for the diagonal stride? If you remember, stand up and show me. That is correct! I see that you have your right arm forward and your left leg forward. If you put your left arm forward, make sure that your right leg is forward. Everyone stand up and copy me. Today we are also going to work on the rhythm of the diagonal stride . . . kick and glide.

We are not going to be using our poles today, so I hope all of you are good balancers. Let's go outside and get started by first practicing scooters.

■ Activities

- Longest Scooter Glide—Students practice performing scooters for several minutes in the track. Halfway through the practice session, the students should switch their ski to the other foot and continue practicing. Once warmed up, students

continued ▶

perform scooters in the track, striving for their longest kick and glide. Mark the distance by setting a cone at the end of their longest glide. Make sure that students repeat the challenge with the other foot.

- Kick and Glide—With both skis on, skiers begin by standing in the tracks and deciding which foot they will kick with first. They then slide that ski backward as the arm on the same side swings forward. As the skiers perform this motion, they should repeat out loud "Kick and glide." Skiers then repeat the action on the other side. Once skiers are confident about the correct arm and leg motion, they can ski back and forth in the parallel set tracks, concentrating on their kick and then shifting weight to the gliding ski. Skiers repeat out loud "Kick and glide" as they perform the actions. Skiers should reach down the track as they swing their arm forward while extending the other arm backward. If skiers lose their rhythm, they should stop, get set again by moving the feet to a side-by-side position, and start with their kick.

- No-pole ski—Take your skiers out for a 2-kilometer (1.2 miles) ski without their poles. Choose a gently rolling terrain for this activity (see figure 4.24).

Figure 4.24 Diagonal stride without poles.

- Hill work—Ski to a moderate hill so students can practice diagonal striding into the hill and transitioning to a herringbone as they continue up and over the crest of the hill. Set up a series of cones and have the skiers practice making snowplow turns around the cones. If the hill is broad enough, after the skiers move over the crest of the hill, they can ski several strides to one side and practice snowplow stops and snowplow turns on the downhill run.

■ Games

- Snowball, Snowball—In this tag game, skiers are safe from being tagged when they are *not* holding a snowball (yarn ball). On flat ground, mark off the playing area by setting a cone at each corner. Depending on the size of your class, select one or two skiers to be It. The skiers who are It will use brightly colored swim noodles to tag skiers (long noodles can be cut into thirds to make the noodle easier to handle). Hand out snowballs to half of the skiers in the class. To avoid being tagged, skiers must underhand toss their snowball to another skier. If a snowball is dropped, both skiers involved must face each other and high step (run in place, lifting their skis high off the ground) for 10 counts. A skier who is holding a snowball and is tagged must also high step in place for 10 counts before skiing off to rejoin game play.

- Longest Glide Team Championship—Divide the class into teams (the number of teams should match the number of parallel tracks you have available). Let students choose which leg they will scooter on first. The first person in line kicks and glides as far as he can. The second person in line starts where the first person ended the glide. Repeat until all team members have had a turn. Use a cone to mark the end distance reached by the team. The team that has the longest cumulative glide wins. Repeat the kick and glide challenge with the opposite leg.

■ Assessment

Formative teacher assessment should be done throughout this lesson. Make sure that skiers use contralateral arm and leg movement and good diagonal stride rhythm when working on the kick and glide and when diagonal striding on the two-kilometer ski. Use the Diagonal Stride No Poles portion of the Intermediate Basic Skills Rubric and Intermediate Basic Skills Checklist to assess skier performance on this skill. Let skiers test themselves by using the self-assessment titled No Poles Kick and Glide for Distance Challenge.

■ Closure

Skiers, it is time for us to head back inside. Raise your hand if you can tell me what we worked on perfecting today. That's correct, having your right arm move forward and your right leg move backward at the same time. What else did we work on? Yes, skiing with a good rhythm that included a kick and a glide. We also practiced using our diagonal stride to ski into the hill before switching to the herringbone. Are you starting to get the feel of when you should switch from the diagonal stride to the herringbone? All of you appear to be doing a great job of skiing under control when doing your snowplows and snowplow turns. Next class session, we will be reviewing the diagonal stride, first without poles and then while using the poles. See you next time!

Interdisciplinary lesson ideas related to science.

DIAGONAL STRIDING WITH RHYTHM AND POLES

In this lesson, you will be continuing the work on the diagonal stride that students began in the previous lesson. In addition, you will be challenging your students to maintain a good diagonal stride rhythm while adding the ski poles to their movement pattern. This is a difficult step for many students, and you will likely see a decrement in their diagonal stride performance when they start to use the ski poles. Many younger skiers are eager to start using poles simply because they see an older sibling using them; these young skiers tend to use the poles for balance, not for propulsion. You should continue to have skiers do plenty of skiing without the poles during each lesson, even after you have incorporated the poles into the students' practice of the diagonal stride.

■ NASPE Content Standards

Standards 1, 2, 4, 6

■ Equipment

Skis, boots, poles, cones

ASSESSMENTS AND REPRODUCIBLES

- Intermediate Basic Skills Checklist (Diagonal Stride With Poles section), page 166
- Intermediate Basic Skills Rubric (Diagonal Stride With Poles section), page 171
- Distance Diagonal Stride With Poles: How Far Can You Go?, page 204

■ Preparation

For this lesson, you will use a groomed or skied-in ski track on a large flat area, an area of flattened snow for games, and a ski trail over gently rolling terrain. Create a start and finish line using paint on the snow, cones, or flags. Set cones in 50-yard (45.7 m) increments down a straightaway for a total distance of 200 yards (182.9 m). Tie crayons to plastic clipboards for each group to use when they are shading in their results.

■ Fitness Development

Students will improve their aerobic fitness and strength.

■ Goal

Having students use poles successfully when performing the diagonal stride

■ Set Induction

Hi, class! For the past few lessons, we have been working on performing the proper rhythm of the diagonal stride without using ski poles. Today we are going to add the poles to our practice of the diagonal stride. Does anyone know what the poles are used for in the diagonal stride?

[Respond to answers.] Yes, the poles are used for balance from time to time, but the main purpose of the poles is for you to push on them. Pushing on the poles will move you forward faster. We are going to start by doing the diagonal stride in the track, holding the poles at the grips but not putting them in the snow.

■ Activities

- Have students ski several laps without poles. Challenge skiers to complete one lap more than they completed in the last class session. Then have the skiers complete one additional lap, this time holding their ski poles in the *middle* of the shaft; they should point the grip parallel to the track as they swing their arms. The skiers' arms should move contralaterally as the skiers kick and glide.

continued ▶

- Skier stride (see chapter 3, page 46)—On a flat, groomed area, have your skiers assume a skier stride position. Skiers should be able to balance on one ski. Have them switch arms and legs several times. While skiers are holding the skier stride position, explain to them that today they will be adding poles to their performance of the diagonal stride. Explain that the poles will be angled backward when stuck into the snow, allowing skiers to push on the poles in a way that helps them to move forward.

- Kick, glide, pole!—Skiers hold their poles by the grips. The skiers will be progressing from holding their poles out of the snow while diagonal striding to pole planting and pushing on the poles to propel themselves forward. Instruct skiers to repeat to themselves "Kick, glide, pole" as they maintain the proper diagonal stride rhythm. When they are ready, they should slowly lower their poles until they are in the snow. If skiers lose the rhythm, they should pull the poles out of the snow, regain the appropriate movement pattern and rhythm, and slowly lower the poles into the snow (see figure 4.25).

- Uphill diagonal—Skiers start their diagonal stride (no poles) approximately 25 feet (7.6 m) from the base of a slight to moderate hill (the hill should not cause skiers to move into a herringbone). Skiers should maintain the diagonal stride rhythm up the hill and over the top, swinging the arms parallel to their skis. Once at the top, skiers can move to one side, assume a downhill tuck position, and glide downhill. They repeat the diagonal stride uphill, working on maintaining good arm swing and rhythm.

- Tour—Take your skiers out for a short ski tour. The skiers should be using poles. Remind them to get their arm swing down and to establish the correct diagonal stride rhythm before lowering the poles into the snow. If skiers lose the rhythm, they should pull the poles out of the snow and begin again. Skiers should start to feel comfortable with the rhythm by the end of your tour.

■ Assessment

Assessment should focus on evaluating whether the skiers are able to maintain the proper diagonal stride rhythm using poles for at least 200 yards when on the flat. You can use the Intermediate Basic Skills Checklist and the Intermediate Basic Skills Rubric to focus on the critical features of the diagonal stride with poles. Videotaping students while they are diagonal striding on the flat is a great way to provide students with immediate feedback. Capture students skiing on the straight section of an oval track. Immediately show the students their video clip and use the Diagonal Stride With Poles checklist to guide your feedback.

■ Closure

Skiers, today we worked on maintaining the diagonal stride rhythm when using poles. All of you are now able to get your arms swinging down the track when not using your poles, and you do a good job with your kick and glide. Who can tell me what you should do if you lose the rhythm when using your poles? That is correct; you should pull your poles out of the snow and begin again, starting with your poles out of the snow and slowly lowering them into the snow. We will continue to work on your "kick, glide, pole" next class session.

Interdisciplinary lesson ideas related to science and physics.

Poles out of the snow

Poles in the snow

Figure 4.25 Poles out of the snow and poles in the snow.

UP AND OVER THE HILL

In this lesson, skiers will be working on performing the diagonal stride into a hill as far as they can before the steepness of the hill forces them to transition to the herringbone. They then use the herringbone to finish moving up and over the crest of the hill, where they transition back to the diagonal stride. If the hill is wide enough, skiers at the top can move to the side, assume an all-purpose sport stance, and glide to the bottom of the hill. When gliding straight downhill, skiers should use their knees as shock absorbers and keep their hands below their waist.

■ NASPE Content Standards

Standards 1, 2, 4, 6

■ Equipment

Skis, boots, poles, cones

ASSESSMENTS AND REPRODUCIBLES

• Uphill Transitions Checklist, pages 193-195

■ Preparation

For this lesson, you need a groomed or skied-in ski track on a large flat area, an area of flattened snow for games, and a moderate hill that is groomed.

■ Fitness Development

Students will improve their strength and aerobic fitness.

■ Goals

• Learning how to diagonal stride uphill and transition into a herringbone (without poles)
• Adding poles to the practice of the herringbone when climbing uphill
• Maintaining balance in a straight downhill run

■ Set Induction

Hello, skiers! Today we are going to work on skiing into a hill using the diagonal stride and then transitioning into the herringbone. [See figure 4.26.] The herringbone looks like a duck walk. [Demonstrate a duck walk.] Your ski tips will be pointed outward, and you will be lifting your ski, taking a step forward up the hill, and setting the ski down on the inside edge of the ski. Edging the ski like that will help keep you from slipping backward. You will also be using your arms and pushing on your ski poles. Once at the top of the hill, you will be using the all-purpose sport stance to glide straight down the hill. [Demonstrate this stance.] When we ski over to the hill, I want you to think about your diagonal stride rhythm—kick, glide, pole! Let's get started!

Figure 4.26 Diagonal stride with transition to herringbone. This skill is accomplished by *(a)* diagonal striding uphill, reducing and eventually eliminating the glide phase and increasing the stride rate, *(b)* transitioning to herringbone with the skis in a V as the hill becomes steeper, and *(c)* increasing the pressure on the inside edge of the ski.

continued ▶

Activities

- Review of the skier stride—Skiers balance on one ski, switching sides of the body. They should then complete several laps without poles before skiing several laps using the ski poles. Watch to make sure that skiers use contralateral arm and leg movements.

- No-Pole Hill—Starting at the bottom of a moderate hill, skiers use good diagonal stride technique to ski into the hill. They transition to the herringbone when the climb becomes too steep to stride up. Skiers using a good arm swing when diagonal striding will have greater success as they move into the hill. Once they transition to a herringbone by creating a V with their skis, the skiers should focus on stepping up the hill and using the inside edge of their skis to help keep them from sliding backward. Skiers should continue to use the herringbone as they move over the top of the hill and should then transition back to the diagonal stride. If space is available on the hill, skiers can use the all-purpose sport stance to glide in a straight downhill run to the bottom of the hill. They should then practice the climb up again.

- Eeek!—In a straight run downhill (with no poles), skiers lift one ski barely off the snow, gliding on the other ski for a short distance (see figure 4.27). They repeat this by lifting the other ski off the snow, balancing on the gliding ski. Skiers should continue switching from leg to leg, trying to increase the distance spent gliding on one ski.

- Speed Skier—Skiers practice moving into a skier's tuck at the start of their straight downhill run. They should bend their knees deeply and put their forearms on their thighs, keeping their hands close together just in front of their knees.

- Herringbone with poles—Skiers diagonal stride into the hill using poles, and they transition to the herringbone when necessary. The poles should alternately be pushed into the snow outside of the angled ski. Remind skiers to edge their skis as they step forward up the hill. As the hill becomes steeper, skiers will have to increase the width of their duck walk and continue to push on the poles as they make their way up the hill. Encourage skiers to stand up fairly straight as they perform the herringbone. Bending forward at the waist will make slipping backward more likely; therefore, skiers should focus their gaze toward the hilltop to make the herringbone more effective.

- Ski Tour—Finish this session by touring over a hilly course. Choose a course that will require skiers to diagonal stride into the hills and transition to a herringbone to finish the climb up and over the top of the hill. Skiers should then transition back to the diagonal stride. They should try to make the transition (from the diagonal stride to the herringbone and back to the diagonal stride) a continuous, smooth movement. Touring over hilly terrain will give skiers plenty of practice with their newly learned skills.

■ Assessment

Assessment should include watching for a smooth transition from the diagonal stride uphill to the herringbone. Have the skiers start several strides away from the base of the hill. Use the Uphill Transitions Checklist to critique the diagonal stride into the hill, the transition to a herringbone, and the transition back to the diagonal stride at the top of the hill.

■ Closure

Class, today you did a great job of mastering the techniques for moving up hills! By the end of our tour, everyone was able to move continually into and up the hills by diagonal striding into the hill as far as possible and then transitioning to the herringbone. In our next class session, we will continue to work on using your poles to help push you up the hill.

Figure 4.27 Lifting one ski off the snow in a downhill run.

Interdisciplinary lesson ideas related to history.

PERFECTING DIAGONAL STRIDING UPHILL AND THE TRANSITION TO THE HERRINGBONE

In this lesson, skiers will continue the work done in the last lesson. They will again be working on performing the diagonal stride as far as they can into a hill before transitioning to the herringbone to finish the climb to the top of the hill. When the skiers reach the crest of the hill, they will be transitioning back to the diagonal stride and continuing on their way down the track. Skiers will be challenged to perform good kicks so that they continue to experience a grip, or purchase, as they move into the hill's slope. As the skiers move into the herringbone, you should watch for correct arm and leg positioning. Instruct skiers to use their arms to push off the hill, a move that will provide propulsion up the hill. When skiers have mastered the transitioning skills, you can challenge them to increase the speed with which they move into and up the hill. In this lesson, you will also review ski and trail etiquette and provide skiers with opportunities to practice good etiquette.

■ NASPE Content Standards

Standards 1, 2, 4, 6

■ Equipment

Skis, boots, poles, cones, a soft soccer ball, flags, and etiquette signs

ASSESSMENTS AND REPRODUCIBLES

- Intermediate Basic Skills Checklist (Herringbone section), page 167
- Intermediate Basic Skills Rubric (Herringbone section), page 173
- Mind Your Manners Quiz, page 178

■ Preparation

For this lesson, you need a groomed or skied-in ski track on a large flat area. You also need an area of flattened snow for games.

■ Fitness Development

Students will improve their strength and aerobic fitness.

■ Goal

Perfecting the diagonal stride uphill and the transition to the herringbone

■ Set Induction

Last class session, we worked on using the diagonal stride to ski as far up the hill as we could before transitioning to the herringbone. Today we will review skiing into the hill and moving into the herringbone to climb up and over the top of the hill before transitioning back to the diagonal stride. I will be encouraging you to step up the hill when doing the herringbone and to really use your arms and poles to help push yourself up the hill. Before we start on the hill work, we are going to warm up with a short tour over a trail I made for you. I have put up several signs along the trail that will remind you of good ski etiquette. Let's go!

continued ▶

Activities

1. Take your skiers on a short tour over varied terrain that will warm them up and allow them to use their ski skills. Be sure to discuss the ski trail etiquette that you expect all skiers to follow (see figure 4.28). Eager skiers will want to ski close to, if not on top of, the skis in front of them, so make sure that you space the skiers out as you begin the tour. Using several sets of parallel tracks will allow skiers to be spaced out while still skiing side by side with friends.

2. Up, Up, and Away!—On an easy to moderate hill, skiers diagonal stride at a slightly faster pace than previously done. The stride will shorten while the stride rate increases. Poling will be quicker, but skiers should still try to push off their poles. Encourage skiers to diagonal stride up and over the top of the hill and to continue with a slightly slower diagonal stride (with an increased glide) once they are over the crest of the hill.

3. Ski and climb—Move to a steeper hill that will force skiers to transition from the diagonal stride to the herringbone in order to keep from slipping backward. Skiers will be able to feel when they need to make the transition from the stride to the herringbone. Skiers should try to keep the movement fluid and keep moving up and over the hill; they need to transition smoothly from the diagonal stride to the herringbone and back to the diagonal stride as they move over the crest of the hill. Skiers should be using their arms contralaterally and pushing off their poles.

4. Half a bone—On a moderate hill, skiers try to keep one ski moving straight ahead up the hill while performing the herringbone with the other ski. Skiers should edge with the herringbone ski to get a grip in the snow that will keep them from slipping backward.

5. Back and forth—Your stronger skiers will have fun trying a gliding herringbone in which they slide their skis up the hill in a V position. Once the skiers get the feel for swinging the hips back and forth as the skis slide forward, they will be zipping to the hilltop with ease.

6. Relay Climb and Glide—Set out three or four cones on the hill for each team; skiers will snowplow turn around these cones. Divide the class into teams of four skiers. Two skiers start at the hill bottom; two skiers start at the top of the hill. The first skier for each team has a stuffed animal to hand off to a teammate. On "Go!" skiers at the bottom of the hill will herringbone up to the top of the hill and hand off the small stuffed animal (the skiers may do any type of herringbone, including a gliding or half herringbone). The skier at the top will ski down, maneuvering through the cones using snowplow turns. The relay continues until all skiers are back to their starting positions.

Assessment

Use the Intermediate Basic Skills Rubric and Intermediate Basic Skills Checklist to assess the skiers' performance of the herringbone. Watch to see if the skiers can move up the hill without stopping or slipping backward. Skiers should be pushing off the poles and edging. Test your skiers on what they remember about etiquette using the Mind Your Manners Quiz.

Closure

Skiers, your hill climbing was much improved today. Who can tell me the names of the two techniques we used to move up the hill? That is correct! We used both the diagonal stride and the herringbone. How did we change the diagonal stride when climbing uphill compared to when we are skiing on the flat? Yes, we shortened the length of our stride and moved our legs more quickly. Next class session, we will have fun working on our downhill ski techniques. See you next time!

Ski in the direction for which the trail is designed.

Be courteous to all other skiers.

If you need to walk on the trail, walk on the side, not in the middle.

Figure 4.28 Ski trail etiquette.

Interdisciplinary lesson ideas related to history.

DOWNHILL FUN!

Your skiers will have a great time working on skiing downhill. All skiers love hills, from the smallest bump to the largest hill! Have fun with this lesson and teach your skiers a variety of ways to move downhill, including kneeling on their skis, sitting on the tails, and assuming a skier's tuck. Emphasize to your skiers the importance of skiing under control when skiing downhill. All of your skiers should be able to perform a snowplow turn and a snowplow stop as a means of controlling speed.

■ NASPE Content Standards

Standards 1, 2, 4, 6

■ Equipment

Skis, boots, poles, cones, soft objects for an obstacle course (such as stuffed animals, hats, and mittens), a small rubber ball

ASSESSMENTS AND REPRODUCIBLES

- Snowplow Turns Draw, page 236
- Intermediate Basic Skills Rubric (Snowplow Turn section), page 176
- Intermediate Basic Skills Checklist (Snowplow Turn section), page 168

■ Preparation

For this lesson, you need an area of flattened snow on a broad, moderate hill. Set several parallel tracks on the downhill.

■ Fitness Development

Students will improve their balance.

■ Goal

Gaining confidence when moving downhill on increasingly steeper terrain

■ Set Induction

Hello, skiers! You are in for an exciting day today! We are going to ski over to the hill and work on gliding down the hill while in your all-purpose sport stance. We will also experiment with several other ways to go downhill. In addition, we will practice snowplow turns and snowplow stops so you will be able to control your speed on the hill. [See figures 3.13 on page 37 and 3.16 on page 40.] Our hill is wide enough so that four of you will be able to ski downhill at the same time. We will be practicing the diagonal stride into the hill and transitioning to the herringbone to climb up the hill. I have created climbing lanes with the cones, so please move over into the climbing lane to ski back up to the top. Please watch where you are going and stay within the lane that I have marked off with cones for your group. Let's go!

■ Activities

- Have skiers warm up by skiing several laps using good diagonal stride technique. Then play Pie Tag. This is a fast-moving tag game that requires skiers to move their skis into a pie-shaped wedge while calling out a name of a type of pie (cherry, blueberry, apple) to avoid being tagged by the person who is It. Skiers must ski off once they have made a pie shape to avoid being tagged. Change taggers frequently. Skiers will be using that same wedge shape once you move to the downhill when they are performing a snowplow stop, a snowplow turn, or a wedge position to control speed (see figure 3.13, page 37).
- Racer's tuck (this is another fun name you can use to refer to the skier's tuck after skiers have grown accustomed to performing the skill; see figure 3.28, page 46)—Skiers assume the racer's tuck (no poles) just as they would the skier's tuck. Skiers should straighten and use a snowplow stop to control their speed at the bottom of their descent.

continued ▶

- Traversing the hill (see page 47)—Traversing a hill is an important safety skill that skiers need to learn.
- Knee Ski—Although this is a fun activity that encourages play on skis and builds confidence on skis, students will also learn a safety maneuver. This activity teaches students that if they end up on a hill that is too difficult for their ability, they can place their knees on their skis in front of the bindings, grab hold of the ski tips, and slide down the hill (see figure 4.29). Once students have mastered this skill, you can let them race each other downhill. *Note:* Allow plenty of space between racers. This will help avoid crashes because some skiers may turn slightly on their way down the hill.

Figure 4.29 Knee Ski fun!

■ Games

- Pizza, French Fries!—Skiers start a straight downhill run with skis parallel. When you call out "Pizza!" the skiers should quickly move their skis into a snowplow wedge, slowing their speed (see figure 4.30). When you call out "French fries!" skiers slide their skis back to a parallel position, continuing their downhill run. You should continue to alternate calling out "Pizza!" and "French fries!" until all skiers have made it to the bottom of the hill.
- Slalom Run—Create slalom courses on the hill using cones or ski poles by spacing the cones or poles out in a straight line down the hill. Leave plenty of space between each pole or cone to allow skiers to perform a snowplow turn around the marker. Students should use snowplow turns to maneuver around the slalom course. See figure 4.31 for a slalom course diagram.

Figure 4.30 Moving the skis from pizza to French fries position on a hill.

Figure 4.31 Slalom course with tight turns.

- Miss Me, Please!—Place small stuffed animals, mittens, hats, or any other soft objects in the downhill ski tracks. The objects should be spaced out at intervals and should alternate between the right and left ski tracks. Make this a "no pole" event. As skiers start their descent, they should balance on one ski and slightly lift the other ski to avoid the stuffed animal in the ski track. Skiers continue to alternate lifting their skis to avoid hitting the stuffed animals. This is a great way for skiers to improve their dynamic balance. You may need to position yourself near the track (or use partners) to replace any animals that get moved; skiers may end up catching the animals with their skis and sliding them along with them as they ski downhill.

■ Assessment

Students can assess their partner's success in weaving around the cones in the Slalom Run. For this evaluation, the students can use the Snowplow Turn Skills Rubric for peer assessment. During the Slalom Run, you can also observe the students' snowplow turn technique and use the

Intermediate Basic Skills Rubric (Snowplow Turn section) to guide your assessment.

■ Closure

Skiers, today you did a super job of controlling your speed when moving downhill. Who can tell me one technique that you can use to slow down when skiing downhill? That's correct! The snowplow stop [or wedge, pizza slice, or piece of pie] will slow you down, and you can even stop by using the snowplow. Why is it important to ski under control when on a hill? What was the most difficult thing you worked on today? I agree! Balancing on one ski when you lifted the other ski to miss the stuffed animals was not easy to do. You can practice balancing on one ski and lifting the other ski even if you do not have stuffed animals to ski over. Next class session, we will work on another fun ski technique you are going to like . . . the double pole! Have a great day!

Interdisciplinary lesson ideas related to reading and history.

Intermediate   **LESSON 8**

DOUBLE-POLE FUN

Double poling (page 31) is a fun, fast, and effective method that skiers can use to easily move from one location to another. Your skiers will enjoy learning this skill and putting it to use when out on the trail. Skiers who have experience downhill skiing will already be familiar with the double-pole technique because alpine skiers frequently use a similar double-pole action to move to and from the ski lift. Once your skiers are able to perform the double pole, the next step will be easy—learning the kick double pole.

■ NASPE Content Standards

Standards 1, 2, 4, 6

■ Equipment

Skis, boots, poles, cones, 5-inch (12.7 cm) snowflakes cut out of foam core board (enough for as many relay teams as you have), Popsicle sticks, small colored balls

ASSESSMENTS AND REPRODUCIBLES

- Intermediate Basic Skills Rubric (Double Pole section), page 172
- Intermediate Basic Skills Checklist (Double Pole section), page 167
- Double-Pole Fun: How Far Can You Go?, page 205
- Kick Double Pole With Alternating Legs: Keeping the Rhythm, page 212
- Power Kicks: Kick Double Pole, page 226
- Snowflake Relay, page 235

continued ▶

Preparation

For this lesson, you need parallel sets of tracks on the flat in a straight line (six sets for a class of 24); a broad, slight to moderate hill with an area of flattened snow; and a large oval track set with multiple tracks. Create a start and finish line using paint on the snow, cones, or flags. Set cones in 3-yard (2.7 m) increments down a straightaway for a total distance of 9 yards (8.2 m). Tie crayons to plastic clipboards for each group to use when shading in their results. For the Snowflake Relay, copy the snowflake, laminate it, and paste it on to a foam core board. Cut out around the circle. Make enough so that each relay team has a snowflake.

Fitness Development

Students will improve their core strength and arm strength.

Goals

- Being able to perform the double pole nonstop on the flat for 9 yards
- Being able to perform the kick double pole nonstop on the flat for 9 yards

Set Induction

Hello, skiers! Today we are going to work on a fun movement called the double pole. Just as the name implies, you will be pushing on both of your ski poles at the same time. As a result, you will move quickly in the ski track. [See figure 3.9, page 31.]

Once you are able to do the double pole, we will work on the kick double pole. The kick double pole adds a kick right before you perform the double pole, making you move forward even faster. Let's get started!

Activities

1. Have students ski two laps around the ski area, first without poles and then with poles. Use this time as a warm-up and an opportunity to observe the skiers' diagonal stride technique. By now your skiers should have a good diagonal stride rhythm and should be able to complete two laps using a continuous diagonal stride. In this lesson, you will be able to combine diagonal stride skiing with double-pole practice once your skiers have had the opportunity to practice the basics of the double pole and kick double pole.

2. Double-pole review (see chapter 3, page 31)—Demonstrate the double-pole action for your skiers by double poling in the track. Let skiers try this movement (double poling back and forth in the tracks) before you provide them with any instruction. You may be surprised at how quickly your skiers pick up on this action and how easily they are able to move just using their arms.

3. Kick double pole (see chapter 3, page 44)—Start this practice by having skiers perform the double pole in parallel sets of track on the flat. Explain to the skiers that they will now be combining the double-pole skill with the same sort of kick that they used when diagonal striding and performing scooters. Skiers should then perform the kick double pole back and forth several times on straight tracks on the flat for a distance of at least 30 feet (9.1 m).

4. Kick double pole with alternating legs (also called "this leg, that leg kick double pole")—Once your skiers have practiced the kick double pole, they can try alternating legs when they kick. This may be challenging for some skiers, especially if they have trouble gliding on their weak leg. Let your skiers know that alternating the kicking leg is a good way to keep their legs from fatiguing. Skiers should perform the kick double pole, alternating leg kicks, back and forth several times on straight tracks on the flat for a distance of at least 30 feet.

5. Downhill double pole—Skiers diagonal stride into a slight downhill, and then near the top of the downhill, they give several strong double-pole pushes to move them with speed down the hill. Students can move into a skier's tuck and glide as far as possible, starting the diagonal stride again at the bottom of the hill before they lose all of their momentum.

Games

- Double-Pole Challenge Ladder—Partners challenge each other to see how far they can go using five double-pole pushes. Give each student a marker to stick in the snow alongside the track at the end of her glide after the fifth double-pole push. Students repeat the five double poles three times. The skier who went the farthest two out of the three trials moves up the challenge ladder to compete against a new partner.

- Distance Double Pole—Skiers see how far they can go when double poling for 10 pushes. Divide the class evenly between the parallel straight tracks. Give each student a marker to place next to the track to mark the distance he travels during the pushes. Allow time for students to have several attempts at improving the distance they travel with 10 double poles.

- Distance Kick Double Pole—On parallel sets of tracks, mark off a start and finish line 30 feet apart. The skiers' goal is to continuously perform the kick double pole for the entire distance. Allow skiers to begin by using two double poles (without the kick) to start the drill.

- Distance Kick Double Pole With Alternating Kicking Legs (see figure 3.22, page 44)—On parallel sets of tracks, mark off a start and finish line 30 feet apart. The skiers' goal is to continuously perform the kick double pole with alternating legs for the entire distance. Allow skiers to begin by using two double poles (without the kick) to start the drill.
- Snowflake Relay—In this double-pole relay, teams will work to move their snowflake around the oval ski track and bring the snowflake back to the starting line. Divide the class into teams of five or six skiers. One skier remains at the starting line while the other skiers ski into positions staggered equal distances around the track. Each skier at the starting line has a snowflake (which can be carried in a pocket or jacket hood). Skiers must double pole to the next skier and hand off their snowflake before that skier can double pole to the next skier. The first team to move their snowflake back to the starting line wins the relay! If your students are in great shape, you can have the teams complete two laps of the racetrack—one lap using only the double pole and the second lap using the kick double pole.

■ Assessment

You can use the Intermediate Basic Skills Rubric and the Intermediate Basic Skills Checklist to assess the double-pole skill and to measure the progress of your skiers. Working alone or with partners, students can use the Double-Pole Fun: How Far Can You Go? assessment to measure how far they can double pole without stopping. The Power Kicks: Kick Double Pole assessment enables students to record the distance they covered when performing 5 and 10 kick double poles. The skiers' ability to alternate kicking legs and maintain the double-pole rhythm is assessed with the Kick Double Pole With Alternating Legs: Keeping the Rhythm handout.

■ Closure

I was impressed with how far and how fast all of you can glide with your double-pole pushes! Who can tell me one thing that you need to remember to do when you are double poling? [Comment on suggestion.] Who can tell me another thing that you need to do when you are double poling? [Comment on suggestion.] Skiers, how does the double pole differ from the kick double pole?

[Comment on answer.] I'm glad all of you enjoyed learning how to double pole. You will be able to practice using it again when we go out on our endurance ski during our next class session. See you then!

Interdisciplinary lesson ideas related to art or science.

Intermediate   **LESSON 9**

ENDURANCE SKI

This ski lesson will challenge your students to use all of the ski skills they have been working on during the ski unit. In addition, when on the endurance ski, the students' aerobic fitness and strength may also be challenged. If possible, you should take your group to a golf course or park with groomed trails. The terrain will provide students with opportunities to use all of their recently learned skills, and trail maps may be available that the students can learn to read. Talk with your class about proper etiquette to follow when on the trail. Encourage your students to drink water before starting the ski and to bring water with them on the trail. Skiers can easily wear a water bottle holder while skiing. A small water bottle tucked into a jacket pocket will also work. Taking a drink of water during the ski will help revive students and will make the remainder of the workout easier.

■ NASPE Content Standards

Standards 1, 2, 4, 6

■ Equipment

Skis, boots, poles, swim noodle

ASSESSMENTS AND REPRODUCIBLES

- Kilometers Skied Record, page 213
- Heart Rate Record, page 211

continued ▶

Preparation

Groom or ski in tracks for a distance ski of 2 to 3 kilometers (1.2 to 1.8 miles) or go to an existing trail.

Fitness Development

Students will improve their aerobic fitness and their arm and leg strength.

Goal

For skiers to ski a longer distance than they previously have over a variety of terrains that require them to use many of the ski skills they have learned

Set Induction

Hello, skiers! Today we will put all of your ski skills to the test as well as challenge your aerobic fitness. We are going to start today's endurance ski by warming up without using poles. Please put your poles off to the side of the trail so they will not be in anyone's way. We are going to ski for five minutes without poles and then return to pick them up and use them for the remainder of our ski tour. During the warm-up, focus on reaching out and swinging your arms down the track. Think about each kick and glide. Try to shift your weight over your gliding ski. Remember to give the person in front of you plenty of room. When we are done with the warm-up, we will head out for our long endurance ski. Let's get started.

Activity

Begin the session with a warm-up ski done without ski poles. If possible, ski a five-minute lap on a loop or ski out and back on a trail. The goal of this warm-up is to make sure that your students are using the proper contralateral arm movement and are reaching down the track with their arms. Focus the students' attention on a good kick and glide. This movement should include shifting weight and balancing on the moving ski (see figure 4.32). Once the warm-up is complete, chal-

lenge your students with an endurance ski that takes them out on a trail that is longer than any previously skied trail. Encourage the skiers to ski further distances than they have done in the past and to take fewer and shorter rest breaks.

Game

Scoot, Scram, Ski!—If enough time remains, you can have the class play this fast-paced tag game that is guaranteed to have your skiers laughing and squealing while increasing their heart rates. Skiers play this game wearing one ski. Skiers find a partner and hook elbows. Together the partners ski around the designated play area while the skier who is It chases the skiers, attempting to tag someone with the swim noodle. When connected to one other skier by hooked elbows, skiers are safe. If a free skier hooks elbows with the pair, the third skier on the other side must ski off and becomes a target for the tagger (the person who is It). Depending on the size of your group, you may want to add a second tagger. The taggers carry a brightly colored swim noodle, which makes it easier for the other skiers to identify them. Change taggers frequently.

Assessment

Depending on where you are skiing, students can record the number of laps they complete as well as the time taken to ski the laps. If trail maps are available, students can calculate the number of kilometers they skied; they can record this distance along with the time taken to ski the distance on the Kilometers Skied Record. The endurance ski is a great opportunity to measure heart rates. Students can wear heart rate monitors, or they can measure their heart rate by counting beats at the wrist. Results can be recorded on the Heart Rate Record.

Closure

Skiers, you did a super job today! This is the farthest that we have ever skied. Did you have fun? What did you enjoy most about skiing on the trail? [Comment on the skills that you thought your skiers did a great job of performing during the ski; for example, "I thought everyone did a good job of controlling their speed on the hills by using their snowplows."] Next class session, we will be having a ski carnival.

Interdisciplinary lesson ideas related to geography or biology.

Figure 4.32 Skier shifting weight to the gliding ski.

SKI CARNIVAL

This lesson will take preparation and planning on the part of the teacher. You will have to make maps, gather equipment, and set up stations. The first time through the ski carnival event will involve a lot of work, so you may want to recruit parents or older students to help. Many of the materials that you create for this event can be reused the following year.

■ NASPE Content Standards

Standards 1, 2, 4, 6

■ Equipment

Skis, boots, poles. Assorted equipment (such as beanbags, tennis balls, foam balls, stuffed animals, hula hoops, and flags) will be needed depending on the activities selected for the carnival.

ASSESSMENTS AND REPRODUCIBLES

- Tell Me!, page 191

■ Preparation

Groom or ski in at least four sets of tracks around a large oval. You also need a large flattened area for games and an obstacle course.

■ Fitness Development

Students will improve their flexibility.

■ Goal

Providing fun activities (races, games, an obstacle course) that challenge the skiers to use all of their newly learned skills

■ Set Induction

Skiers, today we are going to have lots of fun! Today is our ski carnival. You will have the opportunity to participate in a variety of activities. We will be moving clockwise around the activity stations that you see set up. I will let you choose the station you want to start at. Let's get started! Please find three other skiers and stand next to each other. I am going to be staggering your start for the Quiz Race. Some groups will be going to an activity station first and then doing the Quiz Race, and one group will be starting with the Quiz Race. Let's warm up by skiing around to all of the stations, and I will tell you a little bit about each one.

■ Activities

1. As a warm-up, lead the students as they ski in a circle around all of the stations you have set up. This enables the skiers to warm up while you are familiarizing them with the stations. Provide students with the name of the station and a quick idea of what they will be doing at each station.

2. Quiz Race—Before Carnival Day, create a series of quiz cards. Each card should contain a question about material you covered in class (e.g., "Name the muscle that the arrow is pointing at") or a math problem that would be appropriate for your students' age. Use colorful cardstock, print the question on the cardstock, laminate the card, and then punch holes in the top corners. You can run a string through these holes so the card can be easily hung from a tree branch or hoop holder. Tie a crayon, pencil, or marker to the tree branch at each question station. Create a course with a series of 10 cards; the skiers will move around to these cards and answer the questions. You also need to create smaller cards that the skiers will use to record their answers. Skiers will wear these cards hanging around their neck. To create these cards, cut one sheet of cardstock into four equal pieces, and punch holes in the top two corners. Put the numbers from 1 to 10 on the card, providing enough space for a skier to record his answers. Run a string through the holes in the card; the string should be long enough to easily fit over the skier's head and allow the card to hang just above waist level. At the start area, you should create a station that has the correct answer for each of the questions so that skiers can check their own answers once they have completed the course. You can award points for each correct answer.

3. Longest Scooter Glide—At this station, you will need a start line and several parallel set tracks so that more than one student may be competing at a time. This activity works best when students have a partner. One skier will be the competitor; the other skier will write the person's name on a sticky note, put it on a cone, and place the cone at the spot of the partner's longest glide. Each skier gets five tries to achieve her longest glide. The cone set at the spot of the longest glide will stay in place and will represent the distance that the next skier should try to beat. The next skier to glide past the farthest cone places a cone with her name attached to it at the spot of her longest glide.

continued ▶

4. Obstacle Course—Create an obstacle course for skiers to move through. The course can require skiers to ski through a hula hoop set upright in the snow, climb over a hurdle, ski around a circle marked in the snow (use cones or tempera paint), and ski in a track that has Beanie Babies set at intervals so that skiers must lift their ski to avoid skiing over the Beanie Babies. If a hill is available, set up a slalom course with flags (use ski poles or PVC pipe with a colored plastic or fabric square attached). Skiing through a series of hula hoops on a hill is fun, and skiers will also enjoy skiing over a small snow jump. Even a small snow bump will give students a feeling of "catching air" and will be exciting (see figure 4.33).

5. Ski Free Throw—Set up a hoop holder or hang a hula hoop to create a target that a squishy ball can be thrown through. Mark a free-throw line. Put a squishy ball behind the line. Skiers stand behind the free-throw line and try to throw the ball through the hoop. After shooting the ball, the skier skis to retrieve it and returns to the free-throw line as quickly as possible. Each skier gets five free throws. The partner keeps track of the total time taken to shoot all five balls. Students can record the time and the number of made baskets, and you can reward the fastest and most accurate shooter.

6. Treasure Hunt—Your treasure hunt can be as simple as those experienced at children's birthday parties, or it can be more challenging and involve a GPS (if available) for a geocaching experience. To keep it simple, create a list of objects and a map on a piece of cardstock that skiers can take with them as they venture out to find their treasures. Depending on where you are setting up your carnival, you may have skiers find certain types of deciduous leaves, a bird feather, an acorn, or pine needles. It may be easier to hide a variety of Beanie Babies or different colored plastic balls and make a map that the skiers will follow to collect the objects. Remember that you will need to place as many objects at each location as you have students in class. Another option is to put different shaped hole punches at a variety of locations and give each student a cardstock card that has a map on it. The skiers collect their punches on this card.

■ Assessment

You can have skiers record their results for the various events, or you can just let this be a fun day where skiers enjoy their ski skills and continue to gain confidence on skis. Use the Tell Me! assessment to learn more about the ski skills that your skiers are most proud to have mastered during the cross-country ski unit.

■ Closure

Skiers, today is the last day of our ski unit. I am glad that you had such a good time today. I was very impressed with how much each of you has improved your ski skills. If you think back to the first day of this unit, I am sure you will agree. We have learned a lot about skiing this year. I hope that you will borrow the skis and continue to ski this winter. Remember, you can check them out before and after school and at lunch time as well as over the weekend. Next class session, we will be back inside and will move on to our next unit. See you then!

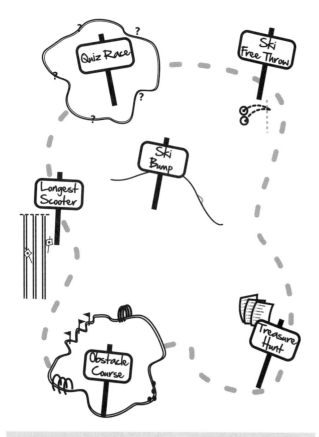

Figure 4.33 Example of an obstacle course layout.

Interdisciplinary lesson ideas related to art.

FIT AND REVIEW EQUIPMENT

In this lesson, you will be fitting all of the ski equipment using the charts and the station format you used in previous years. After these fittings, you will head outside to help everyone get reacquainted with being on their skis on snow. Because your skiers have fit skis, boots, and poles in the past, this should go smoothly and quickly. Therefore, you should have time to move the group outdoors to ski a warm-up loop before working on scooters and the diagonal stride without poles. Before going outside, take a few minutes to review with the skiers how to put on their poles and skis. Go over how to remove the boots from the bindings. Your skiers should be able to ski longer distances this year and should be competent in all of the basic ski skills. You will be challenging them with a variety of new skills throughout the advanced lessons, and they will become real cross-country skiers!

■ NASPE Content Standards

Standards 1, 2, 4, 6

■ Equipment

Skis, boots, poles, cones, extra bright hats or flags

ASSESSMENTS AND REPRODUCIBLES

- Boot Size Record, page 199
- Pole Size Record, page 224
- Ski Size Record, page 228
- Boot Sizer: Boys and Girls, page 200
- Boot Sizer: Men and Women, page 201
- Pole-sizing directions, page 225
- Ski-sizing directions, page 231
- Scooter Count, page 227
- Heart Rate Record, page 211

■ Preparation

For this lesson, you need a groomed or skied-in ski track on a large flat area, as well as six (for a class of 24) rows of set tracks that run approximately the width of a football field.

■ Fitness Development

Aerobic fitness: Students will be skiing a 10-minute warm-up ski.

■ Goals

- Fitting all skiers with skis, boots, and poles
- Reviewing scooters and the diagonal stride without poles
- Having skiers feel comfortable skiing on snow by the end of the lesson

■ Set Induction

Hello, skiers! I see that everyone is dressed for cross-country skiing and that you are ready to get your equipment. Today you will be moving around to the stations I have set up to check out the size charts and get your equipment. Do you remember how we did this last year? You will be working with a partner again to help each other with the sizes. Please write your name and equipment size on the chart by the equipment before you move on to the next station. Once you have all of your equipment, please bring it over to this area and put your boots on.

continued ▶

[Once the class has sized equipment, continue with your instructions.] Today we will be getting back into Nordic skiing. Before we go outside to warm up, I want to review how to put on your ski poles and skis. Once we have done that, we are going outside to ski one lap on the trail for a 10-minute warm-up. We will review and practice scooters and skiing without poles, and we will finish with another long ski. Of course, we will also play a fun game. Does anyone remember how to put your poles on? That's right. [Demonstrate while talking.] Bring your hand from below the strap up through the strap, and then grab the pole. [See figure 4.18, page 69.] Next, let's look at your bindings. Please set your skis flat on the floor. [Again, demonstrate while talking.] You will be putting the toe of your boot into the binding and pressing down until it clicks in. [See figure 2.6, page 12.] Go ahead and try it. To release the boot from the binding, take your ski pole and press the tip of it in the small square on the top of the binding. [Demonstrate this with a ski and boot set on a table so everyone can see.] It looks like everyone has that figured out, so let's go outside, take a quick heart rate reading, and ski!

Activities

1. Have students take a 10-second heart rate count. They should then ski a warm-up loop (using poles) to become familiar with skiing and to get used to being on snow again.

2. Scooters—Students practice scooters (without poles) in a track the width of a football field. The students should remove the right ski and set it aside. They put the left ski into the outer right track and perform scooters down to the end of the track. Skiers should concentrate on using the correct contralateral arm swing and shifting weight completely over the gliding ski. At the end of the track, they switch the ski to the right foot and repeat scooters back to the starting point. Have students repeat "Kick and glide" or "Push and glide" aloud as they perform the scooters. *Note:* Make sure that students perform scooters in a controlled manner. It is easy to rush the movement. When students hurry through the scooters and race down to the other end of the field, they do not shift their body's weight over the gliding ski.

3. Scooter count—Students again perform scooters (without poles) down and back, switching skis at the end of the track. But this time, they count the number of pushes it takes them to ski the length of the track. Good pushes, proper arm swing, and balancing on the gliding ski will help skiers reach the goal of having as few pushes as possible.

4. Slow-Mo Ski—With both skis on, students ski (without poles) down and back on a straight track across the width of the field, concentrating on exaggerating the correct arm swing and shifting weight over the gliding ski in slow motion. Have students repeat "Kick and glide" or "Push and glide" aloud as they ski the track, thinking about what they are doing. This drill forces skiers to shift their weight and commit to the gliding ski. It also focuses their attention on the arm swing position and contralateral action with the legs.

Games

- Jumping Jack Tag (refer to the description on page 80).
- Cool-down ski—Using poles and good diagonal stride technique, skiers complete a cool-down lap.

Assessment

Make sure that all skiers recorded their ski, pole, and boot sizes on the equipment size charts posted in the gymnasium. Use the Scooter Count assessment to track progress on the effectiveness of skiers' scooter pushes. Use the Heart Rate Record to record student heart rates taken before skiing the first warm-up laps and after skiing the cool-down lap.

Have students record their heart rate before beginning activity and immediately after activity; they should record *low* and *high* heart rates. The National Association for Sport and Physical Education (NASPE) does not recommend using training zones for prepubescent children (ages 5 to 12) (Gilbert, 2005). Teachers are encouraged to refer to the article by Gilbert (2005) for the new target heart rate formula and further information on children and target heart rates.

Closure

It feels great to be back outside skiing, doesn't it class? Everyone did a good job of efficiently getting the right size skis, boots, and poles today. Who can tell me one important thing to remember when doing a scooter push? How about a second important thing to remember when doing scooters? When you are doing the diagonal stride and you have your right arm forward, which leg should be forward? When you are doing the diagonal stride and you have your left arm forward, which leg should be forward? Next class session, we will be working on making sure everyone has the correct rhythm down when diagonal striding. We will be skiing two laps on our trail and playing a game of your choice. Please put your skis, boots, and poles back neatly where they belong. See you next time!

Interdisciplinary lesson ideas related to math.

DIAGONAL STRIDE RHYTHM ON THE FLAT

The focus of this lesson is developing good rhythm and correct timing for the diagonal stride. All of the reviewing you will do in this lesson helps your skiers improve their ability to kick and shift weight to the gliding ski. You will be leading skiers through a diagonal stride progression that moves from using no poles to using poles for propulsion. Emphasize to your skiers that it is fine to pull the poles out of the snow and start again if they lose the correct rhythm. Use the Advanced Basic Skills Rubric and the Advanced Basic Skills Checklist to measure the students' progress toward developing a great diagonal stride.

■ NASPE Content Standards

Standards 1, 2, 4, 5

■ Equipment

Skis, boots, poles, cones

ASSESSMENTS AND REPRODUCIBLES

- Slow-Mo Ski Check, page 234
- Scooter Count, page 227
- Heart Rate Record, page 211
- Advanced Basic Skills Rubric (Diagonal Stride sections), pages 143-145
- Advanced Basic Skills Checklist (Diagonal Stride sections), pages 139-140
- Norwegian Words Related to Snow and Skiing, page 223

■ Preparation

For this lesson, you need a groomed or skied-in ski track on a large flat area, six (for a class of 24) rows of set tracks that run approximately the width of a football field, and a large area with flattened snow for game play.

■ Fitness Development

Aerobic fitness: Students will ski a 10-minute warm-up ski.

■ Goals

- Developing correct diagonal stride rhythm when skiing on the flat
- Increasing the length of the glide on one ski when diagonal striding on the flat

■ Set Induction

Hi, skiers! Today we are going to head outside to work on our diagonal strides. We will start by practicing what we did last class session and working on scooters. Then I have a new activity for you to try that will help you develop good diagonal stride rhythm. We will warm up by skiing a 10-minute loop. We will also play a game and finish by skiing a longer loop. Let's go!

■ Activities

1. Have students take a 10-second heart rate count. They should then ski a 10-minute warm-up loop (using poles).

Review the previous lesson by practicing activities 2 through 4 on a flat track without using poles:

2. Scooters—Students practice scooters in a track the width of a football field. Have students repeat "Kick and glide" or "Push and glide" aloud as they perform the scooters. *Note:* Make sure that students perform the scooters in a controlled manner. It is easy to rush the movement. When skiers hurry through the scooters and race down to the other end of the field, they do not shift their body's weight over the gliding ski.

3. Scooter count—Students again perform scooters down and back, switching skis at the end of the track. But this time, they count the number of pushes it takes them to ski the length of the track. Good pushes, proper arm swing, and balancing on the gliding ski will help skiers reach the goal of having as few pushes as possible. Skiers can record their results on the Scooter Count chart.

4. Slow-Mo Ski—With both skis on, students ski down and back on a straight track across the width of the field, concentrating on exaggerating the correct arm swing and shifting weight over the gliding ski in slow motion. Have students repeat "Kick and glide" or "Push and glide" aloud as they ski the track, thinking about what they are doing.

Have students perform the following activities with poles:

5. Skiers hold the poles at the midpoint, one in each hand. The skiers should exaggerate the contralateral arm swing as they move down and back on the straight track the width of a football field.

6. Skiers put the poles on with their hands through the strap. They perform the diagonal stride in the straight track, swinging their arms contralaterally but holding

continued ▶

the poles out of the snow (see figure 4.25, page 84). When skiers feel comfortable with the rhythm, they can lower the poles, putting the pole tips into the snow and pushing on the poles. Skiers continue to diagonal stride the length of the track and back. If they lose the correct rhythm, they should pull the poles out of the snow and start again without planting the poles. Once they can maintain the correct rhythm for several strides, they should lower the poles to the snow and use them to push off.

Teacher note: Watch the gliding foot of the skiers to make sure that they are not sliding the foot forward in front of the knee (see figure 4.34).

■ Games

Play the following games without poles:

- Fast Ski—Skiers ski as fast as they can in the track without running. They must make sure that they are gliding between kicks.
- Elbow Tag—Use cones to mark a large square playing area. Skiers who are It must carry a brightly colored fabric square or a short swim noodle. Players cannot be tagged if they have linked elbows with a partner and are facing opposite directions. A skier can join a group of two, but the person at the other end of the threesome must then leave; this person becomes free to be tagged. To keep the game moving, you can have several skiers be It at the same time. Skiers should

Figure 4.34 Incorrect foot position for the diagonal stride: The gliding foot (left foot) is out in front of the gliding knee.

play this game on one ski. Stop the game from time to time to have skiers switch their ski to the other leg.

- Copycats—Each skier finds a partner (groups of three will also work). One skier is the leader. When the teacher calls out "Go!" the leader moves any way he likes. The partners follow, copying the leader's movements. When the teacher calls out "Copycat!" the leader freezes in a position that the partners must copy. Repeat until every skier has been a leader.

Have students use poles for this final activity:

- Students ski for distance on a loop or trail. The students should take a 10-second heart rate count immediately after they finish skiing.

■ Assessment

Use the Advanced Basic Skills Rubric and the Advanced Basic Skills Checklist to assess the students' diagonal stride rhythm and technique. Skiers can use the Scooter Count chart to record the number of scooter pushes used (with right and left feet) to cover the 50-yard length of flat track. On the Heart Rate Record, students can record their heart rates before and after skiing.

■ Closure

Skiers, today we all got a good workout while improving our diagonal strides. Who remembers the words I asked you to repeat aloud when we were practicing the diagonal stride without using poles? When we practiced the diagonal stride rhythm while using the poles, what did you do when you lost your rhythm? Was it easier to ski the distance loops today? Who had a heart rate that was in their training zone? I am proud of how hard all of you worked today. Next class session, we will be skiing up and over the hill behind the school. We will also work on perfecting our snowplows and will learn how to do a downhill skier tuck. Please put your equipment back where it belongs inside, and I will see you next time.

Interdisciplinary lesson ideas related to science or language.

UPHILLS AND DOWNHILLS

In this lesson, you will help students work on maintaining good rhythm up a hill and increasing diagonal stride tempo as they ascend a hill. You will be leading skiers up a hill that is small enough for them to be successful on, yet large enough to provide a challenge. Skiers will practice transitioning from the diagonal stride to the herringbone while climbing the hill. And of course, for skiers to practice climbing the hill several times, they will have to come down the hill; therefore, downhill skier tucks will also be practiced. Sideslipping is also taught in this lesson to help prepare students for the stem Christie turn that they will learn in the next lesson. Use the Advanced Basic Skills Rubric and the Advanced Basic Skills Checklist to measure students' progress toward developing a great diagonal stride uphill.

■ NASPE Content Standards

Standards 1, 4, 5

■ Equipment

Skis, boots, poles, cones

ASSESSMENTS AND REPRODUCIBLES

- Advanced Basic Skills Rubric (Diagonal Stride Uphill section), page 144
- Advanced Basic Skills Checklist (Diagonal Stride Uphill section), page 139
- Skier Tuck Assessment, page 186
- Heart Rate Record, page 211
- Scooter Count, page 227

■ Preparation

For this lesson, you need multiple sets of parallel groomed or skied-in ski tracks on a flat area. This area should lead up to a hill with room for uphill climbing in and out of the tracks and downhill snowplowing with run-out room at the bottom.

■ Fitness Development

Students will improve their aerobic fitness.

■ Goals

- Maintaining correct diagonal stride rhythm up a hill
- Skiing down the hill successfully using the skier slouch posture
- Skiing a straight downhill run using the skier tuck position

■ Set Induction

Hi, skiers! Today we are going outside to work on taking our diagonal strides straight up the hill! We will spend a few minutes practicing what we did last class session; then we'll work on carrying the diagonal stride rhythm right up the hill before transitioning to a herringbone. We are also going to practice straight downhill runs, first using the skier slouch and then using a skier's tuck. Sideslipping will be the last skill we do on the hill. Sideslipping will help prepare you for the stem Christie turn that we will attempt next class session. Let's start with a warm-up by skiing a 10-minute loop with good classic rhythm. Let's go!

continued ▶

■ Activities

Have students perform the following activities with poles:

- Skiers should take a 10-second heart rate count before skiing the warm-up loop and immediately after finishing the loop.

- Charge the Hill!—Skiers ski up the hill, starting with regular (long) strides and then shortening their strides as they begin to ascend. As they ascend, skiers should pump their arms while poling in order to maintain good timing. The quick tempo promotes good traction, so encourage skiers to keep their arms moving. They should look up the trail well in front of their skis to help keep their hips forward. Skiers glide downhill on a straight run using the skier slouch; they should keep their hands low and poles angled backward.

- Changeover—Skiers diagonal stride up a slope as far as possible, then change to the herringbone to complete the climb up and over the hill (see figure 3.10, page 33).

- Changeover challenge—Challenge your skiers to see how far they can climb up the hill before transitioning to a herringbone. Who can diagonal stride the farthest before switching to the herringbone? Give skiers time to practice several repeats up and down the hill.

- Ski slalom—Use a series of markers (poles or cones) to establish a slalom course on the hill. Set the markers at least 3 yards (2.7 m) apart on a straight line (if the hill is long and steep) to encourage longer, shallower turns. On a short hill, you may have room for only two or three markers. Skiers turn around as many markers as possible on the descent.

- Tuck time—Start by teaching your skiers the skier tuck position (see figure 3.28, page 46) on the flat and without poles. Skiers should stand with skis parallel, flat on the snow. Their weight should be evenly distributed over the skis as they bend forward at the waist and deeply bend their knees. Skiers should rest their forearms on their thighs, keeping their hands near the knees. Next, let the skiers try the skier tuck position when skiing straight down the hill. Explain to the skiers that a straight downhill run is parallel to the fall line of the hill. Once skiers are comfortable with using this position in a downhill run, add the ski poles. The forearms should continue to rest on the thighs with the poles angled backward.

Have students perform the following activities without poles:

- How Low Can You Go?—Set up several sets of limbo poles (make sure that the pole falls off easily) on the downhill track with the bar set at approximately 1.5 yards (1.4 m). Skiers take turns skiing down the hill in a skier tuck, getting low enough to get under the pole without touching it (see figure 4.35). As skiers suc-

Figure 4.35 Skier using a tight tuck position to ski under a pole.

cessfully make it under the bar in a skier tuck position, you should lower the bar in 3- to 6-inch (7.6 to 15.2 cm) increments.

- Sideslipping (see page 44)—Review sideslipping and have students practice this technique on a hill.

- Sideslip traverse—Once skiers are comfortable with sideslipping, you should review the traverse (see chapter 3, page 47) and then combine the two skills to produce the sideslip traverse. When performing the sideslip traverse, the skier will be moving diagonally across the hill while also sliding straight down the hill. Skiers should start the movement with the skis at a slight diagonal to the fall line and edged slightly by rolling the ankles and knees in toward the hill. As skiers start to move forward, they should roll the knees and ankles a bit downhill to a more neutral position. This action will move the skis to the flat bottom of the ski, and the skis should slide down the hill at the same time that the skier is traversing the slope. Explain to skiers that this technique can be used to move safely down a hill that they think is too steep for them to ski down safely and under control. By combining the downhill sliding action of the skis with edging the skis, skiers are able to control the speed of their descent.

■ Games

- Ultimate Frisbee—Play Ultimate Frisbee with players wearing skis. Follow the same rules that are used when the game is played on grass. The goal of Ultimate Frisbee is to move the Frisbee the length of the field and over the end line to score a goal. Divide the class into two teams. Have one team spread out on one half of the field while the other team spreads out on the other half of the field. An offensive player starts play by passing the Frisbee to a teammate (the pass can be made in any direction). Play continues if the pass was complete. An offensive player has 10 seconds to pass the Frisbee and may not ski while holding the Frisbee. The defender counts out the 10 seconds. If the pass is not completed and the Frisbee flies out of bounds or touches the snow, the defense takes possession and then becomes the offense. Players may not touch each other. Try playing the game with players wearing just one ski. Keep teams small to maximize movement for every skier. You can have more than one game being played at a time. Playing Ultimate the width of a football field works well.

- Racing Scooters—Mark a start line and finish line with cones. Students pair up, and each partner removes one ski. Groups of partners then form teams for this relay race. Set out cones for skiers to race to (skiers will scooter around the cones and back), spacing out the cones to provide adequate room for partners to maneuver around. If possible, keep the number of pairs on each team to three in order to allow for maximum activity. Challenge the skiers by requiring them to remove their ski and switch it to the other foot after everyone on the team has gone once. No poles are used.

- Distance ski—If time allows, finish with another 10-minute ski around the trails. Challenge skiers to keep moving using good diagonal stride technique. Skiers can take their heart rates before and after the ski.

■ Assessment

The Advanced Basic Skills Rubric and the Advanced Basic Skills Checklist each have a section on the Diagonal Stride Uphill that you can use to assess skiers' uphill work. In addition, you can use the Skier Tuck Assessment to evaluate the skiers' performance of the skier tuck.

■ Closure

Skiers, today we all got a good workout while improving our diagonal strides. Was it easier to ski the distance loops today? Who had a heart rate that was in their training zone? I am proud of how hard all of you worked today. Next class session, we will be skiing up and over the hill behind the school, working on perfecting our snowplows. I will also teach you another way to turn on your skis called a stem Christie. Please put your equipment back where it belongs inside, and I will see you next time.

Interdisciplinary lesson ideas related to science or physics.

Advanced   **LESSON 4**

TURNING ON HILLS

In this lesson, you will focus on helping students perfect the snowplow turn, and you will introduce stem Christies. Snowplows are used to control speed on downhill runs; they are also used any time a turn is needed. The snowplow and snowplow turn are important fundamental skills that skiers must master in order to be safe skiers who ski under control at all times. Plan on practicing the snowplow and snowplow turns until your skiers have them perfected. Skiers must be able to do a snowplow turn before they try the stem Christie. The stem Christie starts like a snowplow turn and ends like a parallel turn done in alpine (downhill) skiing, making it look like a "hockey stop" done on ice skates. The stem Christie is a fun turn that will challenge your skiers to perfect the snowplow turn so that they can try the flashier stem Christie turn.

■ NASPE Content Standards

Standards 1, 2

■ Equipment

Poles, cones, stopwatch

ASSESSMENTS AND REPRODUCIBLES

- Snowplow Turns, page 237
- Advanced Basic Skills Rubric (Snowplow Turn section), page 150
- Advanced Basic Skills Checklist (Snowplow Turn section), page 141

continued ▶

Preparation

Groom or ski in a track on a broad, moderate hill. Flatten snow for a game area.

Fitness Development

Students will improve their aerobic fitness.

Goals

- Becoming comfortable descending a hill and performing three or four linked snowplow turns
- Being able to demonstrate a stem Christie in both directions

Set Induction

Hi, skiers! Today we are going to spend our class time on the hill again. Our focus today will be on turning while going downhill—but, of course, we will have to go uphill to go down! We will work on perfecting the snowplow turn. Then I will show you how to do another turn called the stem Christie, which is like a hockey stop done on ice skates. Let's head out and ski our 10-minute warm-up loop and then meet at the bottom of the hill.

Activities

- Partner-Push Snowplows—Students pair up with a partner of about the same body size. On a flat, groomed area, one of the partners wears skis, while the other stands behind the skier and does not wear skis. The partner just in boots puts her hand at the top of her partner's hips and pushes the skier. The skier begins with skis parallel and then slides one heel out, creating half a snowplow, which will slow the skier down. The skier should return the skis to parallel before completely stopping. The pushing partner continues

to push steady enough to maintain the skier's speed, and the skier then pushes out the heel of the other ski to experience a snowplow on each side. Repeat the drill, but this time the skier should make a snowplow turn by steering the skis into the turn.

- Linking Snowplows—Skiers descend the hill, using shallow turns to change direction on the hill. On the first descent, skiers should simply steer their skis in a gentle arc to obtain a feel for the pitch of the hill (see the discussion on snowplow turns, including figure 3.16, on page 40). On the second descent, skiers continue to steer the skis in a relaxed fashion, and they count the number of turns during the descent. On the third descent, they steer the skis more sharply in tighter turns, and they increase the number of turns.

- Snow Cones—Use a series of cones to establish a slalom course on the hill. Set the cones at least 3 yards (2.7 m) apart in a straight line (if the hill is long and steep) to encourage longer, shallower turns. On a short hill, you may have room for only two or three cones. Skiers should turn around as many cones as possible on the descent.

- Sideslipping review—Review sideslipping and have skiers practice it on a moderate to steep hill with their skis perpendicular to the fall line. Discuss with skiers how sliding, or skidding, the ski will be used in the stem Christie turn.

- Speed Plows—Skiers practice linked snowplow turns on a moderate to steep hill. Encourage the skiers to make several turns quickly. Adding the element of speed to the snowplow turn will cause skiers to shift to a wide-stance stem Christie. To practice the quick snowplow turn, place a long row of cones more closely together than previously done.

- Stem Christie (see figure 4.36)—A stem Christie is a turn that is performed during a downhill run. The

Figure 4.36 Advanced skier performing a stem Christie. This skill is accomplished by *(a)* beginning with a snowplow turn, *(b)* bringing the uphill ski parallel to the downhill ski , and *(c)* continuing in a new direction traversing the hill.

skier begins the turn by brushing out one ski tail in a snowplow-like move. At this point, the skier's body weight should be shifted to the outside ski, leaving the inside ski free to skid, which happens moments later. The skier skids the inside ski to bring the skis to a parallel position or at least onto corresponding edges. Once skiers have begun the turn from a snowplow, they should sink into the turn by bending the knees. After this sinking motion, skiers should rise upward by straightening the knees. Rising upward helps the skier stand on the outside ski and bring the skis into a parallel position.

Games

- Slalom race—Set up several slalom racecourses on the hillside using cones, ski poles, or flags stuck in the snow (see figure 4.37). Create a start line at the top of the hill. Divide the students into teams and let them practice several trial runs before timing each skier. Total the times for the individual skiers to create a final "team time" for the racecourse. Record team times and let the teams try to better their race times in future lessons.

- Figure Eight Course—On a flat, groomed area, set up two cones approximately 7 yards (6.4 m) apart. Ski a trail around the cones, crossing in the middle and creating a figure eight (see figure 4.38). Have students pair up and play "follow the leader." For a bit of a challenge, have the two skiers start at opposite sides of the two cones. When you call out "Go," the skiers begin a pursuit race, trying to catch each other. Specify the technique that skiers should use or the event will quickly turn to a skating event. For this activity, skiers must be able to steer their skis, which is an important aspect of performing snowplow turns and the stem Christie.

Figure 4.37 Slalom race fun.

- Distance ski—If time remains, finish the class session with a distance ski. Students should try to ski for at least 10 minutes nonstop over terrain with gentle to moderate hills. They should check their heart rates before and after the ski.

Figure 4.38 Figure Eight Course.

continued ▶

■ Assessment

Use the Advanced Basic Skills Rubric and the Advanced Basic Skills Checklist to assess students' performance of snowplow turns and stem Christies. Skiers can use the Snowplow Turns assessment to record the number of cones they are able to continuously turn around.

■ Closure

Skiers, today we all got a good workout and had some fun practicing our turns and stops. You're all getting pretty good at those stem Christies! Why is it important to be able to do good snowplow stops and turns on a hill? That's right, it helps you to ski under control and possibly avoid crashing into someone or something. Next class session, we will work on another turn that is similar to the stem Christies we worked on today. I call it the Nordic swoosh! We will also work on the double pole. The double pole is a fast way to move on skis and will really work your core. See you next time!

Interdisciplinary lesson ideas related to science or physics.

THE POWER OF THE DOUBLE POLE AND KICK DOUBLE POLE

The focus of this lesson is double poling, a cross-country ski technique in which both poles are angled backward and inserted into the snow while the skier pushes simultaneously on both poles. A good double pole is very fast, especially on wet or icy snow. In this lesson, skiers will also review variations of the double pole: the kick double pole and the kick double pole with alternating legs. Both the double pole and the kick double pole are relatively easy skills to learn, but they require good core strength and will be tiring if done nonstop. Skiers will also be challenged to transition from the diagonal stride to double poling and then back to the diagonal stride. (See figure 3.7, page 29.)

■ NASPE Content Standards

Standards 1, 2, 4

■ Equipment

Cones or flags

ASSESSMENTS AND REPRODUCIBLES

- Advanced Basic Skills Rubric (Double Pole section), page 146
- Advanced Basic Skills Checklist (Double Pole section), page 140
- Double-Pole Power!, page 206
- Heart Rate Record, page 211

■ Preparation

For this lesson, you need several skied-in or groomed tracks parallel to each other (or long tracks) on terrain that is flat or slightly uphill. You also need an area of flattened snow for games.

■ Fitness Development

Students will improve their core strength, upper-body strength, and aerobic fitness.

■ Goals

- Understanding and feeling the forward lean into the poles when double poling and kick double poling
- Gaining speed when double poling

- Being able to kick double pole while alternating kicking legs for 13 yards (11.9 m)

■ Set Induction

Hi, skiers! Today we will be working on both the double pole and a variation of the double pole called the kick double pole. The double pole can be very fast, often faster than any other classic technique, so you'll want to master it! Let's head out for a 10-minute warm-up and then meet back at the bottom of the hill.

■ Activities

- Broad jump—Without skis or poles, skiers stand in place and do a standing broad jump without swinging their arms. Then they repeat the jump while swinging both arms. Ask the skiers which method allowed them to jump farther. Discuss the role that the arms play in creating momentum and how this helps move the entire body down the ski track.

- Arm swings—With skis on, skiers stand in the track and flex at the waist so their back is parallel to the ground. In this position, they practice swinging their arms forward and reaching down the track. Skiers should relax their arms and let them swing smoothly down and backward, extending the arms straight. Skiers repeat this several times.

- Free Fall—Without skis or poles, skiers stand facing a partner approximately one yard away. One partner falls forward, bending at the ankles but keeping the heels on the ground, until the other partner catches her. Partners switch roles and repeat. Explain to skiers that this exercise demonstrates the feel of the forward lean that they should try to achieve when double poling.

- Free Fall with poles—With poles, skiers stand with feet together and fall forward so far that they would fall over if they didn't have their poles to catch them (see figure 4.39). Skiers catch themselves using the poles. Again, reinforce that this is the same feel that the skiers should have when double poling.

- Core strength—With poles, skiers stand with their skis in parallel tracks and their arms in proper bent-arm position. The skiers perform a crunch with their core, pushing on the poles, to move forward. They do not swing their arms backward in a follow-through. Skiers should discover that they can propel themselves farther forward when crunching the core than when only using the arms for propulsion.

- Copycats—Demonstrate the double pole on the flat, or have a student who does it well perform the demonstration while the other skiers watch. Provide practice time for skiers to repeat the correct motions in multiple sets of parallel tracks. Review the critical features of the double pole that are listed in the Advanced Basic Skills Rubric.

- Downhill double pole—This drill should initially be performed on a gradual downhill slope. Skiers stand in the track with their skis parallel. They plant their poles just in front of their feet, outside of their skis. With their arms bent approximately 90 degrees, skiers lean on the poles, pushing the poles downward and back to propel themselves forward. Skiers repeat this pole plant with bent arms over and over again to gain momentum all the way to the bottom of the slope and beyond. They then repeat the drill, changing the tempo of the pole plants to experience changes in momentum.

- Stride, double pole, stride—Using parallel sets of track on the flat, skiers start with diagonal striding, then transition to using the double pole for at least three pushes, and then return to diagonal striding. Skiers should repeat this several times until they are comfortable with the transitions.

- Kick double pole—Review the kick double pole, which was covered in Intermediate Lesson 8. Once skiers have the double pole down, adding a kick to the action will be fairly simple. Let skiers experiment with performing repeated kick double poles and alternating double poles with a kick double pole.

- Kick double pole with alternating legs (also called "this leg, that leg kick double pole")—Skiers alternate the foot they are kicking with on each repetition of the kick double pole. Challenge skiers to *continuously* perform kick double poles with alternating legs for a distance of 13 yards.

Figure 4.39 Free Fall with poles.

continued ▶

- Stride, kick double pole, stride—Using parallel sets of track on the flat, skiers start with diagonal striding, then transition to the kick double pole for at least three pushes, and then return to diagonal striding. Skiers should repeat this several times until they are comfortable with the transitions. They can then repeat the drill using the kick double pole with alternating legs.

- Distance ski—Finish the class session with a distance ski over varied terrain that encourages skiers to use all of the skills they have acquired. Identify a portion of the course that will require skiers to transition from the diagonal stride to double poling. Stand off the trail several yards before the transition should be made. As the skiers ski past you, tell them to get ready for the transition to the double pole. Encourage skiers to keep moving for as long as they can when completing the distance ski.

■ Assessment

Use the Advanced Basic Skills Rubric and the Advanced Basic Skills Checklist to assess the students' performance

of the double-pole technique. Skiers can use the Double-Pole Power! worksheet to record the number of double poles they needed to perform to cover a designated distance. This reproducible also allows skiers to mark how far they went with each double-pole push. Using the Heart Rate Record, skiers should record their heart rates before the distance ski and immediately after finishing the ski.

■ Closure

Skiers, today we all got a good workout. How many of you realized that double poling is faster than diagonal striding? It helps to have fast snow. Your abdominal muscles might ache a little tomorrow if you were using them today. Next class session, we will be back to diagonal striding. Have a good day!

Interdisciplinary lesson ideas related to history.

Advanced   **LESSON 6**

POLING PROPULSION AND TIGHT TURNS

In this lesson, you will help your skiers understand the important role that the poles play in creating propulsive forces that aid in moving a skier forward when diagonal striding. Many skiers, particularly beginner skiers, think that the poles are used solely for balance purposes. As the beginner skiers become comfortable with the feeling of moving on skis, their reliance on the poles for balance should decrease. Spending many lessons without using poles will help improve the skiers' balance and comfort level with gliding on a moving ski. When you introduce poles to your skiers, be sure to explain that the pole should be angled backward and planted about even with the ski boot—and that the skier should then push on it!

■ NASPE Content Standards

Standards 1, 2, 4, 5

■ Equipment

Cones or flags

ASSESSMENTS AND REPRODUCIBLES

- Advanced Basic Skills Rubric (Diagonal Stride section), pages 143-145
- Advanced Basic Skills Checklist (Diagonal Stride section), page 139
- Tight Turns!, page 238
- Heart Rate Record, page 211

■ Preparation

For this lesson, you need multiple skied-in or groomed tracks (parallel tracks) on a flat area and going up and down a gradual hill. If you have a steeper hill, create tracks coming down the hill and around a corner.

Fitness Development

Students will improve their upper-body strength.

Goals

- Developing strong propulsion using poles when diagonal striding
- Maneuvering tight turns on the flat and down hills

Set Induction

Hi, skiers! Today we are going to head outside and really give our upper body a workout! We know we can ski without poles, so you might wonder why we use poles when cross-country skiing. We're going to practice without poles for a few minutes, and then we'll add them back in, using skis and poles. After doing this exercise, you should be able to feel how much propulsion the poling action adds to the diagonal stride. Before we are done today, we will also have some fun skiing down the hills and working on turning. Let's head outside and warm up by skiing three laps on the inner trail.

Poling Progression Activity

Have students complete this sequence several times:

1. On a flat track, ski approximately two lengths without poles. Use a nice stride, swinging the arms as if holding poles.
2. On a flat track, ski approximately two lengths using the arms and poles as they are used in a diagonal stride. Do not kick with the legs (see figure 4.40). This arm-only drill is called single sticking.
3. On a flat track, ski two lengths using the diagonal stride with poles and kicking.

Figure 4.40 Single-sticking drill.

Push-Extend Activity

Skiers perform single sticking (use poles, no kick) in the tracks. Skiers should say "Push" out loud when they plant the pole, applying force by pushing on the pole. As the skiers' arms move past their bodies, they should say "Extend," making sure that they are fully extending their arms straight behind them. The skiers should immediately say "Push" and should be applying force to the other pole. They follow this with "Extend" as the arm extends behind the body.

Tight-Turn Activities

1. Figure Eight Course—Create several stations with cones or flags placed approximately 7 yards (6.4 m) apart. Skiers ski a figure eight around the cones without using their poles.
2. Pursuit eights—Continuing on the figure eight course, skiers participate in a pursuit race against a partner. One skier starts three seconds ahead of his partner. The following skier tries to catch the partner before two laps are finished. Skiers should exchange roles so the lead skier becomes the pursuer.

Activities

1. Pole Maze—On the hill, place poles or cones randomly across the hill. Skiers descend the hill, weaving in and out of as many poles as possible.
2. Tight Hill Turns—Create several lines of five or six cones (or flags) in a straight line down the hill. Put the cones slightly closer together than you have for previous activities (see figure 4.37 on page 105). This will challenge the skiers to make quicker, tighter turns and will encourage skiers to use the stem Christies that they learned several lessons ago.
3. Classic Relay—Prepare an out-and-back course or a loop course that is short and fairly flat. Divide the class into teams of three skiers each. The first skier skis the assigned distance doing the diagonal stride. The second skier skis using only the kick double pole. The third skier finishes the relay using only the double pole.
4. Distance ski—Finish the class session with a distance ski over varied terrain that will require skiers to use their ski skills. Try to have skiers go farther than they have in previous sessions. Skiers should take their heart rates before and after the ski.

Assessment

Observe and assess the skiers' pole position during the diagonal stride. Use the Advanced Basic Skills Rubric and the Advanced Basic Skills Checklist to evaluate important

continued ▶

aspects related to poling (e.g., pole angled backward, pole plant alongside the boot, arm applying force initially in a bent position, arm then extending in back of the body). Use the Tight Turns! assessment form to evaluate skier progress on maneuvering and controlling skis when turning on the flat. Skiers can record heart rates before and after the distance ski using the Heart Rate Record.

■ Closure

Skiers, today you worked hard on using your poles correctly to help move you forward by applying force to the pole and pushing on it. Now, everyone give yourself some personal space and get into the skier's stride position with your right leg back and your right arm forward. Your left leg should be forward and your left arm extended backward. Using your poles, show me where you should plant the right pole. That's right, it should be across from your right boot. Where should your left pole be? Yes, extended in back of you. Next class session, we will continue to work on turning around tighter corners, and we will go for a longer distance ski. Have a great day!

Interdisciplinary lesson ideas related to history.

CORNERING

The focus of this lesson is cornering while going down hills. Most young adults will enjoy the opportunity to ski down hills—the steeper the better. Young skiers love speed and are willing to fly down hills beyond their abilities. In previous lessons, skiers learned skills such as snowplow turns and stem Christies on gentle to moderate hills; these skills can also be used on steeper hills. When skiing on trails at a city, county, or state park, skiers will be experiencing trails that require the ability to turn, or corner, in a fairly narrow space. In this lesson, you will be creating situations for your skiers that will help them learn how to safely corner a tighter turn like the ones they will experience when out skiing on a trail.

■ NASPE Content Standards

Standards 1, 2, 3

■ Equipment

Cones, flags, Beanie Babies

ASSESSMENTS AND REPRODUCIBLES

- Advanced Basic Skills Rubric (Snowplow Turn and Stem Christie Turn sections), pages 150-151
- Advanced Basic Skills Checklist (Snowplow Turn and Stem Christie Turn sections), pages 141-142
- Heart Rate Record, page 211

■ Preparation

For this lesson, you need a broad area of flattened snow on a moderate to steep hill; several sets of parallel tracks should be set from the top to the bottom of the hill.

■ Fitness Development

Students will improve their agility.

■ Goals

- Gaining the ability to ski down steeper hills and to corner tighter turns
- Being able to turn around a series of objects smoothly, comfortably, and with confidence

■ Set Induction

Hi, skiers! Today we are going to be on the hill working on making tighter turns around corners. I have set up several slalom courses using cones and flags. Notice that on one of the courses I have used the cones to create two rows on either side of the flags. You will have to stay inside the aisle as you make your turns around the cones. If everyone goes up the hill on the left and skis down the hill on the right, we will avoid collisions and have a lot of fun. Let's start with two warm-up laps around the loop trail and then ski up the hill and meet at the top.

■ Activities

1. **Tight-Turn Slalom**—Use a series of poles to create a slalom course on a moderate to steep hill. Use cones placed approximately 2.5 yards (2.3 m) from the flags and in a line parallel to the flags to create aisles on either side of the flags (see figure 4.41). Skiers will try to stay inside of the aisles as they make their tight turns around the flags. Allow time for repeated practice. No poles are used in this activity.

2. **Turn Time!**—Facing downhill, skiers stand in two rows at the top of the hill, with plenty of space between skiers so they have room to turn. The traffic controller stands near the bottom of the hill; this person is facing the skiers and holding a brightly colored flag that all skiers can see. The traffic controller starts the skiers downhill by shouting "Racers, start your engines. Go!" Once the skiers have started to descend, the traffic controller directs the skiers' turns by pointing the flag in the direction he wants the skiers to turn. Skiers should complete the turn and then turn back downhill, watching the traffic controller for the next turn command. Skiers continue to obey the traffic controller until everyone reaches the bottom of the hill.

3. **Teaching trail turns**—Locate a twisty trail or create one that will require skiers to make multiple turns as they ski the trail. Demonstrate turning technique on the trail, emphasizing the need for skiers to be looking and planning ahead of the actual turn. Ski sections of the trail again, providing skiers with practice time to learn what to expect and to figure out how to maneuver around the corners.

4. **Up, Down**—Alongside the downhill parallel tracks, space out Beanie Babies approximately 3 yards apart. Skiers start at the hilltop and descend, bending their knees to pick up the Beanie Babies as they approach them. Once at the bottom, skiers should herringbone up to the top, placing the Beanie Babies alongside the track for the next skier to pick up. This is a no-poles activity that encourages skiers to bend the knees, sinking down and then straightening; these are the same movements that the skiers use when turning.

5. **Jumps!**—If you have the opportunity to create jumps the day before class, a few small "lumps" added to your hill will become the highlight of the skiers' season. (The best method is to form the jumps and allow the snow to freeze up and harden overnight.) This fun activity is best done initially without ski poles, but poles can help increase speed later on. As skiers gain confidence and improve their ski-jumping ability, they can use their poles and assume a tight skier's tuck when going over the jump (see figure 4.42).

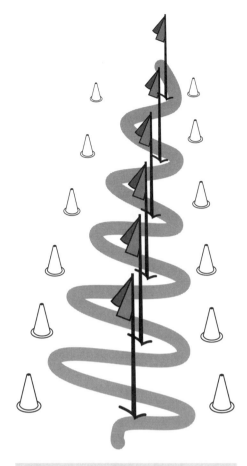

Figure 4.41 Tight-turn slalom course layout.

Figure 4.42 Skier going over a jump.

continued ▶

6. Distance ski—Finish the class session with a distance ski over varied terrain that will require skiers to use their turning skills. Try to have skiers go farther than they have in previous sessions. Skiers should take their heart rates before and after the ski.

■ Assessment

Use the Advanced Basic Skills Rubric and the Advanced Basic Skills Checklist to evaluate the skiers' performance of snowplow turns and stem Christie turns. Students can record their heart rates before and after the distance ski on the Heart Rate Record.

■ Closure

Skiers, today I challenged you with making much tighter turns when skiing downhill. Being able to perform a good turn is an important ski skill. As you saw when we practiced turns on the trail, the trail is much narrower than the space we practice in on our hill. Why is it important to be able to execute a good turn on your skis? That's right! Being able to turn will make you a safer skier and allow you to ski on more difficult, fun trails. Next class session, we will be working on the Nordic swoosh and marathon skate techniques as well as practicing your diagonal stride up and over the hilltop. Have a great day!

Interdisciplinary lesson ideas related to history or industrial arts.

SKI SKILL CHALLENGES

In this lesson, skiers will be using the diagonal stride technique to ski up and over the crest of a hill without losing momentum. Developing this skill demands that skiers be in fairly good aerobic condition and be able to keep the arms and legs moving contralaterally while moving up a moderate hill. Stress to the skiers that they should not slow down as they approach the top of the hill; rather, they should keep moving over the crest of the hill before stopping. Skiers will continue to work on their stem Christies, and if ready, they will move on to try the flashier Nordic swoosh. Skiers who are also ice skaters and know how to do a hockey stop will be well on their way to accomplishing the Nordic swoosh. The swoosh starts like a stem Christie—or for the more advanced skiers, like a parallel turn—and finishes like a hockey stop with skis together and sliding across the snow, shooting up a plume of snow. Skiers will also have fun learning how to marathon skate. The marathon skate is a fast method of moving that involves keeping one ski in the track while the other ski angles outward and pushes against the snow.

■ NASPE Content Standards

Standards 1, 2, 4

■ Equipment

Cones, flags

ASSESSMENTS AND REPRODUCIBLES

- Advanced Basic Skills Rubric (Stem Christie Turn and Diagonal Stride Uphill sections), pages 151 and 144
- Advanced Basic Skills Checklist (Stem Christie Turn and Diagonal Stride Uphill sections), pages 142 and 139
- Heart Rate Record, page 211
- Marathon Skate Checklist, page 177

■ Preparation

For this lesson, you need parallel sets of tracks across a flat area, multiple sets of tracks going up and over the top of a hill, and a flattened playing area for games.

■ Fitness Development

Students will improve their aerobic fitness.

■ Goals

- Being able to diagonal stride up and over the top of a moderate hill
- Being able to marathon skate on the flat for at least three pushes with good rhythm
- Being able to perform a stem Christie with good form
- Learning and attempting the Nordic swoosh

■ Set Induction

Hello, skiers! Today we are going to do a variety of things. After warming up, we will be working on the marathon skate, a technique that combines the double pole and skate skiing, all while staying in the tracks! We will also practice diagonal striding up the hill, making sure that we keep striding over the top of the hill. On the first several downhill runs, you will be practicing your stem Christies. I will then show you how to do the Nordic swoosh. The Nordic swoosh looks like a hockey stop done on skates. Let's get started with two laps on the inner loop.

■ Marathon Skate Activities

Complete the marathon skate exercises in the following order:

1. Double-pole review—Have skiers practice the double pole on the flat in multiple sets of parallel tracks. Skiers should go down and back at least once, concentrating on good double-pole form.

2. Skate time—As skiers begin to swing their arms forward in a double-pole action, they should pull one ski out of the track; the ski should be angled outward so that the tips of the skis are wide apart and the ski tails are close together. The angled ski is set on the snow, weight is transferred to the angled gliding ski, and poles are planted for the push-off. To get a feel for the rhythm of the marathon skate, skiers can repeat "Plant, push" aloud as they simultaneously plant their poles and push off of the angled gliding ski.

3. Shift push—Skiers can first try the marathon skate without poles. They should take two or three diagonal strides to gather momentum before moving one ski into the angled position. Encourage skiers to focus on shifting their body weight to the angled ski while unweighting the ski that is gliding in the ski track. Skiers then push off the angled ski and shift weight back to the gliding ski in the track. The arms should move through the same double-pole motion that they would if holding poles. Skiers then repeat the drill with poles, concentrating on the weight shift, the push, and the weight shift back to the gliding ski.

■ Hill Climb Activity

Up and over!—Skiers start performing the diagonal stride seven yards away from the base of a moderate hill. Encourage the skiers to diagonal stride all the way to the hilltop and *over* the crest of the hill without stopping (see figure 4.43). This will certainly get the heart rates up and require good arm and leg strength. Skiers can practice the Nordic swoosh on the way back down the hill. They should repeat the hill climb several times.

Figure 4.43 Diagonal stride up and over the hilltop.

continued ▶

Nordic Swoosh Activities

1. Snowplow turns review (see figure 3.16, page 40)—Take your skiers through a review of snowplow turns on a moderate hill. Have the skiers perform snowplow turns while moving down a slalom course. Encourage skiers to make tight turns, as close to the cone as possible.

2. Stem Christie review (see figure 4.36, page 104)—Set up aisles of cones 2.5 yards from the center line of slalom flags on both sides of the flags. Skiers start the stem Christie with a snowplow wedge and then bring the inside ski alongside the outside ski as they skid. Encourage skiers to make tight turns around the cones.

3. Nordic swoosh—Encourage your skiers to think about what a hockey stop on ice skates looks like before they try this dramatic stop. For more skilled skiers, the Nordic swoosh will be similar to a parallel turn in which the skis are kept parallel to each other throughout the turn (making it one that is carved rather than one that starts as a snowplow and involves more skidding). For the less skilled skiers, you can encourage them to move the skis into a parallel position earlier in the stem Christie turn. Sinking into the turn by bending the knees helps to unweight the skis, making it easier to turn the skis as the knees straighten. Skiers will finish this stop with the skis parallel and edged into the hill. With increased pressure put on the inside ski edges, the stop will be more abrupt, and snow will fly into the air (see figure 4.44). When less pressure is put on the inside ski edges, the skis will skid across the snow and gradually come to a stop.

Game

Distance ski—Lead skiers on a distance ski over varied terrain for a longer length of time than they have skied in previous sessions. Encourage skiers to use the double-pole technique and marathon skate in appropriate spots on the trail.

Assessment

Use the Advanced Basic Skills Rubric and the Advanced Basic Skills Checklist to assess the skiers' performance of the diagonal stride uphill and stem Christie. Use the Marathon Skate Checklist to assess the marathon skate technique. Students should use the Heart Rate Record to record their heart rates before the hill climb repeats and after all repeats are done.

Closure

Skiers, I am impressed with how hard you worked today. Using the diagonal stride to ski all the way to the top and over the crest of our hill is not an easy thing to do. I noticed that many of you were able to increase your speed when doing the marathon skate. What helped you to increase your speed? Yes, pushing off the angled ski gave you increased speed, as did using both arms to pole. Next class session, we will go on an endurance ski that will keep us on the trails the entire class time. Have a great day!

Interdisciplinary lesson ideas related to science or biology.

Figure 4.44 Nordic swoosh stop. This skill is accomplished by *(a)* beginning the stop with a snowplow turn or a stem Christie (more advanced skiers will be able to carve a parallel turn), *(b)* bringing the uphill ski parallel to the downhill ski , and *(c)* skidding to a stop. The skier can come to a gradual stop with less edging of the skis or make a dramatic, sudden stop that will make the snow fly by increasing pressure on the inside edge of the skis.

ENDURANCE SKI

For this lesson, you will take your skiers on an endurance ski that will require them to use all of the skills they have learned in previous class sessions. If you are able to take a field trip to a local ski trail, choose one with a variety of terrain and a trail approximately 5 kilometers (3.1 miles) long. Before starting your ski tour, talk with your class about proper etiquette to follow when on the trail. Encourage your students to drink water before starting the ski and to take water with them on the trail. Skiers can easily wear a water bottle holder while skiing, and unless it is bitter cold out, the water bottle shouldn't freeze up in the length of time you will be out. A small water bottle tucked into a jacket pocket will also work. If you've got a competitive group of skiers, provide the option of timing the skiers on the course.

■ NASPE Content Standards

Standards 3, 5

■ Equipment

Cones or flags to mark the start and finish line, a stopwatch, and a helper to serve as the timer if students want to be timed. (The helper should dress appropriately, knowing that she will be standing around for a long period.) It is always helpful for the leader to carry a pack with a few emergency items, such as a water bottle, first aid supplies, cell phone, and extra hats and mittens. The leader may want to bring a small, healthy snack along in case of an emergency.

ASSESSMENTS AND REPRODUCIBLES

- Ski Trail Time, page 233
- Etiquette Check, page 164
- Ski Trail Etiquette, page 232

■ Preparation

If you are unable to travel to a groomed trail system, you should set or groom your own trail approximately five kilometers long. Include a variety of terrain, turns, and hills of various lengths and heights (followed by sufficient flat area for skiers to catch their breath).

■ Fitness Development

Students will improve their aerobic fitness.

■ Goal

For skiers to complete the entire course using all of the ski skills they have learned

■ Set Induction

Hi, skiers! Today we are going on a ski tour on a trail that will require you to use the skills you have learned this season. Find a partner to ski with and make sure that both of you make it back to the end of the trail where we will meet. Please use all of the etiquette and courtesy rules that we have discussed. Everyone should take a marked trail map with them that shows the route we will be following. Please stay on the trail, and if you come to a junction where you are unclear about which way to go and can't figure it out by looking at your map, please wait at that spot for someone who knows the way. If anyone wants to be timed on this course, let me know and we'll send you out first. Everyone should take it easy as you begin the tour so you can warm up your muscles. I will bring up the rear, so I will see you at the end of the trail! Have a great time!

continued ▶

■ Activity

Here are some steps you should take to help smooth your skiers' experience on the trail:

1. Before the trip, review a trail map marked with the trail you will be following. Also review etiquette and courtesy rules (see figure 4.28, page 88).

2. Talk with your skiers about how to best prepare for the ski tour. Discuss things such as eating, drinking water, dressing appropriately, and bringing extra dry clothing. You may want to provide water at the end of the tour (see figure 4.45).

Figure 4.45 Ready for a ski tour.

3. Before going to the trail, cover any other rules you want skiers to follow. Review these once again at the trail.

4. When at the trail, set out on the course as a group, trying to organize the skiers by ability and speed. Have the faster skiers go out first so they do not "run over" the slower skiers.

■ Assessment

Because the group will be spread out, you will have difficulty trying to evaluate every skier on specific skills. If you position yourself at a spot near a portion of the trail where all students will be using the same technique, you may be able to evaluate each skier on one or two skills. You can assess the students' knowledge of etiquette by having the students complete the Etiquette Check form. Student self-assessment can be done using the Ski Trail Time assessment.

■ Closure

Skiers, you did a great job today! What did you think was the most challenging part about skiing on a trail? You can see why we spent so much time practicing our turns . . . that came in handy today, didn't it? Next class session, we will be back at our usual spot, and we will have a great time doing a Ski-O!

Interdisciplinary lesson ideas related to geography, math, and biology.

Advanced   **LESSON 10**

SKI-O!

In this class session, your skiers will use their ski skills to complete a Ski-O course. Ski-O is orienteering on skis, so students will need to use the orienteering, compass, and map skills that they learned in previous classes. If your skiers do not have an orienteering background, you should spend time in a previous class (maybe during a fall orienteering unit) discussing how to use a compass and read a map (these make great interdisciplinary activities that a geography teacher can help with). Ski-O can be done at a trail system, or you can create a Ski-O course on a golf course or even on the school grounds. You may use a variety of designs for this Ski-O lesson, from having students complete a challenging course that requires off-trail skills to letting students make their own maps of school grounds for a Ski-O course.

■ NASPE Content Standards

Standards 6, 7

■ Equipment

Compasses, maps, orienteering controls (hole punches of various shapes or colored pencils or crayons), control flags (see figure 4.46), cones, stopwatch

Figure 4.46 Orienteering control flag.

ASSESSMENTS AND REPRODUCIBLES

- Ski-O Quiz, page 188
- Ski-O Quiz Answers, page 189
- Ski-O!, page 229
- Ski-O Terminology, page 230

■ Preparation

Set up a Ski-O course by placing controls tied to a control flag. You can use the Ski-O! information sheet to learn about ski orienteering.

■ Fitness Development

Students will improve their aerobic fitness.

■ Goal

For skiers to be able to complete a Ski-O course by reading a map and locating controls while on skis

■ Set Induction

Hello, skiers! Today we are going to take part in a Ski-O competition. I have set up a course with 10 different controls placed all over this section of the trail system. With a partner, you will be reading your map and using your compasses to figure out the fastest way to reach the control. You will then ski to the control and punch the bottom edge of your map with the hole punch you find at the control. Once you have found all of the controls and punched the corresponding control numbers on the bottom of your map, you should ski back here as fast as you can! I will be starting groups at 20-second intervals after you take 3 minutes to study your map with your partner. Good luck and let's get started!

■ Activities

Here are a few Ski-O variations that you can try with your class:

- Divide the class into groups of three and let each group design their own Ski-O course (and make a corresponding map). In the next class session, groups should exchange maps and ski each other's courses.

- Have your upper-level students make a Ski-O challenge for the younger skiers. The older students can design courses, make maps, and if possible, assist the younger skiers when they try the courses (see figure 4.47).

- Geocache—Geocaching is a great way to encourage high levels of physical activity, and it can be done as easily on skis as on foot. If you are close to a state or county park, check to see if the site already has coordinates and caches set up for geocaching. Some state parks even have GPS units that people may borrow. If necessary, you can hide your own caches and create coordinates to enter into the GPS units. Geocaching can also be used to create an interdisciplinary lesson with help from a geography teacher who can teach students terms such as *latitude* and *longitude*.

Figure 4.47 An older skier helping a younger skier study the Ski-O map before setting off.

continued ▶

■ Game

Favorite game—If time remains and a flat area is available, let the skiers choose their favorite game to play.

■ Assessment

Use the Ski-O Quiz to test the students' knowledge about Ski-O.

■ Closure

Congratulations, skiers! You have just successfully completed your first Ski-O course! You all look as if you got a good workout today. Everyone made it around to all of the controls. I hope you enjoyed yourself and learned a lot about cross-country skiing in the past few weeks. I hope to see you out on the trails!

Teacher's note: If you are not familiar with ski orienteering (Ski-O), you can find many resources (in print or on the Internet) that will help you learn more about the sport. You may want to include an orienteering unit in your curriculum during the fall. This way, the students will have skills that they can build on in the winter Ski-O lesson. Ski-O also lends itself to interdisciplinary lessons with your geography, math, or science teachers. So plan ahead and work with others to make this event a memorable one.

Interdisciplinary lesson ideas related to art

CHAPTER 5

Games and Activities

To make cross-country skiing even more fun, you can use additional games and activities to supplement the ones already included within the lessons in chapter 4. Many of the games that you play in the gymnasium or on a grass field can be adapted to be played on snow. Changes you make in game play will either increase or decrease the difficulty of the activity. To keep play safe, do not use ski poles unless doing a poling activity where you really need them.

For many activities, you can try the following variations with your skiers:

■ Remove one ski.
■ Pair with a partner.
■ Increase or decrease distance.
■ Add hills.
■ Include turning.
■ Include stopping.
■ Add an object to be manipulated (ball to catch, Frisbee to throw, and so on).

Including game play in each lesson not only adds an element of fun, but also allows skiers to experiment with moving on skis. Through game play, skiers will teach themselves basic skills as well as increase their confidence when moving on skis. You can expect students to acquire the following as a result of regular game play:

■ Improved ability to shift weight to a gliding ski
■ Improved ability to glide for longer distances on one ski
■ Increased strength of the kick
■ Improved ability to steer and control the direction of the ski
■ Improved ability to stop
■ Increased confidence with ski skills
■ Improved self-esteem as confidence and skill improve

When playing games, holding a relay race, or doing an activity, you should be aware that students' technique will often suffer at the expense of speed and fun. Don't expect skiers to perform the ski techniques perfectly, or even well, when engaged in game play. Game play still serves many purposes, so you should include game play in every lesson you teach. The benefits will become immediately apparent.

Games

AROUND THE WORLD

■ Equipment

Cones to use for creating a 5-by-5-foot (152 by 152 cm) square home base; a tracked ski trail loop between 100 and 400 meters (109 and 437 yards).

■ Description

This is a chase game that is played with three or more skiers. No poles are used. The skiers gather at home base. One skier is It and stands several feet away from the group at home base. All the skiers at home base think of names of a state. Each skier whispers his selection to the others so that everyone but the skier who is It knows everyone else's state. Once the states are selected, the skier who is It calls out states. When a skier's state is called, the skier must leave home base and ski around the established ski loop (between 100 and 400 meters). The skier tries to make it back to home base before being tagged by the It. If many skiers are involved, you can assign several skiers to be It so that no one is standing around too long. The skiers assigned to be It should be changed frequently so the activity continues and everyone gets to ski the loop.

The It and the skier must ski in the same direction. A lead zone—about three yards or meters extended from home base in the direction of the skiing route—may be used as an area for the skier to get ready to ski or to toy with the It. The It may tag the skier in this zone, but within this zone, the skier may quickly get back to home base (like a baseball player leading off a base). When skiers step outside the boundaries of the lead zone, they must commit to the chase. The It should be far enough away from home base that he would have to be very fast to tag someone in the lead zone; however, this can happen, especially if the skier falls trying to get back to home base. The skier can only go back to home base from the lead zone three times; on the fourth move into the lead zone, the skier must ski the entire loop. If a skier gets tagged, the skier becomes another It and helps the original It tag skiers. If the It doesn't tag anyone, that person remains It, but they won't have additional help from others they might have tagged.

CANADIAN BORDER

■ Equipment

Cones or markers to mark a field; a flag that can be stuck in the snow

■ Description

Divide skiers into teams of five and play with no poles. Flip a coin to determine which team plays defense. The defending team tries to block the offense from capturing their flag, while the offensive team tries to avoid being tagged by the defending team. When a skier is tagged by a member of the opposite team, the skier becomes a member of that team.

FOX AND GEESE

■ Equipment

Large, brightly colored fabric squares or short swim noodles for taggers to carry; a large circle to ski in that is divided into six or eight wedges

■ Description

In this tag game, skiers (geese) must ski in the existing tracks as they move around the circle attempting to avoid being tagged by the It (fox). See figure 5.1 for the setup. Select several skiers to be foxes and identify them with either swim noodles or brightly colored fabric squares. The center of the circle is the safety zone (goose nest); one skier at a time can ski into this zone and stand until another skier wants to come in. The first skier must then leave. The last skier to be tagged becomes the next fox. No poles are used. This game can be played with skiers wearing both skis or just one ski.

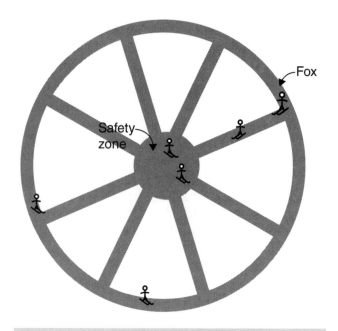

Figure 5.1 Setup diagram for Fox and Geese.

FRISKI

■ Equipment

Frisbee, cones to mark bases

■ Description

This game is baseball played with a Frisbee and on skis! To start the game, the at-bat skier throws the Frisbee as far as she can and then skis off to first base. A caught Frisbee on the fly is an out. To tag a skier out, another skier holding the Frisbee must tag the skier. A run is scored when the skier makes it safely around the bases. No poles are used.

GERM TAG

■ Equipment

Cones to mark playing area

■ Description

In this tag game, one person is "The Germ" who tries to tag other skiers moving around the playing area. When "The Germ" tags another skier, the body part tagged is rendered useless. For example, if a leg is touched by "The Germ," that skier must ski on one ski. Skiers may be tagged more than once. If skiers run out of forearms, shoulders, legs, and equipment, they run in place until another skier frees them by tagging them.

HILL HILL

■ Equipment

Cones or other markers to mark a finish line at the base of the hill

■ Description

This works best when you have a small hill where skiers can circle the bottom of the hill all the way around (see figure 5.2). Choose someone to be It. This person stands in the middle of the top of the hill. The remaining skiers line up at the bottom of the hill behind the line. When the It shouts, "Hill, hill, come over the hill!" everyone skis up and over the top of the hill and down the other side, crossing over the line at the bottom. Anyone tagged becomes an It and stays at the hilltop to help tag skiers. The game ends when all skiers have been tagged. The first person tagged becomes It to begin the next round.

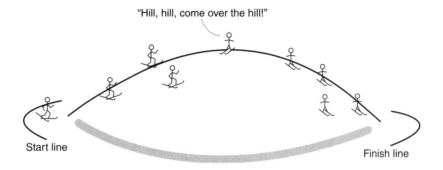

Figure 5.2   Diagram of Hill Hill.

KEEP-AWAY

■ Equipment

Flags (like those used in flag football) or colored fabric squares to tie on an arm or leg

■ Description

Create several groups of five or six skiers. Identify teams with flags tied on the skiers' arms or legs. Space groups well apart to allow for lots of action. Let each group play Keep-Away against another group using a soft spongy ball (such as a Nerf ball). After teams have played for a bit, rotate teams so every group has a new opponent. No poles are used.

■ Variations

This game can also be played with skiers wearing just one ski.

KEEP THE BALL

■ Equipment

Soft, easy-to-catch ball; cones to mark the playing area

■ Description

Divide skiers into two teams. There is no limit on the number of skiers per team. Before starting the game, determine the size of the field and the length of time you will play the game. The goal of this game is for a team to keep the ball and pass it around to teammates for as long as possible.

The game starts when the teacher throws the ball up to the sky. The skier who catches the ball tosses the ball to a teammate, who then tosses it to another teammate, while the opposing team tries to steal the ball. Teammates continue to toss the ball to each other until the opposing team manages to take it away from them. Skiers cannot return the ball to the skier who tosses it to them. When the time is up, the team that has possession of the ball wins.

SKIER TAG

■ Equipment

Cones or flags to mark the playing area; brightly colored swim noodles or large fabric squares

■ Description

This tag game can be played with one or two skis on. Depending on the size of your class, select one or two people to be It. The people who are It will carry a brightly colored swim noodle or large fabric square, which gets handed off to the person they manage to tag. To avoid being tagged, players must call out a ski technique such as "Herringbone" or "Stride" and assume the position of the technique they called out. They can only stay in place for five seconds before they must move again to avoid being tagged. Suggested techniques that skiers may call out include snowplow stop, snowplow turn, star turn, kick turn, double pole, kick double pole, skate ski, and dead bug. No poles are used.

SKISERS

■ Equipment

Cones to mark the playing area; flag football flags

■ Description

This chase game is played on a large open field that has a line drawn across the width of the field at either end, creating a safe zone for each team (see figure 5.3). The area between the two end lines is "no-man's land." The game begins with each team standing in their safe zone. On a signal from the teacher, teams take turns sending out one member at a time from their safe zone until all players are in no-man's land. Once out of the safe

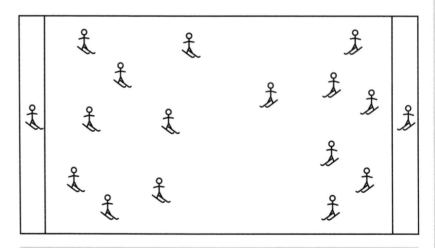

Figure 5.3 Setup diagram for Skisers.

zone, any player can be tagged by a member of the opposing team. The goal of each team is to collect as many players as possible by tagging out a player from the opposite team, at which point both tagger and tagged player return to the tagger's safe zone and stay there until the end of the game, or until one of the tagged player's teammates makes it across the no-man's land to collect them. If that happens, both players leave the safe zone to continue playing. Game play continues until all skiers are back in one safe zone or the other, or until the teacher calls time. The winning team is the one who has collected the most players. Teams can strategize early on in the game by sending out the team's fastest skiers to get close to the other team's safe line, making it difficult for the other team to leave their safe zone without being tagged. No poles are used.

■ Variations

Once tagged, skiers ski around the perimeter of the game field and then rejoin their team behind the safe line. Another option is to have tagged skiers immediately perform five jumping jacks and then return to their own team behind the safe line.

SNOWBALL FIGHT!

■ Equipment

Cones to mark the playing area; white yarn balls (or any soft and squishy ball that will not freeze; enough for half of the class to each have one); and large, brightly colored fabric squares or short swim noodles for taggers to carry

■ Description

Depending on your class size, assign one or two students to be It. These students hold the fabric squares or noodles. Divide the rest of the class in half and give one group the white yarn balls (snowballs). The Its try to tag skiers holding snowballs. To avoid being tagged, players may underhand toss their snowball to another skier who does not have a snowball; however, if the snowball is dropped, the tosser and catcher must face each other and perform five jumping jacks together. The Its may hand off their fabric square or swim noodle when they choose to. No poles are used.

SNOWFLAKE MELTERS

■ Equipment

Two or three white yarn balls (or any soft and squishy ball that will not freeze) to represent snowflakes and two or three red yarn balls (or any soft and squishy ball that will not freeze) to represent melters; cones to mark the playing area

■ Description

In this freeze tag game, the melters try to melt and unfreeze the skiers frozen by the snowflakes. Skiers tagged by the snowflakes freeze in place in a skier's stride (diagonal stride position) and wait to be "melted" by being handed a red yarn ball by a melter. Melters will be handing off their red yarn balls to the frozen skiers when they unfreeze them. Snowflakes do not hand off their white yarn balls when they freeze a skier. Switch the snowflake taggers frequently. No poles are used.

STEAL THE BACON

◼ Equipment

A baseball or softball glove; a Nerf football or other object of similar size

◼ Description

The object of Steal the Bacon is for players to ski the "bacon" back to their team's side without being caught. In this game, two teams are formed. The members of each team stand in a row facing each other across the field. Each team numbers their players. The bacon is placed in the exact center between the lines. The teacher then calls out several numbers. Skiers whose numbers were called ski to the center where the bacon is located while their teammates remain standing on their sideline. Skiers may not touch the other players until someone touches the bacon. Once a skier touches the bacon, the other players may tag that skier. If a player is able to grab the bacon and ski it back over to his own side, that player's team scores a point. If a player is tagged after grabbing the bacon and before returning to his own side, the tagging team scores a point. The game is over when a team scores a predetermined number of points or when all numbers have been called.

SWAP TIME

◼ Equipment

15 balls of one color; 15 balls of another color; cones to mark the field

◼ Description

Each team tries to move all of their team's balls from one circle to the other. The circles may be guarded. Both teams work at the same time, tossing the balls underhand to a partner (no overhand throws are allowed) or skiing with the ball. A dropped ball can be picked up by either team and remains in play. Game play continues for the length of time determined by the teacher. At the end of the playing time, the team that moved the most balls from one circle to the other wins the round. Once the balls are reset in their respective circles, a new round starts. This game can be played with either one or two skis on. No poles should be used.

TEAM VOLLEYBALL

◼ Equipment

Multiple volleyball nets or ropes stretched between poles at standard volleyball net height; beach balls or other large, soft balls that students can safely hit with their hands; tempera paint to mark court areas

◼ Description

In this cooperative game of volleyball, two teams of four or five players are working together to move the ball over the net as many times as possible. The server stands behind the end line to put the ball into play with a serve. The serve may be to teammates, who will then hit the ball over the net. Teams are allowed three hits on their side of the court before the ball is hit over the net. If the ball touches the ground, the ball goes to the other team; that team serves the ball back into play, and the counting of hits starts over again at zero. Teams should rotate position when they lose serve. Teams should record the highest number of times they have hit the ball back and forth over the net. After five minutes of play, the teams with the greatest number of consecutive hits over the net should rotate to court 1, the court that all teams are striving to be in.

DOUBLE-POLE CHARIOT RACES

■ Equipment

Cones or flags to mark a starting line and finish line

■ Description

Skiers pair up with a partner close to their own size. Partners start both facing the same direction, one right behind the other. The front skier has poles. The second skier (without poles) puts her skis between the front skier's legs and holds on to her waist. The front skier then performs the double pole, propelling both skiers forward. This activity can be done as a relay race. The activity works best on an area of flat, packed snow.

DOUBLE-POLE RELAY

■ Equipment

Soft foam balls (one for each team); cones to mark off the relay area, which should be a large flat oval

■ Description

Form teams based on how many skiers you have; in colder weather, use a smaller number of skiers per team to increase the activity level of each skier. In this relay, all skiers double pole. Skiers using another technique will have to stop and turn around once using a star turn before continuing. Skiers hold a softball-size foam ball between their thighs or knees. This will help the skiers keep their legs together while double poling (see figure 5.4). When skiers reach their teammate, they hand the ball to the next skier, who puts it between his legs and skis on. The first team to ski each leg of the relay and successfully move the ball to the finish line wins.

Figure 5.4 In the Double-Pole Relay, students are challenged to hold a ball with their legs while they perform the double pole. This is a fun way to teach students to keep their legs together when they double pole.

HILL OVER RELAY

■ Equipment

Cones or flags to place at the midpoint of the hill, the top of the hill, and the finish line at the bottom of the hill

■ Description

Form teams with four or fewer skiers per team. Use a hill that is wide enough for each team to climb and descend at one time; the hill should also be steep enough to require some herringboning. Skier 1 starts at the bottom and skis to the hilltop, around a cone or flag, and halfway down the hill to where skier 2 waits. Skier 1 must come to a complete stop and then tag off to skier 2. Skier 2 then skis to the bottom of the hill, around another cone or flag, and up to the midway point, where skier 3 waits for the tag-off. Depending on how many skiers are on each team, this routine continues with the tag-off happening at the midway point of the hill. The final skier will finish the race by using a tight tuck all the way to the finish line.

MITTEN RELAY

■ Equipment

Large, flat area with multiple pairs of set tracks (for older skiers, the area should be the size of a football field)

■ Description

Form teams based on how many skiers you have. In colder weather, use a smaller number of skiers per team to increase the activity level of each skier. Divide each team so that half the team is on one end of the tracks and half is on the other end. The first skier skis 100 yards (91 m) to his teammate waiting at the other end of the track. The first skier trades mittens with the second skier, who then skis back to the third skier and again trades mittens, and so on. No poles are used. The teacher can determine how many lengths of track the relay race will include.

OLYMPIC BIATHLON RACE

■ Equipment

Five brightly colored hula hoops, five balls or beanbags to toss for each station, and cones to mark two separate ski loops

■ Description

For this race, you will need to set up a long loop, a shorter penalty loop, a toss area, and a throw area (see figure 5.5). Skiers start by skiing a longer ski loop and then skiing into the toss area. In the toss area, they stand behind a line 5 to 10 yards (4.6 to 9.1 m) from a hula hoop (adjust the distance based on age and skill) and toss five balls or beanbags at the hoop target lying flat on the snow. If skiers miss any tosses, they ski one penalty lap for each missed toss. Skiers then exit the toss area to ski one lap of the longer loop before entering the throw area, where they will throw balls or beanbags through a target (hula hoop or smaller hoop on a stand). If any throws are missed, skiers ski one penalty lap for each missed throw before completing the final long loop. Skiers exit the throw area to ski the last lap of the long loop. No poles are used.

■ Variations

Skiers can toss beanbags into a bucket, or they can use tennis rackets to hit tennis balls underhand to a target.

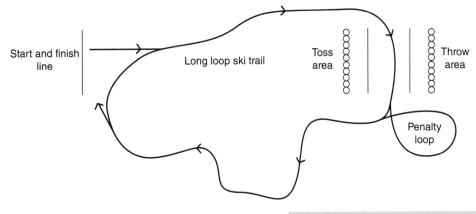

Figure 5.5 Setup diagram for Olympic Biathlon Race.

OLYMPIC NOODLE RELAY RACE

■ Equipment

One 20-inch (51 cm) swim noodle for each team (cut the longer 60-inch [152 cm] noodle into three equal portions); multiple pairs of set tracks in a large oval (for older skiers, the oval should be the size of a football field)

■ Description

This relay race is conducted similar to a running relay race. Create teams of four skiers and position the skiers equal distances from each other around the oval track. Use cones (or painted lines in the snow) to mark the spots on the oval where each skier should start. The first skiers hold the swim noodle and pass it to the next skier. Teams should practice the handoff with the skiers standing several ski strides apart; this will help skiers learn how to avoid skiing on top of their teammates' skis. Using the 20-inch swim noodle allows skiers to maintain a bit of distance during the exchange. No poles are used in this race.

PUZZLE RACE

■ Equipment

Maps of the ski area or ski trail. The maps can be of one trail or various trails in the same vicinity. You need to print or paste the maps onto tagboard and cut them apart into puzzle shapes; all maps should have controls marked on them. You also need to hang color crayons or hole punches with different shapes at each control corresponding to the controls marked on the students' map.

■ Description

Start the class indoors with skiers dressed and ready to ski. For each team, you will need a map printed on tagboard or cardstock and cut apart into puzzle pieces. Divide the class into teams of four students and give each team an envelope with their puzzle pieces. On "Go," the teams put their puzzle together, tape the pieces in place, and then head outside to ski their course. For each control, the students will punch their map (or copy a shape with the color crayon on the map). The first team that returns with all controls correctly marked wins the race.

THE SKI SHOP RELAY

■ Equipment

A flat, oval loop with multiple sets of track

■ Description

Form teams based on how many skiers you have; in colder weather, use a smaller number of skiers per team to increase the activity level of each skier. A short loop works well for this relay. With one ski on and no poles, skier 1 performs a scooter around the loop for the first leg of the relay, tagging off to skier 2. Skier 2 skis the loop while wearing two skis and not using poles. Skier 2 tags off to skier 3, who skis with two skis and two poles. From this point, the relay could end after this leg of the race, or the relay could work in reverse, reducing equipment to one ski.

SNOWBALL RELAY

■ Equipment

One plastic bucket for each team; enough white yarn balls (or any soft and squishy ball that will not freeze; to represent snowballs) for each team member to have a snowball

■ Description

Set up a start line and a finish line 17 yards (15.5 m) away (make this distance shorter for younger skiers). Place a bucket filled with the team's snowballs at the finish line. (See figure 5.6 for the setup.) Divide the class into teams. Start the relay race by calling out "Skiers take your mark! Go!" Skiers will ski down to their team's bucket, pick up a snowball, and ski back to the start line. The first group to return all of their snowballs to the start line wins the relay. No poles are used.

■ Variations

Conduct the race with skiers performing scooters (one ski on, one ski off), or have skiers use both skis but no poles. In another variation, once the skiers pick up their snowball, they ski one lap around the perimeter of the playing area and then ski back to their team; in this variation, the second skier starts once the first skier has picked up her snowball and has started to ski the perimeter.

Start
line

Buckets with snowballs

Figure 5.6 Setup diagram for Snowball Relay.

UPS AND DOWNS RELAY

■ Equipment

Cones or flags for skiers to ski around at the top of the hill

■ Description

This relay is a great workout as well as an excellent skill builder. Relay teams can have any number of skiers, but two-person teams work best. The teacher decides how many times each skier will go up and down the hill. The race begins with skier 1 skiing up the hill, around a cone or flag, and down the hill. Skier 1 tags off to skier 2 (probably at full speed), and skier 2 then skis to the top and back down. Skiers are penalized with an extra half a hill climb if the skier skiing down the hill is going too fast or out of control and misses the tag-off.

WATER BOTTLE RELAYS

■ Equipment

A belt pack with a water bottle carrier for each skier (if you do not have water bottle carriers for each skier, use an 8-ounce bottle of water and have skiers tuck it into a jacket pocket); one water bottle for each team

■ Description

A short loop is best for this relay, but an out-and-back course can also be used. Four-person teams work well. Mark off transition zones for each lane. The first skiers are given a water bottle to carry in a pocket or a belt pack. The first skier skis the assigned loop and returns to hand off the water bottle to the second skier while skiing through the transition zone. The second skier continues on, skiing the course and handing the bottle to the third skier, who then skis and hands off to the fourth skier, and so on. If the bottle is dropped, the skier must simply pick it up and continue on. Have enough water bottles for everyone at the finish.

Activities

COUNTDOWN!

■ Equipment

Cones to mark the start and finish lines (or tempera paint to draw the start and finish lines); multiple sets of groomed tracks that are straight and parallel

■ Description

This is a scooter challenge that provides skiers with the opportunity to practice their kicks and glides. Skiers will work to improve the distance they can glide on one ski. With one ski on, skiers start at the starting line with the ski in the outside track. Skiers kick and glide as they use their scooter pushes to propel them to the finish line. Skiers should count the number of pushes it takes for them to make it from the start line to the finish line. When they reach the finish line, skiers turn around and return to the start line, trying to make it back using one less scooter push than it took them to make it to the finish line. Encourage skiers to move their arms in the correct movement pattern when they kick and to work on holding their diagonal stride position when they are gliding. Skiers repeat the activity using the other leg.

DANCE, DANCE, SKI DANCE!

■ Equipment

Boom box with music that is appropriate for dancing and has an easy and strong beat for students to follow

■ Description

Divide the class into small groups of three or four. Each group will be creating their own dance routine (on skis) that includes a 12-count series of movements, a connector 4-count series of movements, and then another 12-count series of movements. Once the groups have practiced, let them perform their "ski dances" for the rest of the class.

DOUBLE-POLE CHASE

■ Equipment

Cones or paint lines to mark a start and finish line (these lines should be 17 to 23 yards apart depending on skier skill); multiple sets of straight tracks

■ Description

Divide the class into teams of four or five. On the teacher's command of "Ready! Set! Race!" the first skier in each line double poles toward the finish line. After the first skiers have completed about five double poles, the teacher starts the second skiers, who then attempt to catch the first skiers. The third and fourth skiers are started one after another as done with the first and second skiers. When the whole team has made it to the finish line, the first skier goes to the end of the line and becomes the last skier. The second skier moves up to become the first skier. Repeat the exercise in the opposite direction, again starting the skiers at intervals. If your skiers are in good condition, repeat the exercise until each skier has had the chance to be the lead skier.

HOT SNOW

■ Equipment

Long jump ropes or tempera paint to draw parallel lines in the snow

■ Description

In this activity, skiers will be sidestepping over five or more ropes stretched out straight on the snow (or long lines made with tempera paint on the snow). Skiers stand with their side to the rope and sidestep over the rope, placing their ski far enough away from the rope that there is room for the other ski to be set down beside it (the skier is now standing between the ropes with skis parallel to the ropes). Skiers continue to work their way across the lines and then reverse directions and return to their starting point.

■ Variations

- Encourage skiers to pick up the pace and move quickly through the lines and back again, pretending that the snow is hot sand. The skiers need to lift their knees and quickly move over the lines.
- Lay out lines on a hill so skiers will sidestep up the hill and back down.

PARACHUTE CIRCLES

■ Equipment

Large, brightly colored parachute; beach ball

■ Description

The youngest skiers will enjoy playing with the parachute outside. Space the skiers out around the edge of the parachute, giving each skier room to slide his skis forward without running into the skier in front of him. Skiers should grasp the edge of the chute with their right hand. On the teacher's command, skiers ski clockwise until they have completed one full circle. Skiers then set the chute on the snow and perform a counterclockwise star turn. Skiers pick the chute up with their left hand; on the teacher's command, the skiers ski counterclockwise around the circle, returning to their home position. Then they perform a clockwise star turn. To finish, the teacher tosses snowballs (white yarn balls) onto the chute, and the skiers raise and lower their arms to bounce the snowballs on the chute.

■ Variations

- Start with skiers spaced around the edge of the chute, holding on to the chute with their left hand. The skiers complete one full circle and then set the chute on the snow. Skiers perform a quarter of a star turn so they now face away from the circle. They ski five strides away from the circle. Next, skiers perform half a star turn so they now face the circle, and they ski five strides back to the chute.
- Place a beach ball on the parachute. Skiers stand facing into the center of the parachute with their ski tips close together and ski tails wide apart, creating a snowplow. Skiers grasp the edge of the parachute and then lean back and raise their arms as necessary to move the ball around the parachute in a circle.
- Place a beach ball on the parachute. Skiers face clockwise and grasp the edge of the parachute with their right hand, keeping their skis parallel. Skiers lean out away from the parachute, allowing their skis to edge. They raise their arms as necessary to move the ball around the parachute in a circle.

PLEASE PASS THE SNOWBALL!

■ Equipment

Cones or tempera paint to mark a start and finish line; yarn balls (or any soft and squishy ball that will not freeze) or other soft balls that are easy to catch with mittens on

■ Description

Skiers stand side by side with their partner; the two skiers are approximately two arm lengths apart. As they ski across the playing area, they toss the ball back and forth to each other, counting the number of tosses and catches they make. If one of the partners drops the ball, both partners return to the start line and begin again.

■ Variations

Reverse the goal of trying to make many tosses and catches so that the skiers are trying to make fewer tosses and catches.

PART III

Teaching Aids

Assessments

ADVANCED BASIC SKILLS CHECKLIST

Name _____ Date _____

Put a check mark in the "Yes" column if the skier is able to satisfactorily complete the skill. Put a check mark in the "No" column if the skier does not perform the skill correctly.

Diagonal Stride No Poles

	Yes	No	Comments
Start with feet side by side			
Kick with right foot			
Right arm swings forward			
Left arm swings backward			
Glide on left ski			
Right foot returns to side-by-side position next to left foot			
Kick with left foot			
Left arm swings forward			
Right arm swings backward			
Left foot returns to side-by-side position next to right foot			

Diagonal Stride Uphill

	Yes	No	Comments
Stride shortens as hill gets steeper			
Glide disappears			
Increase tempo			
Eyes focused on hill in front of skis			
Elbows very bent			
Poles planted across from heel or slightly farther back			
Skier pushes off of poles			
Stride is continuous up and over hill crest; no break in momentum			

Diagonal Stride With Poles

	Yes	No	Comments
Start with feet side by side			
Kick with right foot			
Right arm swings forward			
Poles held angled backward			
Left arm swings backward			
Glide on left ski			
Right pole is planted even with left foot			
Skier pushes on right pole			
Right foot returns to side-by-side position next to left foot			
Kick with left foot			

continued ▶

Diagonal Stride With Poles *(continued)*

	Yes	No	Comments
Left arm swings forward			
Poles held angled backward			
Right arm swings backward			
Glide on right ski			
Left pole is planted even with right foot			
Skier pushes on left pole			
Left foot returns to side-by-side position next to right foot			

Double Pole

	Yes	No	Comments
Feet side by side			
Arms extended in front of body			
Elbows slightly bent			
Poles angled backward			
Skier bends at waist, crunching core; back parallel to ground			
Poles planted slightly forward of feet with hands approximately shoulder high			
Skier pushes back on poles			
Hands brush past knees			
Arms extend in back of skier			
Skier starts to stand			
Hands are swung to in front of skier			

Kick Double Pole

	Yes	No	Comments
Feet side by side			
Kick starts simultaneously with arm swing			
Arms swing forward, extended in front of body			
Elbows slightly bent at approximately 90 degrees			
Poles angled slightly backward			
Poles planted slightly forward of feet with hands approximately shoulder high			
Skier flexes at waist, crunching core; back parallel to ground			
Skier pushes back on poles			
Kick leg moves forward to side-by-side position with other foot			
Hands brush past knees			
Arms extend in back of skier			
Skier's trunk moves upright			
Hands are swung to in front of skier; feet are side by side			
Kick starts simultaneously with arm swing			

continued ▶

Herringbone

	Yes	No	Comments
Head up and eyes looking at hilltop			
Begin with skis in V position			
Step forward with one ski			
Poles angled backward			
Skier pushes off of poles			
Contralateral pole and leg motion			
Ski tail clears other ski			
Edge ski as ski is set on snow			
Step forward with other ski			

Snowplow Stop

	Yes	No	Comments
Start with skis parallel when moving downhill			
Slide skis into a wide V with tips together, tails spread			
Hands held low in front of body			
Poles angled backward			
Upper body upright			
Knees and ankles bent			
Skis are edged			
Skier comes to a stop			

Snowplow Turn

	Yes	No	Comments
Move downhill with skis parallel			
Slide skis into a narrow V with tips together, tails spread			
Skis are on inside edges			
Knees and ankles bent			
Trunk upright			
Weight balanced between skis			
Hands slightly in front of body with poles angled backward off the snow			
Knee and foot rotate in direction of turn			
Weight shifts to the ski opposite the direction of turn (to turn to the left, weight is put on the right ski)			
Skier is able to link a turn to the right with a turn to the left in a continuous, smooth pattern			

continued ▶

Stem Christie Turn

	Yes	No	Comments
Skis start parallel and move into a narrow V position as skier moves down a moderate hill			
Skier has an upright posture; knees and ankles bent			
Weight is transferred to the downhill ski			
Skier straightens knees and ankles slightly			
The uphill ski slides into a position parallel to the downhill ski			
Skis skid in a parallel position near the end of turn			
Skier sinks into the finish by flexing knees and ankles			

Advanced Lessons 2, 3, 4, 5, 6, 7, and 8.

From B.A. Duoos and A.M. Rykken, 2012, *Teaching Cross-Country Skiing* (Champaign, IL: Human Kinetics).

ADVANCED BASIC SKILLS RUBRIC

Use the following rubric to assess student progress toward competency in the basic skills:

1 = Skier does not perform critical features correctly; skier is not competent at the skill.

2 = Skier performs some of the critical features correctly; many errors still exist.

3 = Critical features are performed satisfactorily; a few errors still exist.

4 = Skier performs most of the critical features correctly; minor errors exist.

5 = Skier performs critical features correctly; skier is competent at the skill.

Diagonal Stride No Poles

Name																						
Start with feet side by side																						
Kick with right foot																						
Right arm swings forward																						
Left arm swings backward																						
Glide on left ski																						
Right foot returns to side-by-side position next to left foot																						
Kick with left foot																						
Left arm swings forward																						
Right arm swings backward																						
Left foot returns to side-by-side position next to right foot																						
TOTAL SCORE																						

continued

Advanced Basic Skills Rubric (continued)

Diagonal Stride Uphill

Name																			
Stride shortens as hill gets steeper																			
Glide disappears																			
Increase tempo																			
Eyes focused on hill in front of skis																			
Elbows very bent																			
Poles planted across from heel or slightly farther back																			
Skier pushes off of poles																			
Stride is continuous up and over hill crest; no break in momentum																			
TOTAL SCORE																			

continued ►

Advanced Basic Skills Rubric (continued)

Diagonal Stride With Poles

Name																						
Start with feet side by side																						
Kick with right foot																						
Right arm swings forward																						
Poles held angled backward																						
Left arm swings backward																						
Glide on left ski																						
Right pole is planted even with left foot																						
Skier pushes on right pole																						
Right foot returns to side-by-side position next to left foot																						
Kick with left foot																						
Left arm swings forward																						
Poles held angled backward																						
Right arm swings backward																						
Glide on right ski																						
Left pole is planted even with right foot																						
Skier pushes on left pole																						
Left foot returns to side-by-side position next to right foot																						
TOTAL SCORE																						

continued ▲

Advanced Basic Skills Rubric (continued)

Double Pole

Name																			
Feet side by side																			
Arms extended in front of body																			
Elbows slightly bent																			
Poles angled backward																			
Skier bends at waist, crunching core; back parallel to ground																			
Poles planted slightly forward of feet with hands approximately shoulder high																			
Skier pushes back on poles																			
Hands brush past knees																			
Arms extend in back of skier																			
Skier starts to stand																			
Hands are swung to in front of skier																			
TOTAL SCORE																			

continued

Herringbone

Name																				
Head up and eyes looking at hilltop																				
Begin with skis in V position																				
Step forward with one ski																				
Poles angled backward																				
Skier pushes off of poles																				
Contralateral pole and leg motion																				
Ski tail clears other ski																				
Edge ski as ski is set on snow																				
Step forward with other ski																				
TOTAL SCORE																				

continued ▲

Kick Double Pole

Name																			
Feet side by side																			
Kick starts simultaneously with arm swing																			
Arms swing forward, extended in front of body																			
Elbows slightly bent at approximately 90 degrees																			
Poles angled slightly backward																			
Poles planted slightly forward of feet with hands approximately shoulder high																			
Skier flexes at waist, crunching core; back parallel to ground																			
Skier pushes back on poles																			
Kick leg moves forward to side-by-side position with other foot																			
Hands brush past knees																			
Arms extend in back of skier																			
Skier's trunk moves upright																			
Hands are swung to in front of skier; feet are side by side																			
Kick starts simultaneously with arm swing																			
TOTAL SCORE																			

continued

Advanced Basic Skills Rubric (continued)

Snowplow Stop

Name																				
Start with skis parallel when moving downhill																				
Slide skis into a wide V with tips together, tails spread																				
Hands held low in front of body																				
Poles angled backward																				
Upper body upright																				
Knees and ankles bent																				
Skis are edged																				
Skier comes to a stop																				
TOTAL SCORE																				

continued ▲

Snowplow Turn

Name																					
Move downhill with skis parallel																					
Slide skis into a narrow V with tips together, tails spread																					
Skis are on inside edges																					
Knees and ankles bent																					
Trunk upright																					
Weight balanced between skis																					
Hands slightly in front of body with poles angled backward off the snow																					
Knee and foot rotate in direction of turn																					
Weight shifts to the ski opposite the direction of turn (to turn to the left, weight is put on the right ski)																					
Skier is able to link a turn to the right with a turn to the left in a continuous, smooth pattern																					
TOTAL SCORE																					

Advanced Basic Skills Rubric (continued)

Stem Christie Turn

Name																	
Skis start parallel and move into a narrow V position as skier moves down a moderate hill																	
Skier has an upright posture; knees and ankles bent																	
Weight is transferred to the downhill ski																	
Skier straightens knees and ankles slightly																	
The uphill ski slides into a position parallel to the downhill ski																	
Skis skid in a parallel position near the end of turn																	
Skier sinks into the finish by flexing knees and ankles																	
TOTAL SCORE																	

Advanced Lessons 2, 3, 4, 5, 6, 7, and 8

From B.A. Duoos and A.M. Rykken, 2012, *Teaching Cross-Country Skiing* (Champaign, IL: Human Kinetics).

BEGINNER BASIC SKILLS CHECKLIST

Name _____ **Date** _____

Put a check mark in the "Yes" column if the skier is able to satisfactorily complete the skill. Put a check mark in the "No" column if the skier does not perform the skill correctly.

Dead Bug

	Yes	No	Comments
Fall to side or back			
Skier's bottom hits first			
Roll to back			
Skis parallel in air			
Skier tips to one side, keeping skis parallel			
Skier moves to one knee			
Skier stands			

Herringbone

	Yes	No	Comments
Begin with skis in V position			
Step forward with one ski			
Ski tail clears other ski; skier sets ski on snow			
Step forward with other ski			
Ski tail clears other ski; skier sets ski on snow			

Ski Handling—Carrying Skis, One in Each Hand

	Yes	No	Comments
Skier carries one ski and one pole in each hand			
Skis and poles are under control			

Ski Handling—Carrying Skis, Both Under One Arm

	Yes	No	Comments
Skier carries both skis with one hand and both poles with the other			
Skis and poles are under control			

Ski Handling—Putting Skis On

	Yes	No	Comments
Skier puts toe of boot into binding, raises heel			
Skier pushes down with toe so binding clicks in place			

Ski Handling—Taking Skis Off

	Yes	No	Comments
Skier uses tip of pole to push down on binding to release boot			

continued ▶

Sidestepping

	Yes	No	Comments
Pick up right ski			
Ski clears ground			
Set ski down 6 to 8 inches to right side			
Pick up left ski			
Ski clears ground			
Set ski down next to right ski			

Snowplow (Wedge Shape)

	Yes	No	Comments
Start with skis parallel (French fries)			
Move skis into V with tips together, tails spread			
Return skis to parallel (French fries)			

Star Turn

	Yes	No	Comments
Start with ski tails together, tips apart			
Move right ski tip to right, keeping ski tail on snow			
Move left ski tip to right, keeping ski tail on snow			
Repeat, moving in a complete circle clockwise			
Repeat to the left, moving in a complete circle counterclockwise			

Beginner Lessons 2, 3, 9, and 10; Intermediate Lessons 1 and 2.

From B.A. Duoos and A.M. Rykken, 2012, *Teaching Cross-Country Skiing* (Champaign, IL: Human Kinetics).

BEGINNER BASIC SKILLS RUBRIC

Use the following rubric to assess student progress toward competency in the basic skills:

1 = Skier does not perform critical features correctly; skier is not competent at the skill.

2 = Skier performs some of the critical features correctly; many errors exist.

3 = Critical features are performed satisfactorily; a few errors still exist.

4 = Skier performs most of the critical features correctly; minor errors exist.

5 = Skier performs critical features correctly; skier is competent at the skill.

Dead Bug

Name																				
Fall to side or back																				
Skier's bottom hits first																				
Roll to back																				
Skis parallel in air																				
Skier tips to one side, keeping skis parallel																				
Skier moves to one knee																				
Skier stands																				
TOTAL SCORE																				

continued ▲

Herringbone

Name																		
Begin with skis in V position																		
Step forward with one ski																		
Ski tail clears other ski; skier sets ski on snow																		
Step forward with other ski																		
Ski tail clears other ski; skier sets ski on snow																		
TOTAL SCORE																		

continued

Beginner Basic Skills Rubric (continued)

Ski Handling—Carrying Skis, One in Each Hand

Name																			
Skier carries one ski and one pole in each hand																			
Skis and poles are under control																			
TOTAL SCORE																			

Ski Handling—Carrying Skis, Both Under One Arm

Name																			
Skier carries both skis with one hand and both poles with the other																			
Skis and poles are under control																			
TOTAL SCORE																			

continued

Beginner Basic Skills Rubric (continued)

Ski Handling—Putting Skis On

Name		
Skier puts toe of boot into binding, raises heel		
Skier pushes down with toe so binding clicks in place		
TOTAL SCORE		

Ski Handling—Taking Skis Off

Name		
Skier uses tip of pole to push down on binding to release boot		
TOTAL SCORE		

continued

Beginner Basic Skills Rubric (continued)

Sidestepping

Name																			
Pick up right ski																			
Ski clears ground																			
Set ski down 6 to 8 inches to right side																			
Pick up left ski																			
Ski clears ground																			
Set ski down next to right ski																			
TOTAL SCORE																			

continued

Beginner Basic Skills Rubric (continued)

Snowplow

Name																					
Start with skis parallel (French fries)																					
Move skis into V with tips together, tails spread																					
Return skis to parallel (French fries)																					
TOTAL SCORE																					

continued

Beginner Basic Skills Rubric (continued)

Star Turn

Name																					
Start with ski tails together, tips apart																					
Move right ski tip to right, keeping ski tail on snow																					
Move left ski tip to right, keeping ski tail on snow																					
Repeat, moving in a complete circle clockwise																					
Repeat to the left, moving in a complete circle counterclockwise																					
TOTAL SCORE																					

Beginner Lessons 2, 3, 9, and 10

From B.A. Duoos and A.M. Rykken, 2012, *Teaching Cross-Country Skiing* (Champaign, IL: Human Kinetics).

DIAGONAL STRIDE WITH POLES RUBRIC

Watch each skier perform the diagonal stride using poles. Look for the critical features listed, and score the skier's performance according to the rubric. Put your score in the space provided.

5 = Critical feature is present and performed correctly.

4 = Critical feature is present and nearly correct.

3 = Critical feature is present but needs work.

2 = Critical feature is sometimes present; much work is needed.

1 = We need to review! I will go over this with you so you can learn how to perform this correctly.

Name																
1. Skier starts in skier slouch position, poles angled backward																
2. Skier kicks, arms move contralaterally																
3. Body weight shifts over the gliding ski																
4. Pole is planted near foot																
5. Pole is planted angled backward																
6. Legs move back together																
7. Skier kicks, arms move contralaterally																
TOTAL SCORE																

Beginner Lesson 7

From B.A. Duoos and A.M. Rykken, 2012, *Teaching Cross-Country Skiing* (Champaign, IL: Human Kinetics).

DOUBLE-POLE FUN PEER EVALUATION

Name _____ **Date** _____

Peer you are observing _____

Your ski partner needs your help with the double pole. Your job is to watch your partner very carefully to see if he or she is doing the six moves listed below. If you see your partner making the correct move, put a check mark in the "Yes" column. If you do not see your partner making the correct move, put a check mark in the "No" column.

Double Pole

	Yes	No
1. Skier begins in skier's slouch.		
2. Both arms swing forward at same time with poles angled backward.		
3. Poles are angled backward.		
4. Poles are planted in snow near bindings.		
5. Skier pushes on poles.		
6. Skier compresses torso so back is parallel to ground.		
7. Arms swing down and past pockets, with poles extended.		

Beginner Lesson 7

From B.A. Duoos and A.M. Rykken, 2012, *Teaching Cross-Country Skiing* (Champaign, IL: Human Kinetics).

DRAW ME!

Name _____ **Date** _____

In the space below, draw a picture (a stick figure is OK) of what you should look like when you are doing the skier slouch *walk*. Label the following on your drawing:

1. Right arm
2. Left arm
3. Right leg
4. Left leg

Check Your Work

When you are done with your drawing, give it to your partner. Your partner will stand in the same position that you just drew. Look carefully at how your partner is standing. Is your partner standing in a contralateral position? (In this position, the right arm is forward when the right leg is back, and the left arm is forward when the left leg is back.) If yes, give yourself a star at the top of your picture. If not, draw your picture again so your arms and legs are in the right position.

Intermediate Lesson 1

From B.A. Duoos and A.M. Rykken, 2012, *Teaching Cross-Country Skiing* (Champaign, IL: Human Kinetics).

ETIQUETTE CHECK

Name _____ **Date** _____

Neatly print your answers in the space provided. Point values are given in the parentheses. You can earn up to five points total.

1. You are skiing in the only ski track in the state park when a faster skier comes up behind you and wants to pass you. What words should the faster skier call out so that you know the skier is there and wants to move around you? (1)

   _____

2. What should *you* do when you hear the faster skier call out the words you wrote down for question number 1? (1)

   _____

   _____

3. Oh no! Your ski binding breaks while you are out skiing on a trail in your city park. Your ski boot will not stay in the binding, so you will have to walk back to the ski center. Where should you walk on your way back to the ski center? (1)

   _____

4. You love to cross-country ski so much that you want to teach your younger brother and sister how to ski. List two rules of etiquette, or courtesy rules, that you will tell them they must follow when on the ski trails. (1 point for each rule, 2 points total)

   a. _____

   b. _____

Advanced lesson 9
From B.A. Duoos and A.M. Rykken, 2012, *Teaching Cross-Country Skiing* (Champaign, IL: Human Kinetics).

I CAN TEACH YOU THE SNOWPLOW STOP

Name _____ **Date** _____

Peer you are observing_____

Skiers, today we worked on using the snowplow stop to control your speed when moving down a hill. When we learned how to do a snowplow stop, we practiced at least five different things that helped you control your speed when moving down a hill. Now it is your turn to teach your friend how to do a snowplow stop. In the following spaces, list five things you would tell your friend so that he or she can learn how to do a snowplow stop.

1. _____

2. _____

3. _____

4. _____

5. _____

Scoring

Each line is worth one point. Your work will be scored based on the following:

    5 points—Five correct critical features of the snowplow stop are given.

    4 points—Four correct critical features of the snowplow stop are given.

    3 points—Three correct critical features of the snowplow stop are given.

    2 points—Two correct critical features of the snowplow stop are given.

    1 point—One correct critical feature of the snowplow stop is given.

Beginner Lesson 8

From B.A. Duoos and A.M. Rykken, 2012, *Teaching Cross-Country Skiing* (Champaign, IL: Human Kinetics).

INTERMEDIATE BASIC SKILLS CHECKLIST

Name _____ **Date** _____

Put a check mark in the "Yes" column if the skier is able to satisfactorily complete the skill. Put a check mark in the "No" column if the skier does not perform the skill correctly.

Diagonal Stride No Poles

	Yes	No	Comments
Start with feet side by side			
Kick with right foot			
Right arm swings forward			
Left arm swings backward			
Glide on left ski			
Right foot returns to side-by-side position next to left foot			
Kick with left foot			
Left arm swings forward			
Right arm swings backward			
Left foot returns to side-by-side position next to right foot			

Diagonal Stride Uphill

	Yes	No	Comments
Stride shortens as hill gets steeper			
Glide disappears			
Increase tempo			
Eyes focused on hill in front of skis			
Poles planted across from heel or slightly farther back			
Stride is continuous up and over hill crest			

Diagonal Stride With Poles

	Yes	No	Comments
Start with feet side by side			
Kick with right foot			
Right arm swings forward			
Poles held angled backward			
Left arm swings backward			
Glide on left ski			
Right pole is planted even with left foot			
Right foot returns to side-by-side position next to left foot			
Kick with left foot			
Left arm swings forward			
Poles held angled backward			
Right arm swings backward			

continued ▶

	Yes	No	Comments
Glide on right ski			
Left pole is planted even with right foot			
Left foot returns to side-by-side position next to right foot			

Double Pole

	Yes	No	Comments
Feet side by side			
Arms extended in front of body			
Elbows slightly bent			
Poles angled backward			
Skier bends at waist, crunching core			
Poles planted alongside feet			
Skier pushes back on poles			
Hands brush past knees			
Arms extend in back of skier			
Skier starts to stand			
Hands are swung to in front of skier			

Herringbone

	Yes	No	Comments
Begin with skis in V position			
Step forward with one ski			
Poles angled backward			
Contralateral pole and leg motion			
Ski tail clears other ski			
Edge ski as ski is set on snow			
Step forward with other ski			

Kick Double Pole

	Yes	No	Comments
Feet side by side			
Kick starts simultaneously with arm swing			
Arms swing forward, extended in front of body			
Elbows slightly bent			
Poles angled slightly backward			
Poles planted slightly forward of feet			
Skier flexes at waist, crunching core			
Skier pushes back on poles			
Kick leg moves forward to side-by-side position with other foot			
Hands brush past knees			
Arms extend in back of skier			
Skier's trunk moves upright			

continued ▶

Kick Double Pole *(continued)*

	Yes	No	Comments
Hands are swung to in front of skier; feet are side by side			
Kick starts simultaneously with arm swing			

Snowplow Stop

	Yes	No	Comments
Move downhill with skis parallel			
Slide skis into V with tips together, tails spread			
Knees and ankles bent			
Trunk upright			
Skis are edged			

Snowplow Turn

	Yes	No	Comments
Move downhill with skis parallel			
Slide skis into a narrow V with tips together, tails spread			
Skis are on inside edges			
Knees and ankles bent			
Trunk upright			
Hands slightly in front of body with poles angled backward off the snow			
Knee and foot rotate in direction of turn			
Weight is put on the ski opposite the direction of turn (to turn to the left, weight is put on the right ski)			

Intermediate Lessons 2, 3, 4, 6, 7, and 8

From B.A. Duoos and A.M. Rykken, 2012, *Teaching Cross-Country Skiing* (Champaign, IL: Human Kinetics).

INTERMEDIATE BASIC SKILLS RUBRIC

Use the following rubric to assess student progress toward competency in the basic skills:

1 = Skier does not perform critical features correctly; skier is not competent at the skill.

2 = Skier performs some of the critical features correctly; many errors still exist.

3 = Critical features are performed satisfactorily; a few errors still exist.

4 = Skier performs most of the critical features correctly; minor errors exist.

5 = Skier performs critical features correctly; skier is competent at the skill.

Diagonal Stride No Poles

Name																				
Start with feet side by side																				
Kick with right foot																				
Right arm swings forward																				
Left arm swings backward																				
Glide on left ski																				
Right foot returns to side-by-side position next to left foot																				
Kick with left foot																				
Left arm swings forward																				
Right arm swings backward																				
Left foot returns to side-by-side position next to right foot																				
TOTAL SCORE																				

continued ▲

Intermediate Basic Skills Rubric (continued)

Diagonal Stride Uphill

Name																			
Stride shortens as hill gets steeper																			
Glide disappears																			
Increase tempo																			
Eyes focused on hill in front of skis																			
Poles planted across from heel or slightly farther back																			
Stride is continuous up and over hill crest																			
TOTAL SCORE																			

continued ▲

Diagonal Stride With Poles

Name																
Start with feet side by side																
Kick with right foot																
Right arm swings forward																
Poles held angled backward																
Left arm swings backward																
Glide on left ski																
Right pole is planted even with left foot																
Right foot returns to side-by-side position next to left foot																
Kick with left foot																
Left arm swings forward																
Poles held angled backward																
Right arm swings backward																
Glide on right ski																
Left pole is planted even with right foot																
Left foot returns to side-by-side position next to right foot																
TOTAL SCORE																

continued

Double Pole

Name																			
Feet side by side																			
Arms extended in front of body																			
Elbows slightly bent																			
Poles angled backward																			
Skier bends at waist, crunching core																			
Poles planted alongside feet																			
Skier pushes back on poles																			
Hands brush past knees																			
Arms extend in back of skier																			
Skier starts to stand																			
Hands are swung to in front of skier																			
TOTAL SCORE																			

continued

Intermediate Basic Skills Rubric (continued)

Herringbone

Name																						
Begin with skis in V position																						
Step forward with one ski																						
Poles angled backward																						
Contralateral pole and leg motion																						
Ski tail clears other ski																						
Edge ski as ski is set on snow																						
Step forward with other ski																						
TOTAL SCORE																						

continued ▲

Intermediate Basic Skills Rubric (continued)

Kick Double Pole

Name																			
Feet side by side																			
Kick starts simultaneously with arm swing																			
Arms swing forward, extended in front of body																			
Elbows slightly bent																			
Poles angled slightly backward																			
Poles planted slightly forward of feet																			
Skier flexes at waist, crunching core																			
Skier pushes back on poles																			
Kick leg moves forward to side-by-side position with other foot																			
Hands brush past knees																			
Arms extend in back of skier																			
Skier's trunk moves upright																			
Hands are swung to in front of skier; feet are side by side																			
Kick starts simultaneously with arm swing																			
TOTAL SCORE																			

continued

Intermediate Basic Skills Rubric (continued)

Snowplow Stop

Name																			
Move downhill with skis parallel																			
Slide skis into V with tips together, tails spread																			
Knees and ankles bent																			
Trunk upright																			
Skis are edged																			
TOTAL SCORE																			

continued ▲

Snowplow Turn

Name																		
Move downhill with skis parallel																		
Slide skis into a narrow V with tips together, tails spread																		
Skis are on inside edges																		
Knees and ankles bent																		
Trunk upright																		
Hands slightly in front of body with poles angled backward off the snow																		
Knee and foot rotate in direction of turn																		
Weight is put on the ski opposite the direction of turn (to turn to the left, weight is put on the right ski)																		
TOTAL SCORE																		

Intermediate Lessons 2, 3, 4, 6, 7, and 8

From B.A. Duoos and A.M. Rykken, 2012, *Teaching Cross-Country Skiing* (Champaign, IL: Human Kinetics).

MARATHON SKATE CHECKLIST

Name _____ **Date** _____

Watch the skier perform several repetitions of the marathon skate. Put a check mark in the box if the critical feature is present and being performed correctly. Put an NW (for needs work) in the box if the critical feature is present but needs to be improved. Leave the box blank if the critical feature is absent.

	Date	Date	Date	Date	Date
One ski in the track, one ski angled outward					
Ski tips wide apart					
Ski tails close together					
Weight on the ski in the track					
Weight shifts to angled ski					
Skier performs the double pole					
Skier pushes off the angled ski					
Arms swing forward					
Weight shifts to ski in track					

Your score for the marathon skate is based on your improvement in performing the critical features listed. You will earn points as follows:

5 points = You correctly performed all critical features.

4 points = You correctly performed four critical features.

3 points = You correctly performed three critical features.

2 points = You correctly performed two critical features.

1 point = You correctly performed one critical feature.

Advanced Lesson 8

From B.A. Duoos and A.M. Rykken, 2012, *Teaching Cross-Country Skiing* (Champaign, IL: Human Kinetics).

■ 177

MIND YOUR MANNERS QUIZ

Name _____ **Date** _____

You have read about how to be a courteous skier in your handout, and we have practiced good etiquette when we have been on the ski trail. List five important things that you should remember to do in order to practice good etiquette on the ski trail.

Neatly print your answers on the lines. Each line is worth one point (five points total).

1. _____

2. _____

3. _____

4. _____

5. _____

Intermediate Lesson 6

From B.A. Duoos and A.M. Rykken, 2012, *Teaching Cross-Country Skiing* (Champaign, IL: Human Kinetics).

178 ■

ON AND OFF

Putting Skis On and Taking Skis Off Assessment

Observe the skier putting skis on and taking skis off. Put a check mark in the appropriate column.

Name	Date	Steps into binding and easily secures ski	Has difficulty putting skis on	Cannot put skis on without help	Easily removes skis	Has difficulty removing skis	Cannot remove skis without help

Beginner Lesson 2

From B.A. Duoos and A.M. Rykken, 2012, *Teaching Cross-Country Skiing* (Champaign, IL: Human Kinetics).

SCOOTER ARMS

Watch each skier perform scooters back and forth in the track on the flat. Focus on the arm swing and leg kick, looking for contralateral action. As the right arm swings forward, the right leg should move backward. As the left arm swings forward, the left leg should move backward. Place a check mark in the appropriate column.

Name	Date	Can maintain contralateral arm and leg action for the following distance:			Cannot maintain contralateral action
		10 yards	15 yards	20 yards	

Beginner Lesson 5

From B.A. Duoos and A.M. Rykken, 2012, *Teaching Cross-Country Skiing* (Champaign, IL: Human Kinetics).

SCOOTER COUNTDOWN

Name _____ **Date** _____

Count the number of scooter kicks it takes you to ski the distance between the cones. Record the number of kicks for each trial in the following boxes.

Date_____ Distance_____

Trial 1	Trial 2	Trial 3	Trial 4	Trial 5	Trial 6

Date_____ Distance_____

Trial 1	Trial 2	Trial 3	Trial 4	Trial 5	Trial 6

Date_____ Distance_____

Trial 1	Trial 2	Trial 3	Trial 4	Trial 5	Trial 6

Date_____ Distance_____

Trial 1	Trial 2	Trial 3	Trial 4	Trial 5	Trial 6

Beginner Lesson 5
From B.A. Duoos and A.M. Rykken, 2012, *Teaching Cross-Country Skiing* (Champaign, IL: Human Kinetics).

SCOOTER SHIFT CHALLENGE

Watch skiers as they perform scooters in the tracks on a flat area. Look for a complete weight shift from the kicking leg to the gliding ski. Place a check mark in the appropriate column.

Name	Date	Complete weight shift occurs; glide is present	Skier straddles track; quick weight shift occurs

Beginner Lesson 4

From B.A. Duoos and A.M. Rykken, 2012, *Teaching Cross-Country Skiing* (Champaign, IL: Human Kinetics).

SCOOTER SKILLS PARTNER CHECKLIST

Name _____ **Date** _____

Partner

It is your turn to help your partner perfect his or her scooter skills. You will watch your partner perform scooters and then give feedback on the partner's performance of the technique. Watch your partner scooter back and forth, and look for the critical features listed in the checklist. Put a check in the appropriate box if you see your partner perform the skill.

Skier

Remove the right ski and use the right foot to push while gliding on the left ski. The left ski should be in the right track (outer track) so the pushing foot is not destroying the ski track. You should kick with the right foot and transfer weight to the gliding ski. As the right foot kicks, the right arm should swing forward; the left arm swings back. Do not use poles. Once your partner has observed you several times and has completed the checklist for the right foot, you should switch your ski to the left foot and repeat the activity.

Name of skier _____

	DATE:		DATE:		DATE:		DATE:	
	Right-foot kick	Left-foot kick	Right-foot kick	Left-foot kick	Right-foot kick	Left-foot kick	Right-foot kick	Left-foot kick
RIGHT KICK								
Start with feet side by side								
Kick with right foot pushing backward								
Weight transfers to gliding ski (left ski)								
Right arm swings forward down the track when skier kicks								
Left arm swings backward when skier kicks								
Glide on left ski								
Feet return to side-by-side position								
LEFT KICK								
Start with feet side by side								
Kick with left foot pushing backward								
Weight transfers to gliding ski (right ski)								
Left arm swings forward down the track when skier kicks								
Right arm swings backward when skier kicks								
Glide on right ski								
Feet return to side-by-side position								

Intermediate Lesson 2

From B.A. Duoos and A.M. Rykken, 2012, *Teaching Cross-Country Skiing* (Champaign, IL: Human Kinetics).

SHUFFLE COUNTDOWN

Name _____ **Date** _____

Count the number of shuffles or kicks it takes you to ski the distance between the cones. Record the number of shuffles (kicks) for each trial in the following boxes.

Date_____ Distance_____

Trial 1	Trial 2	Trial 3	Trial 4	Trial 5	Trial 6

Date_____ Distance_____

Trial 1	Trial 2	Trial 3	Trial 4	Trial 5	Trial 6

Date_____ Distance_____

Trial 1	Trial 2	Trial 3	Trial 4	Trial 5	Trial 6

Date_____ Distance_____

Trial 1	Trial 2	Trial 3	Trial 4	Trial 5	Trial 6

Beginner Lesson 5

From B.A. Duoos and A.M. Rykken, 2012, *Teaching Cross-Country Skiing* (Champaign, IL: Human Kinetics).

SHUFFLE, SHUFFLE, GLIDE

Weight Shift

Watch skiers as they perform the "shuffle, shuffle, glide" movement in the tracks on a flat area. Look for a weight shift from the kicking leg to the gliding ski. Place a check mark in the appropriate column.

Name	Date	Complete weight shift occurs; glide is present	Skier straddles track	No weight shift occurs; no glide is present; skier shuffles continuously

Beginner Lesson 4

From B.A. Duoos and A.M. Rykken, 2012, *Teaching Cross-Country Skiing* (Champaign, IL: Human Kinetics).

SKIER TUCK ASSESSMENT

Observe your students performing a tuck on a moderate hill. Look for the listed critical features. Write the skier's name in the column that most accurately describes the skier's performance of the skills.

▶ The skier maintains the skis parallel and flat on the snow most of the time. ▶ The skier is flexed at the waist. ▶ The skier's knees are bent. ▶ The skier's arms are not consistently held on the thighs. ▶ The skier's poles may move around.	▶ The skis bounce around. ▶ The skier does not maintain waist flexion. ▶ The skier's knees bend and straighten. ▶ The skier's arms move around. ▶ The skier's poles move around.	▶ The skier maintains the skis parallel and flat on the snow. ▶ The skier's body weight is evenly distributed over both skis. ▶ The skier is deeply flexed at the waist. ▶ The skier's knees are deeply bent. ▶ The skier's forearms rest on the thighs with the hands near the knees. ▶ The skier's poles are angled backward.

Advanced Lesson 3

From B.A. Duoos and A.M. Rykken, 2012, *Teaching Cross-Country Skiing* (Champaign, IL: Human Kinetics).

SKIER WALK ASSESSMENT

Contralateral Arm and Leg Movement

Does the skier's *right leg* move backward when the *right arm* moves forward? Place a check mark in the appropriate column.

Name	Date	Yes, all of the time	Half of the time	Less than half of the time	No, none of the time

Beginner Lesson 2

From B.A. Duoos and A.M. Rykken, 2012, *Teaching Cross-Country Skiing* (Champaign, IL: Human Kinetics).

SKI-O QUIZ

Name _____ **Date** _____

Think about your Ski-O experience when answering the following questions. Each question is worth one point (five points total).

1. The red and white markers that you were looking for (and that you found at each point marked on your map) are called _____.

2. On the map below, label the directions of north, west, east, and south using N, W, E, and S.

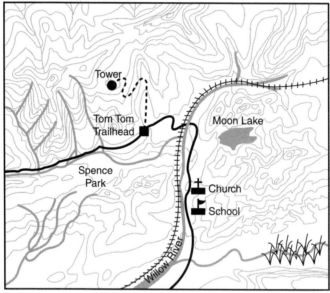

Reprinted, by permission, from C.J. Bunting, 2005, *Interdisciplinary teaching through outdoor education* (Champaign, IL: Human Kinetics), 113.

3. The distance between two controls is called a _____.

4. Provide an example of a *catching feature:* _____.

5. Draw the symbol for a small hill:

Advanced Lesson 10

From B.A. Duoos and A.M. Rykken, 2012, *Teaching Cross-Country Skiing* (Champaign, IL: Human Kinetics).

188 ■

SKI-O QUIZ ANSWERS

1. controls

2. North is at the top of the map, south is at the bottom of the map, west is on the left side of the map, and east is on the right side of the map.

3. leg

4. lake, huge tree, crater

5. ◯

Advanced Lesson 10

From B.A. Duoos and A.M. Rykken, 2012, *Teaching Cross-Country Skiing* (Champaign, IL: Human Kinetics).

■ 189

SNOWPLOW TURN SKILLS RUBRIC

Name _____ **Date** _____

Use the following rubric to assess student progress toward competency in the basic skills:

1 = Skier does not perform critical features correctly; skier is not competent at the skill.
2 = Skier performs some of the critical features correctly; many errors still exist.
3 = Critical features are performed satisfactorily; a few errors still exist.
4 = Skier performs most of the critical features correctly; minor errors exist.
5 = Skier performs critical features correctly; skier is competent at the skill.

Snowplow Turn

	Date	Date	Date	Date	Date	Date	Date
Move downhill with skis parallel							
Slide skis into a narrow V with tips together, tails spread							
Skis are on inside edges							
Knees and ankles bent							
Trunk upright							
Hands slightly in front of body with poles angled backward off the snow							
Knee and foot rotate in direction of turn							
Weight is put on the ski opposite the direction of the turn (to turn to the left, weight is put on the right ski)							

Beginner Lesson 8

From B.A. Duoos and A.M. Rykken, 2012, *Teaching Cross-Country Skiing* (Champaign, IL: Human Kinetics).

TELL ME!

Name _____ Date _____

I would like to know which ski skill you think you are best at and which skill you found most difficult to learn. Please neatly print your answers to the first three questions on the lines provided.

I would also like to know which ski skill you think you could teach a friend. What will you tell that friend when you are teaching the skill? Critical features are important body positions that help to define a technique. Here's an example of a critical feature of the snowplow stop:

Your skis are in a V position when performing a snowplow stop.

1. The cross-country ski skill that I think I can perform the best is the _____.

2. The ski skill that I had the most trouble learning was the _____.

3. I could teach my best friend how to do this ski skill: _____.

4. When teaching my friend how to do this skill, I would be sure to describe the following three critical features:

    a. _____

    b. _____

    c. _____

Scoring

You will earn points based on listing three critical features of the skill you chose.

3 points—All three critical features that you listed for your chosen skill are correct.

2 points—Two of the critical features that you listed for your chosen skill are correct.

1 point—One of the critical features that you listed for your chosen skill is correct.

Intermediate Lesson 10

From B.A. Duoos and A.M. Rykken, 2012, *Teaching Cross-Country Skiing* (Champaign, IL: Human Kinetics).

UPHILL HERRINGBONE PEER EVALUATION

Name _____ **Date** _____

Peer you are observing_____

Your ski partner needs your help in making it up the hill using the herringbone. Your job is to watch your partner's skis very carefully to see if your partner is making the skis do the six moves that are listed below. Place a check mark in the appropriate column.

Herringbone

	Yes	No
1. Begin with skis in V position		
2. Step forward with one ski		
3. Ski tail clears other ski; skier sets ski on snow		
4. Step forward with other ski		
5. Ski tail clears other ski; skier sets ski on snow		
6. Ski is edged so inside edge of ski bites into snow		

Beginner Lesson 6

From B.A. Duoos and A.M. Rykken, 2012, *Teaching Cross-Country Skiing* (Champaign, IL: Human Kinetics).

192 ■

UPHILL TRANSITIONS CHECKLIST

For this activity, skiers start diagonal striding for a few strides on the flat before diagonal striding up a moderate hill. Skiers should diagonal stride as far as they can up the hill before they transition to using the herringbone to climb to the top of the hill, where they will transition back to using the diagonal stride. Watch each skier and place a check mark in the appropriate column.

Diagonal Stride Uphill

Name																				
Glide shortens but is still present																				
Tempo increases																				
Arms pull on pole plant																				
Arm extension in back of body is shorter																				

continued ▲

Uphill Transitions Checklist (continued)

Transition to Herringbone

Name																			
Skier feels when hill becomes too steep to continue diagonal stride																			
Rhythm of diagonal stride continues with smooth change to herringbone																			
Skier edges skis and continues to move uphill																			

continued ▲

Uphill Transitions Checklist (continued)

Transition Back to Diagonal Stride

Name																				
Skier crests hill and transitions back to the diagonal stride																				
Skier smoothly changes technique and continues to diagonal stride																				

Scoring

Use the following to score the skier skills:

5 points—Looks great! All critical features are present.

3 points—Good work! Most critical features are present. Let's work on skills that are in this row.

1 point—Needs work. Critical features are missing. Let's work on skills that are in this row.

From B.A. Duoos and A.M. Rykken, 2012, *Teaching Cross-Country Skiing* (Champaign, IL: Human Kinetics).

CHAPTER 7

Reproducibles

BOOT SIZE RECORD

Name	Boot size

Beginner Lesson 1, Intermediate Lesson 1, and Advanced Lesson 1

From B.A. Duoos and A.M. Rykken, 2012, *Teaching Cross-Country Skiing* (Champaign, IL: Human Kinetics).

Place heel here

Boot sizer:
Boys and girls

23.5 (7)
24.5 (8)
25.5 (9)
26.5 (10)
27.5 (11)
28.5 (12)
30 (13)
31 (1)
32.5 (2)
33.5 (3)
34.5 (4)
35.5 (5)

Beginner Lesson 1, Intermediate Lesson 1, and Advanced Lesson 1

From B.A. Duoos and A.M. Rykken, 2012, *Teaching Cross-Country Skiing* (Champaign, IL: Human Kinetics).

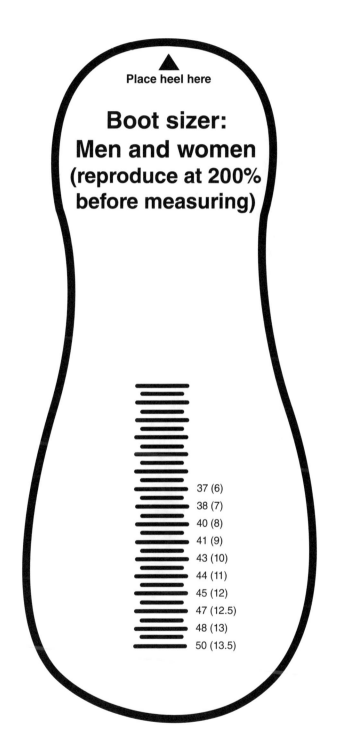

Place heel here

Boot sizer:
Men and women
(reproduce at 200%
before measuring)

37 (6)
38 (7)
40 (8)
41 (9)
43 (10)
44 (11)
45 (12)
47 (12.5)
48 (13)
50 (13.5)

Beginner Lesson 1, Intermediate Lesson 1, and Advanced Lesson 1

From B.A. Duoos and A.M. Rykken, 2012, *Teaching Cross-Country Skiing* (Champaign, IL: Human Kinetics).

CLOTHING GUIDE FOR CROSS-COUNTRY SKIING

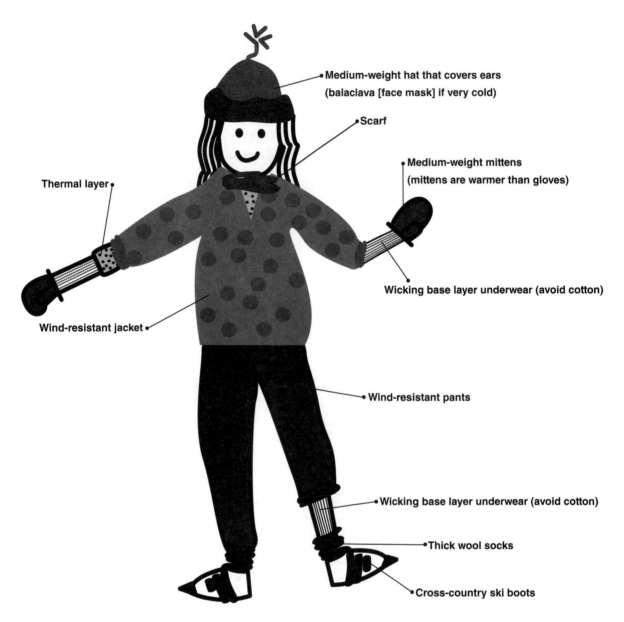

Medium-weight hat that covers ears (balaclava [face mask] if very cold)

Scarf

Medium-weight mittens (mittens are warmer than gloves)

Thermal layer

Wicking base layer underwear (avoid cotton)

Wind-resistant jacket

Wind-resistant pants

Wicking base layer underwear (avoid cotton)

Thick wool socks

Cross-country ski boots

Skier Clothing

To dress successfully for Nordic skiing, people must take many factors into account. Making poor clothing selections can make skiing miserable. Skiers should choose clothing that will help them meet these goals:

- Remaining dry
- Being able to freely move
- Maintaining a comfortable body temperature (not too hot, not too cold)

Layering clothing is a better option than wearing heavy jackets or snowsuits.

continued ▶

Clothing Guide for Cross-Country Skiing

Base Layer

The base layer is designed to pull moisture off the skin (wicking) and allow it to evaporate as quickly as possible. The thickness of the material will affect the amount of insulation that it provides. A thicker material works well for colder weather, as long as it still wicks. The best materials are polypropylene-based fabrics such as poly-pro, dri-lete, dri-fit, and Therma-Pro. Poly-pro comes in various thicknesses (weights), so skiers may want to own a thin and thick version of each piece. This gives the skier several options when dressing for the weather. Skiers should avoid wearing cotton, because cotton absorbs moisture, holds on to it, and becomes damp and cold. Knowing if you are generally a cold person or a warm person will help when making a decision between one type of fabric or the other.

Skiers will need the following:

- Long-sleeved top
- Long underwear bottom
- Thin socks and medium-weight socks

Outer Layer

The outer layer is designed to break the wind, breathe (allow moisture to evaporate), and allow as much freedom of movement as possible. Thicker is not necessarily better, because a thicker material traps moisture, gets wet, and restricts movement. Jackets with heavy linings are discouraged.

Skiers will need the following:

- Wind jacket (unlined or thinly lined)
- Wind pants or wind tights

Hand Coverings

Gloves and mittens with a leather palm specifically made for Nordic skiing are the best option. Mittens will be warmer than gloves, but cross-country skiers should avoid using downhill ski mittens because they are usually too bulky. Fleece-backed mitts or gloves with a leather palm and minimal bulk will provide warmth and will be comfortable.

Skiers will need the following:

- Gloves
- Mittens (or lobster-style mittens)

Head Wear

You may have heard this before: "If your feet are cold, put on a hat." This is definitely true for Nordic skiing. A good hat is essential—ideally, the hat will be thin, warm, and comfortable. Many skiers wear earmuffs underneath a thin hat to help prevent cold or frostbitten ears. You will get hot and eventually wet wearing a big, thick hat. Using only earmuffs is usually not sufficient. Headbands worn under hats work well, as do balaclavas (face masks) for extreme cold or windy conditions. Scarves are often too bulky and may get tangled in poles, so skiers should try a fleece neck warmer if additional warmth and protection are needed.

Skiers will need the following:

- Hat
- Balaclava, breathable face mask, or neck warmer

Beginner Lesson 1

From B.A. Duoos and A.M. Rykken, 2012, *Teaching Cross-Country Skiing* (Champaign, IL: Human Kinetics).

DISTANCE DIAGONAL STRIDE WITH POLES:
HOW FAR CAN YOU GO?

Name _____ Date _____

Ski as far as you can with the correct diagonal stride rhythm using your poles. Mark off your progress on the ski trail below by shading in the distance you skied on the ski track for each trial.

	Trial 1	Trial 2	Trial 3	Trial 4	Trial 5	Trial 6	Trial 7	Trial 8	Trial 9	Trial 10

Start
0 yards

50 yards

100 yards

150 yards

200 yards
Finish

Intermediate Lesson 4

From B.A. Duoos and A.M. Rykken, 2012, *Teaching Cross-Country Skiing* (Champaign, IL: Human Kinetics).

204 ∎

DOUBLE-POLE FUN

How Far Can You Go?

Name _____ **Date** _____

How far can you double pole without stopping? Begin double poling behind the start line and see if you can make it to the finish line without stopping to rest. Mark off your progress on the ski track below by shading in the distance you double poled without stopping.

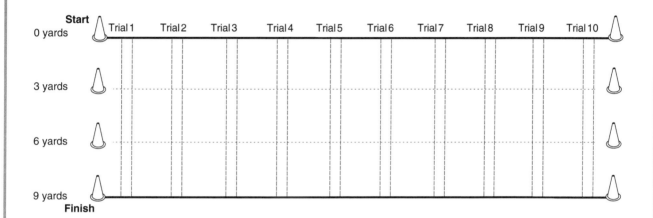

Intermediate Lesson 8

From B.A. Duoos and A.M. Rykken, 2012, *Teaching Cross-Country Skiing* (Champaign, IL: Human Kinetics).

DOUBLE-POLE POWER!

Name _____ **Date** _____

Shade in the distance you covered with your first double-pole push and draw in a horizontal line at the end of the shading. Repeat for each push until you have made it to the finish line. Write in the total number of pushes it took you to double pole from the start to the finish line for each trial.

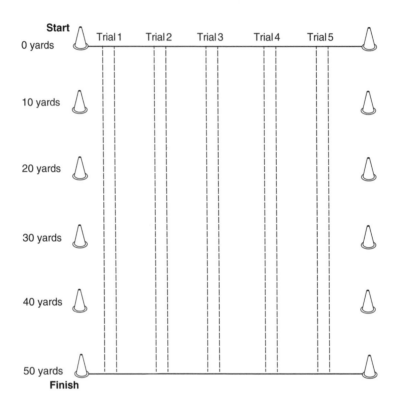

Total number of pushes _____ _____ _____ _____ _____

Scoring

You will earn points based on the following:

    4 points = Decreased the number of double-pole pushes from start to finish by four pushes

    3 points = Decreased the number of double-pole pushes from start to finish by three pushes

    2 points = Decreased the number of double-pole pushes from start to finish by two pushes

    1 point = Decreased the number of double-pole pushes from start to finish by one push

Advanced Lesson 5

From B.A. Duoos and A.M. Rykken, 2012, *Teaching Cross-Country Skiing* (Champaign, IL: Human Kinetics).

Exaggerated Arm Swings

Beginner Lesson 1, Intermediate Lesson 1

From B.A. Duoos and A.M. Rykken, 2012, *Teaching Cross-Country Skiing* (Champaign, IL: Human Kinetics).

Repetitive Standing Broad Jumps

Beginner Lesson 1
From B.A. Duoos and A.M. Rykken, 2012, *Teaching Cross-Country Skiing* (Champaign, IL: Human Kinetics).

Diagonal Side-to-Side Jumps

Beginner Lesson 1
From B.A. Duoos and A.M. Rykken, 2012, *Teaching Cross-Country Skiing* (Champaign, IL: Human Kinetics).

Gorilla Walk

Beginner Lesson 1

From B.A. Duoos and A.M. Rykken, 2012, *Teaching Cross-Country Skiing* (Champaign, IL: Human Kinetics).

HEART RATE RECORD

Name _____ **Date** _____

Date	10-second heart rate before exercise	10-second heart rate after exercise

Intermediate Lesson 9 and Advanced Lessons 1, 2, 3, 5, 6, 7, and 8.

From B.A. Duoos and A.M. Rykken, 2012, *Teaching Cross-Country Skiing* (Champaign, IL: Human Kinetics).

KICK DOUBLE POLE WITH ALTERNATING LEGS

Keeping the Rhythm

Name _____ Date _____

Can you perform the kick double pole while alternating your leg kicks continuously the entire distance without stopping? Begin your kick double pole with alternating leg kicks behind the start line and see if you can make it to the finish line without stopping to rest. Can you alternate the leg you are kicking with for the entire distance?

Mark off how far you are able to continuously kick double pole with alternating leg kicks on the ski track below by shading in the distance you double poled without stopping.

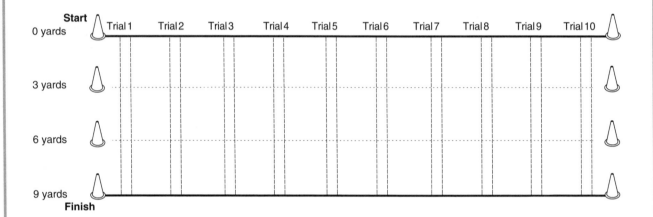

Intermediate Lesson 8
From B.A. Duoos and A.M. Rykken, 2012, *Teaching Cross-Country Skiing* (Champaign, IL: Human Kinetics).

212 ▪

KILOMETERS SKIED RECORD

Name _____ Date _____

Fill in the following chart with the name of the trail you skied, the length of time it took you to ski the distance, and your 10-second heart rate count before and after you skied the distance.

Date	Trail skied	Distance skied	Time	10-second heart rate before skiing	10-second heart rate after skiing

Beginner Lesson 9 and Intermediate Lesson 9

From B.A. Duoos and A.M. Rykken, 2012, *Teaching Cross-Country Skiing* (Champaign, IL: Human Kinetics).

Sidestepping

Beginner Lesson 2

From B.A. Duoos and A.M. Rykken, 2012, *Teaching Cross-Country Skiing* (Champaign, IL: Human Kinetics).

Herringbone

Beginner Lesson 2

From B.A. Duoos and A.M. Rykken, 2012, *Teaching Cross-Country Skiing* (Champaign, IL: Human Kinetics).

Star Turn

Beginner Lesson 2

From B.A. Duoos and A.M. Rykken, 2012, *Teaching Cross-Country Skiing* (Champaign, IL: Human Kinetics).

French Fries and Pizza

Beginner Lesson 2
From B.A. Duoos and A.M. Rykken, 2012, *Teaching Cross-Country Skiing* (Champaign, IL: Human Kinetics).

Dead Bug

Beginner Lesson 2

From B.A. Duoos and A.M. Rykken, 2012, *Teaching Cross-Country Skiing* (Champaign, IL: Human Kinetics).

Taking Skis Off and Walking With Skis and Poles

Beginner Lesson 2
From B.A. Duoos and A.M. Rykken, 2012, *Teaching Cross-Country Skiing* (Champaign, IL: Human Kinetics).

Taking Skis Off and Walking With Skis and Poles

Beginner Lesson 2
From B.A. Duoos and A.M. Rykken, 2012, *Teaching Cross-Country Skiing* (Champaign, IL: Human Kinetics).

Putting Skis On and Balancing on One Ski

Beginner Lesson 2
From B.A. Duoos and A.M. Rykken, 2012, *Teaching Cross-Country Skiing* (Champaign, IL: Human Kinetics).

NO POLES KICK AND GLIDE FOR DISTANCE CHALLENGE

Name _____ **Date** _____

Use both skis but no poles for this challenge. Count the number of kicks and glides it takes you to ski the distance between the cones. If you lose your rhythm, stop and start again with your feet side by side. Continue counting kicks from where you left off. Record the number of kicks for each trial in the boxes below. Record the number of times you had to start over.

Date_____ Distance_____

Trial	Number of kicks	Did you have to start over?		If yes, number of times you started over
1		Yes	No	
2		Yes	No	
3		Yes	No	
4		Yes	No	
5		Yes	No	

Intermediate Lesson 3

From B.A. Duoos and A.M. Rykken, 2012, *Teaching Cross-Country Skiing* (Champaign, IL: Human Kinetics).

NORWEGIAN WORDS RELATED TO SNOW AND SKIING

Norwegian word	English translation
Snoflak	Snowflake
Snø	Snow
Snøkjerring	Very large snowflake
Snøkrystall	Snow crystal
Snøkorn	Snow grain
Slaps	Slush; wet, melting snow
Puddersnø	Powder snow
Snødett	Light snowfall
Snørok	Medium snowstorm
Ski (pronounced shee)	Ski
Gå på ski	Go for a ski
Skihopp	Ski jump
Skiløype	Ski track or trail
Langrenn	Cross-country skiing
Snøballkrig	Snowball fight

Beginner Lesson 2, Intermediate Lesson 2, and Advanced Lesson 2

From B.A. Duoos and A.M. Rykken, 2012, *Teaching Cross-Country Skiing* (Champaign, IL: Human Kinetics).

POLE SIZE RECORD

Name	Pole size

Beginner Lesson 1, Intermediate Lesson 1, and Advanced Lesson 1

From B.A. Duoos and A.M. Rykken, 2012, *Teaching Cross-Country Skiing* (Champaign, IL: Human Kinetics).

POLE SIZING

Tape a measuring tape (showing the metric side) to a wall so skiers can see what the height of their poles should be.

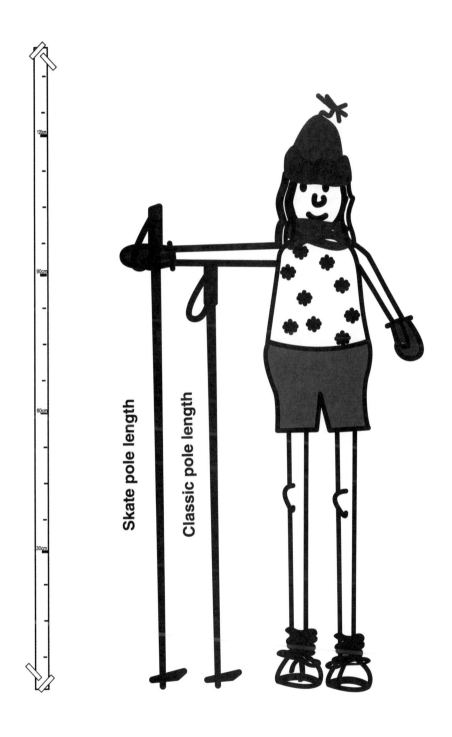

Beginner Lesson 1, Intermediate Lesson 1, and Advanced Lesson 1
From B.A. Duoos and A.M. Rykken, 2012, *Teaching Cross-Country Skiing* (Champaign, IL: Human Kinetics).

■ 225

POWER KICKS

Kick Double Pole

Name _____ Date _____

How far can you go with 5 kick double poles? Ten kick double poles? Start several strides behind the start line and take a couple of double-pole pushes to get you to the start line where you will begin your kick double pole. Perform 5 kick double poles, glide as far as you can with the last kick double pole, and then mark the spot alongside the track where you stopped gliding. Mark off your progress on the ski tracks below by shading in the distance you covered using 5 kick double poles. Repeat for a total of five tries using 5 kick double poles. Then repeat another five trials, this time using 10 kick double poles.

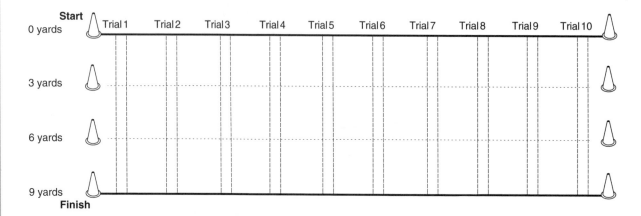

Intermediate Lesson 8

From B.A. Duoos and A.M. Rykken, 2012, *Teaching Cross-Country Skiing* (Champaign, IL: Human Kinetics).

226 ■

SCOOTER COUNT

Name _____ **Date** _____

Write down the number of kicks you used to cover the marked distance. Then answer the question.

Trial 1	Trial 2	Trial 3	Trial 4	Trial 5

Circle the trial on which you used the fewest number of kicks. List two things that you did in that trial that helped you glide farther.

a. _____

b. _____

Scoring

You will earn points based on the improvement you have shown from the first lesson to the third lesson.

5 points = Decreased kicks by *five* from the worst trial in lesson 1 to the best trial in lesson 3

4 points = Decreased kicks by *four* from the worst trial in lesson 1 to the best trial in lesson 3

3 points = Decreased kicks by *three* from the worst trial in lesson 1 to the best trial in lesson 3

2 points = Decreased kicks by *two* from the worst trial in lesson 1 to the best trial in lesson 3

1 point = Decreased kicks by *one* from the worst trial in lesson 1 to the best trial in lesson 3

Beginner Lesson 5 and Advanced Lessons 1, 2, and 3
From B.A. Duoos and A.M. Rykken, 2012, *Teaching Cross-Country Skiing* (Champaign, IL: Human Kinetics).

SKI SIZE RECORD

Name	Ski size

Beginner Lesson 1, Intermediate Lesson 1, and Advanced Lesson 1

From B.A. Duoos and A.M. Rykken, 2012, *Teaching Cross-Country Skiing* (Champaign, IL: Human Kinetics).

SKI-O!

Ski-O can be described as the following:

- Orienteering on skis
- Getting your bearings in unfamiliar territory
- Moving from point to point using map and compass
- A challenging cardiovascular and mental activity
- A great interdisciplinary activity that can involve biology, earth science, geography, or math

Students must understand the following:

- A map is a picture of the ground.
- Geographical features of the ground are represented by lines and symbols on the map.
- A map must be held so it corresponds directly with the surrounding ground.

Students must be able to do the following:

- Correctly use a compass.
- Understand standard orienteering symbols.

If possible, conduct an orienteering unit in the fall so your students will learn how to use a compass and GPS unit. Visit the website www.learn-orienteering.org/old/ for easy-to-follow instructions on how to read a compass as well as information on the compass and map interaction. Instructional help for designing lessons for young children and a brief list of orienteering terms can be found at http://orienteeringusa.org/youth-leaders/materials/o-young. The U.S. Orienteering Federation (USOF) also provides a wealth of information on orienteering. Contact your nearby county and state parks to see if they have contour maps and orienteering maps of the park available that you could incorporate into your lessons.

The following is a teaching progression that will take your students through a series of orienteering experiences that will help them to be better prepared for the Ski-O lesson.

- Track tag: Play tag on the lines on the gym floor. The person who is It calls out the direction of travel when tagging another person.
- Direction call-out: Form circles of four to six students. Students bounce pass a ball to a teammate and call out the direction that the ball is passed.
- Compass rose: Students label the directions on a stick compass.
- Gym map: Students draw a map of your gym with controls marked.
- School ground map: Students draw a map of your school grounds and mark controls.
- Map puzzle relay: Cut apart copies of real maps (contour or orienteering) and have teams put the maps together. Increase the difficulty of this exercise by having the team work with the map to identify directions or to circle a land feature.
- Make a ski trail: Let students design and draw a ski trail on graph paper. Ski the trail.
- Contour maps: Teach students how to read a contour map. Work with the classroom teacher to have students learn how to use the computer to generate a map.

Advanced Lesson 10

From B.A. Duoos and A.M. Rykken, 2012, *Teaching Cross-Country Skiing* (Champaign, IL: Human Kinetics).

SKI-O TERMINOLOGY

This is a brief listing of orienteering terminology to get you started. Complete glossaries of terminology can be found at the references listed on the Ski-O information sheet.

bearing—The direction of travel read from the compass.

catching feature—A catching feature is an obvious feature that is slightly beyond the control. When you approach this feature, you know that you have probably overshot the control.

checkpoints—Features on the map or the ground that help you determine that you are on the correct course.

contour—Topographic maps are marked with contour lines that indicate elevation of the land features.

control—The point that you are looking for, which is identified on the orienteering map.

control marker—The orange and white (or red and white) marker identifying the control.

control punch—A punch found at each control that is used to indicate that the control has been visited.

course—A series of controls make up a course.

housing—A compass needle is inside the housing, which sits on the compass base plate.

knoll—A knoll is a small hill.

leg—The area between two consecutively set markers is called a leg.

legend—The legend shows the symbols that are used on the map and defines what they mean. The legend is also called a key.

linear feature—A fairly straight feature such as a straight trail or fence.

string course—An orienteering course set with one continuous piece of string. This type of course is usually set up for young beginners.

Advanced Lesson 10

From B.A. Duoos and A.M. Rykken, 2012, *Teaching Cross-Country Skiing* (Champaign, IL: Human Kinetics).

230 ■

SKI SIZING

Tape a measuring tape (showing the metric side) to a wall so skiers can see what the height of their skis should be. Note the size range that is suitable for a skier.

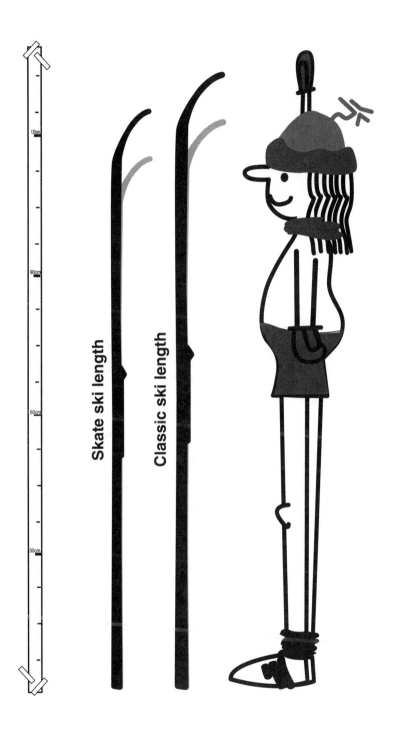

Beginner Lesson 1, Intermediate Lesson 1, and Advanced Lesson 1

From B.A. Duoos and A.M. Rykken, 2012, *Teaching Cross-Country Skiing* (Champaign, IL: Human Kinetics).

SKI TRAIL ETIQUETTE

Here are 10 rules to follow while on the ski trail. These rules will help ensure that everyone has a good time and returns safely.

- Be kind, courteous, and as helpful as you can to all other skiers.
- If another skier asks to pass you, step aside so the skier can get by. Skiers may say "track" or "excuse me" or "on your left" (or right) as they come up from behind.
- If the trail is marked, ski in the direction it is designed for. If it is not marked, try to determine the direction that most people are skiing, and ski the same way. If you do meet another skier head on when on a hill, the skier going uphill should yield the right-of-way. On level ground, the slower skier should yield the right-of-way.
- Avoid walking on the trail at all costs. If you must walk, do so on the side, not in the middle.
- If you have trash, carry it out with you.
- Be responsible for your equipment. Do not leave it lying in anyone's way. Set it aside neatly when you are not using it. Have all your own equipment marked with your name on it.
- If you choose to skate, do not skate on the tracks; skate off to the side of the set track.
- If you fall, move off the track and fill in any holes left behind so the track is safe for the next skiers.
- Respect the wildlife. Enjoy watching the animals, but don't hassle them.
- Respect other people on the trail. Ski with quiet voices; avoid shouting and loud careless behavior.

Advanced Lesson 9

From B.A. Duoos and A.M. Rykken, 2012, *Teaching Cross-Country Skiing* (Champaign, IL: Human Kinetics).

232 ■

SKI TRAIL TIME

Name _____ **Date** _____

Today you had the opportunity to ski over real ski trails. Please neatly print your responses to the questions below on the lines provided.

1. List three rules of etiquette that you followed today when on the trails.

    a. _____

    b. _____

    c. _____

2. Think about the clothing that you had on today when you were skiing. Circle yes or no.

    a. Were you too hot?   Yes   No

    b. Were you too cold?   Yes   No

    c. Were you comfortable?   Yes   No

3. List two things you would change about your clothing if you were either too hot or too cold today. If you were comfortable, skip to the next question.

    a. _____

    b. _____

4. Using your trail map, add up the number of kilometers you skied today. Record that number here: _____

5. On the trail map, draw a line over the trails you followed. Turn your map in to your instructor.

Scoring

You will earn points based on the following:

5 points = All five questions have been answered.
4 points = Four questions have been answered.
3 points = Three questions have been answered.
2 points = Two questions have been answered.
1 point = One question has been answered.

Advanced Lesson 9

From B.A. Duoos and A.M. Rykken, 2012, *Teaching Cross-Country Skiing* (Champaign, IL: Human Kinetics).

SLOW-MO SKI CHECK

Name _____ **Date** _____

Your job is to put the statements below in the correct order by numbering them from 1 to 8. You need to put the movements in the order they should be done when performing the Slow-Mo Ski. Write the number in the box. Read each statement carefully before making your decisions. Then try it out! Have your partner read the statements in the order you selected as you perform the movement. If it is not quite right, try again and change the order around. Start with a right-foot kick.

Here are your choices:

Feet are side by side.	Left foot kicks.
Right foot kicks.	Right arm swings backward.
Glide on the left ski.	Glide on the right ski.
Right arm swings forward down the track.	Left arm swings forward down the track.

Scoring

You will earn points based on the following:

    5 points = You were able to put the critical features in the correct order on the first try. Congratulations!

    3 points = You put the critical features in the correct order on the second try. Good job!

    1 point = It took you more than two tries to put the critical features in the correct order. Let's practice Slow-Mo Skier.

Advanced Lesson 2

From B.A. Duoos and A.M. Rykken, 2012, *Teaching Cross-Country Skiing* (Champaign, IL: Human Kinetics).

234 ■

SNOWFLAKE RELAY

SNOWPLOW TURNS DRAW

Name _____ **Date** _____

After you have practiced your snowplow turns, draw the curving path around the cones that you snowplowed continuously around for each trial.

Start _____

Finish _____

Scoring

You will earn points based on the number of continuous snowplow turns you can make in a row.

    4 points = Skier has made four continuous snowplow turns.

    3 points = Skier has made three continuous snowplow turns.

    2 points = Skier has made two continuous snowplow turns.

    1 point = Skier has made one snowplow turn.

Intermediate Lesson 7

From B.A. Duoos and A.M. Rykken, 2012, *Teaching Cross-Country Skiing* (Champaign, IL: Human Kinetics).

SNOWPLOW TURNS

Name _____ **Date** _____

After you have practiced your snowplow turns, draw the curving path around the cones that you snowplowed continuously around for each trial.

Start

Finish

Scoring

You will earn points based on the number of continuous snowplow turns you can make in a row.

   5 points = Skier has made five continuous snowplow turns.

   4 points = Skier has made four continuous snowplow turns.

   3 points = Skier has made three continuous snowplow turns.

   2 points = Skier has made two continuous snowplow turns.

   1 point = Skier has made one snowplow turn.

Advanced Lesson 4

From B.A. Duoos and A.M. Rykken, 2012, *Teaching Cross-Country Skiing* (Champaign, IL: Human Kinetics).

TIGHT TURNS!

Name _____ **Date** _____

Skiers, you are challenged to complete the double figure eight as fast as possible. You will have time to practice the course during several class sessions. In this fun exercise, you will be starting at the top of the large figure eight. You will continue on the outside course until you cross back over to the top loop, where you will then cross to the inside loop. Complete the inside loops and finish on the outside loop at the starting point. Your partner can serve as timer and recorder.

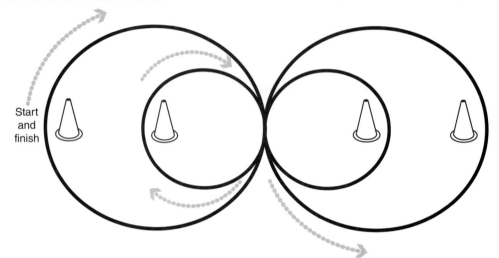

Please record your time in seconds and neatly print it in the space provided.

Date_____

Trial 1	Trial 2	Trial 3	Trial 4	Trial 5

Date_____

Trial 1	Trial 2	Trial 3	Trial 4	Trial 5

Date_____

Trial 1	Trial 2	Trial 3	Trial 4	Trial 5

Scoring

Your score will be based on your *improvement* from one trial to the next.

   5 points = You decreased your time by five seconds or more from a trial on the first day to a trial on the last day.

   4 points = You decreased your time by four seconds from a trial on the first day to a trial on the last day.

   3 points = You decreased your time by three seconds from a trial on the first day to a trial on the last day.

   2 points = You decreased your time by two seconds from a trial on the first day to a trial on the last day.

   1 point = You decreased your time by one second from a trial on the first day to a trial on the last day.

Advanced Lesson 6

From B.A. Duoos and A.M. Rykken, 2012, *Teaching Cross-Country Skiing* (Champaign, IL: Human Kinetics).

Glossary

all-purpose sport stance—This position is commonly used in many sports. In this position, the feet are shoulder-width apart, the arms are relaxed and hanging, the shoulders are relaxed and slumped somewhat forward, and the knees are slightly bent.

bindings—The hardware that attaches the ski boot to the ski.

camber—The amount of vertical curvature in the middle of the ski when the ski sits on its base on the floor; camber is crucial for creating a kick zone.

contralateral—The right arm swings forward as the left leg steps forward. The left arm swings forward as the right leg steps forward.

diagonal stride—A striding technique in which the skier's contralateral arm and leg move simultaneously, as when walking. When this technique is executed efficiently, each stride includes kick, pole, and glide phases.

double pole—A technique in which the skier plants both poles simultaneously and pushes down and back on them to produce a powerful forward thrust.

downhill ski—When the skis are positioned diagonally or perpendicular on the slope, the downhill ski is the ski that is closest to the bottom of the hill.

edging—Tilting one or both skis onto either edge, usually to prevent slipping.

fall line—The line that a rolling ball would take down a given slope; the steepest, shortest, and fastest line down any given hillside.

gliding ski—The weighted ski; the ski that is gliding on the snow while the other ski is kicking or recovering.

herringbone—A technique used for climbing hills with skis in a V position. No glide is used, and the poles are planted alternately behind the skis. A distinctive herringbone pattern is left in the snow.

inside ski—The ski closest to the center of the circle that the skier is turning about.

in the track—Skiing in the ski tracks that have been either skied in or set by a machine.

kick—A kick is a quick downward movement of the foot that causes the skier to propel forward. During the kick, after the push down, the leg extends rearward, providing a strong push forward to the skier's whole body. The kick leg is then relaxed and recovers forward while the skier glides by balancing on the other ski.

kick double pole—In this technique, both poles are angled backward and planted simultaneously to give a powerful thrust. As the poles swing forward, the skier performs a single leg kick. This technique is used when the skier is moving too quickly to diagonal stride but is having difficulty double poling (it is typically used on slight uphills or at the bottom of a long hill, just before switching to the diagonal stride).

kick turn—An about-face turn that a skier performs while stationary by lifting one ski and reversing its direction, followed by the other ski.

locomotor—Motor skills (running, hopping, jumping, skipping, galloping, sliding, leaping) that are used to move the body from one location to another.

marathon skate—With one ski continually gliding in a set track, the skier angles the other ski (the pushing ski) out of the track and pushes against it. The ski is recovered and the movement is repeated. A double-poling action with the poles coincides with the push.

Nordic skiing—This encompasses all forms of skiing involving free-heel skiing, where the foot is only attached to the ski at the toe region. It includes biathlon, cross-country skiing, ski orienteering, ski racing, ski touring, ski jumping, telemarking, and bushwacking on skis.

Nordic swoosh—A parallel turn out of the fall line to a position perpendicular to the fall line, which brings the skier to a complete stop. This technique is similar to a hockey stop.

no-wax ski—A ski with a base that has a texture in the kick zone so no kick wax is necessary.

on the flat—This phrase is used to indicate that you will be skiing on flat ground.

outside ski—The ski farthest away from the center of the circle that the skier is turning about.

poling—The act of driving the ski pole into the snow at an angle, either to aid turning or as a method of propulsion.

scooter—With one ski on, the skier pushes off with the booted foot while gliding forward on the ski.

set track—Tracks made by a machine.

sideslipping—A method of controlled descent that skiers can use on steeper slopes. The skier keeps the skis perpendicular to the fall line and allows the skis to flatten out onto the snow, sliding down the slope. The skis slide along the fall line (sideslipping) or at an angle to the fall line (diagonal sideslipping).

sidestepping—A technique that skiers can use to safely ascend or descend any slope by keeping the skis perpendicular to the fall line, edging the skis, and stepping the skis sideways one at a time.

single sticking—An exercise that helps develop upper-body strength. To perform this exercise, skiers use the diagonal stride arm movement while poling, but they keep their feet side by side. No kick is used.

skied-in track—Skiers create a ski trail by skiing through snow that has not been previously skied in.

Ski-O—Ski orienteering is a sport that involves navigation using a map and compass. The object is to ski to a series of controls shown on the map, choosing routes—both on and off trail—that will help you find all of the controls and get back to the finish in the shortest amount of time.

snowplow—A braking and turning technique. The front tips of the skis are brought together, and the tails are pushed wide apart to form a wedge; the knees are rolled inward slightly. By applying pressure against the snow with the edges of the skis, the skier can reduce speed or stop completely.

snowplow stop—Performing a snowplow glide with the inside edges of the skis biting into the snow to produce a braking force that slows and then stops the skier.

snowplow turn—A technique used to change direction and reduce speed while descending a hill. The skier places the skis in a position with the tips together and tails spread, or snowplow position, and then turns by shifting weight from one ski to another.

stem Christie—A ski technique used for turning. Before the turn, the skier stems the uphill ski by skidding the tail outward, and as the turn is made, the skier brings the uphill ski to a position parallel with the downhill ski.

step turning—A technique that skiers use to change direction while descending without reducing speed. The skier turns by stepping each ski independently in small steps toward the desired direction of travel.

straight run—Descending directly down the fall line of a hill with skis parallel.

traverse—To descend a slope diagonally, reducing the rate of descent, by setting the skis parallel and across the fall line at the desired angle of descent.

tuck—An aerodynamic method of gliding downhill. The skier crouches in a tuck position with the forearms resting on the thighs and with the ski poles tucked under the arms.

uphill ski—Refers to the ski that is in a position higher up the hill.

waxable ski—A ski with a base that has a smooth bottom, allowing the ski's kick zone to be waxed for kick, while the glide zone is waxed for glide.

References

Aarnio, M., Winter, T., Peltonen, J., Kujala, U.M., and Kaprio, J. (2002). Stability of leisure-time physical activity during adolescence: A longitudinal study among 16-, 17- and 18-year-old Finnish youth. *Scandinavian Journal of Medicine & Science in Sports,* 12(3), 179-185.

Bays, T. (1980). *Nine thousand years of skis: Norwegian wood to French plastic.* Ishpeming, MI: National Ski Hall of Fame Press.

Flemmen, A., and Grosvold, O. (1982). *Teaching children to ski.* Champaign, IL: Leisure Press.

Fox, E., Bowers, R., and Foss, M. (1993). *The physiological basis for exercise and sport.* Madison, WI: Brown and Benchmark.

Fraioli, F., Moretti, C., Paolucci, D., Alicicco, E., Crescenzi, F., and Fortunio, G. (1980). Physical exercise stimulates marked concomitant release of β-endorphin and adrenocorticotropic hormone (ACTH) in peripheral blood in man. *Cellular and Molecular,* 36, 987-989.

Gilbert, J. (2005). Using target heart rate zones in your class. *Journal of Physical Education, Recreation and Dance,* 76(3), 22-26.

Gullion, L. (1990). *The cross-country primer: The complete beginner's guide to equipment, fundamentals, and techniques.* New York: The Lyons Press.

Gullion, L. (1990). *Ski games: A fun-filled approach to teaching nordic and alpine skills.* Champaign, IL: Leisure Press.

Gullion, L. (1993). *Nordic skiing: Steps to success.* Champaign, IL: Human Kinetics.

Haukelid, K. (1989). *Skis against the atom.* Minot, ND: North American Heritage Press.

Hindman, S. (2005). *Cross-country skiing: Building skills for fun and fitness.* Seattle, WA: The Mountaineers Books.

Lovell, O. (1984). *The promise of Norway: A history of the Norwegian-American people.* Minneapolis: University of Minnesota Press.

Lunge-Larsen, L. (2001). *The race of the Birkebeiners.* Boston, MA: Houghton Mifflin Company.

McSwigan, M. (2005). *Snow treasure.* New York: Dutton's Children's Books.

Mustoe, G. (1998). Cross-country skis, the easy way. In *Fine woodworking on bending wood,* ed. Fine Woodworking Editors, 82-83. Newton, CT: The Taunton Press, Inc.

Saltin, B., and Astrand, P.O. (1967). Maximal oxygen uptake in athletes. *Journal of Applied Physiology,* 23, 353.

Smith, G. (2002). Biomechanics of cross country skiing. In H. Rusko (Ed.), *The Handbook of Sports Medicine and Science.* Oxford: Blackwell Publishing.

Starr, R. (1998). Cross-country skis, Norwegian style. In *Fine woodworking on bending wood,* ed. Fine Woodworking Editors, 84-85. Newton, CT: The Taunton Press, Inc.

About the Authors

Bridget A. Duoos, PhD, is an associate professor in the health and human performance department at the University of St. Thomas in St. Paul, Minnesota.

Dr. Duoos has done extensive research in the biomechanics of cross-country skiing skills, pedagogy of skiing skills, skill progressions, and methods of assessing students' progress. She has presented her research on both the biomechanics and the teaching of cross-country skiing at state, district, and national American Alliance for Health, Physical Education, Recreation and Dance (AAHPERD) conferences. She holds a bachelor of arts degree in physical education teaching and health education teaching and both a master's and doctorate in biomechanics.

An experienced and passionate instructor, Dr. Duoos has taught cross-country skiing to children, youth, and adults as a coach for the Minnesota Youth Ski League (MYSL) and as an instructor at the University of Minnesota and the University of St. Thomas. Dr. Duoos is a past member of the MYSL board of directors and coauthor (with Anne Rykken) of the MYSL curriculum, used by hundreds of instructors throughout the upper Midwest.

Dr. Duoos has been a member of AAHPERD since 1975. In 1999 she received the Presidential Award for Physical Education from the Minnesota Association for Health, Physical Education, Recreation and Dance and recently received the Lou Keller award for outstanding contributions to the field. She is also a member of the International Society of Biomechanics in Sports (ISBS), the Biomechanics Academy of AAHPERD, and the American College of Sports Medicine (ACSM).

Dr. Duoos and her husband, Armen Hitzemann, reside in North Branch, Minnesota. When the snow melts, she spends her free time running, golfing, and reading.

Anne M. Rykken, BFA, is a graphic designer and Nordic ski coach. She has been the head coach for 14 years at Minnehaha Academy in Minneapolis, Minnesota.

Anne is a founding member of the Minnesota Youth Ski League (MYSL), where she spent 15 years as executive director developing a nearly 1,000-member youth ski club from the ground up. During the same time, Rykken led the MYSL Como Park club, which remained the largest cross-country ski club in the United States for the duration of her leadership.

Rykken coauthored (with Bridget Duoos) the current MYSL curriculum. She recently received the Lifetime Achievement Award from the Minnesota Nordic Ski Association for her work in developing youth skiing in Minnesota. She is frequently invited to help leaders in the ski community develop vibrant family-oriented ski clubs.

In addition to skiing, Rykken enjoys biking and most other outdoor activities. She and her husband, Scott, live in St. Paul, Minnesota. Nearby are their two grown children, who are accomplished Nordic skiers and coaches as well.

You'll find other outstanding
physical education resources at
www.HumanKinetics.com